AF560003

SOYBEAN AND ITS DISEASES

SOYBEAN
AND
ITS DISEASES

By

Dr. Renuka Sharma

DISCOVERY PUBLISHING HOUSE PVT. LTD.
NEW DELHI-110 002

Published by:
Tilak Wasan

DISCOVERY PUBLISHING HOUSE PVT. LTD.
4383/4B, Ansari Road, Darya Ganj
New Delhi-110 002 (India)
Phone : +91-11-23279245, 43596064-65
Fax : +91-11-23253475
E-mail : discoverypublishinghouse@gmail.com
sales@discoverypublishinggroup.com
parul.wasan@gmail.com
web : www.discoverypublishinggroup.com

***First Edition:* 2014**

ISBN: 978-93-5056-447-9

Soybean and its Diseases

Printed at:
Aditi Fine Art Press
Delhi

Preface

Soybean (*Glycine max* (L.) Merr. Family : Fabaceae) is known as the *"Golden Bean"* of the 20th Century. Though, Soybean is a legume crop, yet it is widely used as oilseed. Due to very poor cookability on account of inherent presence of trypsin inhibitor, it cannot be utilized as a pulse. It is now the second largest oilseed in India after groundnut. It grows in varied agro-climatic conditions. It has emerged as one of the important commercial crop in many countries. Due to its worldwide popularity, the international trade of Soybean is spread globally. Several countries such as Japan, China, Indonesia, Philippines, and European countries are importing Soybean to supplement their domestic requirement for human consumption and cattle feed.

Soybean crop is vulnerable to different insect pests and diseases, which results into considerable loss in yield. It is, therefore, necessary to adopt integrated plant protection measures such as Cultural Measures, Biological Control of Insects Diseases, Harvesting and Post-harvest Care.

There are hundreds of non viral pathogens known to attack soybean, of which 35 are economically important. Soybean is also prone to be attacked by viruses or viral strains. Among the viral diseases, six viral diseases are believed to have some economic significance in India. These are Soybean mosaic potyvirus (SMV), Mungbean yellow mosaic geminivirus (MVMV), Cowpea mild mottle carlavirus (CPMMV), Chlorotic mottle bromovirus (CMV), Peanut bud Necrosis tospo Virus (PBNV) & Tobacco ring spot nepovirus (TRSV). Currently the emerging viral disease is bud blight of soybean. In India, the virus causing bud blight of soybean was identified as Tobacco ring spot virus. Researchers from Maharashtra also reported as Tobacco ring spot virus. But in the upcoming years there have been a lot of controversial statements and arguments regarding the exact etiology of bud blight disease of soybean.

Disease often goes unnoticed in soybean fields, although it may be causing significant yield losses. Most major soybean diseases are associated with cool, wet conditions and heavier soils. The most cost-effective means of controlling disease is through genetic resistance.

Growers who use Integrated Pest Management (IPM) try to increase profits by reducing production costs and keeping pest losses low. Scouting is the best way to know what pests are in the field and whether or not they will threaten yields and profits.

Information on disease names, pathogen, symptoms, economic importance, disease distribution, other hosts, cultural and pathogenic variability of the pathogen, disease control, whether the pathogen is seedborne and/or seed transmitted, effect on seed quality, pathogen transmission, seed treatments and seed health tests is provided for all diseases of soyabeans caused by fungi, bacteria, mycoplasma-like organisms and viruses.

We hope that this book is useful to soybean researchers as well as to people working with other crop species.

—Author

Contents

1

Introduction

Soybean (*Glycine max* (L.) Merr. Family: Fabaceae) is known as the *"Golden Bean"* of the 20th Century. Though, Soybean is a legume crop, yet it is widely used as oilseed. Due to very poor cookability on account of inherent presence of trypsin inhibitor, it cannot be utilized as a pulse. It is now the second largest oilseed in India after groundnut. It grows in varied agro-climatic conditions. It has emerged as one of the important commercial crop in many countries. Due to its worldwide popularity, the international trade of Soybean is spread globally. Several countries such as Japan, China, Indonesia, Philippines, and European countries are importing Soybean to supplement their domestic requirement for human consumption and cattle feed.

Soybeans are legumes, native to East Asia, that are grown for oil and protein around the world. Cultivated primarily in warm and hot climates, soybeans were originally used as nitrogen fixers in early systems of crop rotation – ancient farmers would plant a field of soybeans on an exhausted or depleted field and then plow the crop under to replenish the soil. Development of use technologies such as fermentation and processing for oil has led to many new applications of this useful plant.

Soybean has great potential as an exceptionally nutritive and very rich protein food. It can supply the much needed protein to human diets, because it contains above 40 per cent protein of superior quality and all the essential amino acids particularly glycine, tryptophan and lysine, similar to cow's milk and animal proteins. Soybean also contains about 20 per cent oil with an important fatty acid, lecithin and Vitamin A and D. The 4 per cent mineral salts of soybeans are fairly rich in phosphorous and calcium.

Taxonomy and Natural History

Soybeans are native to East Asia, where they appear to have been cultivated from a wild species known as *glycine soja* starting about 5000 years ago. The semi-legendary Emperor Shennong, the "Divine Farmer" who is believed to have introduced agriculture to the peoples of China and Vietnam, is said to have listed soybeans as one of the "Five Sacred Plants," a list that also includes rice, wheat, barley and millet. Soybeans were also cultivated in Korea no later than 1000 BC, and in Japan from the time of the Roman Empire.

Soy belongs to the *fabaceae* or *leguminosae* (legume) family which also includes peanuts, chickpeas and other beans and pulses. This constitutes the third largest family of flowering plants, with well over 19,000 distinct species. Soybeans themselves are hard and rounded, and range in color from black to pale yellow. Although classified as a bean, a soybean is actually an oilseed like the peanut. Because of their high oil and protein content, soybeans are particularly useful for a variety of purposes.

Soybeans were introduced to Europe and the United States from colonial times. However, the plant was not cultivated in significant amounts outside of Asia until 1910. Since then, the balance of production has shifted; 55 per cent of the world soybean crop is harvested in the Americas.

Botany

Soybean belongs to family fabaxeae and sub-family papilionaceae. The soybean is an erect, bushy annual plant of great norphological diversity. The important morphological characters are described below:

Root

Soybean consists of tap root formed by the radical. Numerous secondary roots, arranged in four rows along the tap root, and several highly branched adventitious roots arising from lower portion of the hypocotyls are found in soybean plants, however, tap root has somewhat larger diameter. The root consists of nodules on their surface which are visible about 10 days after sowing and the root system becomes extensively nodulated at maturity. The depth of root system becomes extensively nodulated at maturity. The depth of root system depends upon soil type and cultural practices viz. in open soil types the tap roots may go as deep as 2 metres and the laterals up to 2.5 metres.

Stem

Stems are formed as a result of hypocotyls elongation of the seed axis which forms the lower portion of the stem. The height of stem and its branching habit depends upon variety. The forage types are very profusely branched with long prostate or horizontal creeping branches whereas they are short and erect in grain types. The stems are hairy or purbescent due to which they look whitish in colour and the hairs remain throughout life cycle of the plant.

Leaves

Soybean has four different types of leaves:

1. cotyledons or seed leaves which emerge with seedlings;
2. two simple primary leaves;
3. trifoliate leaves, and about;
4. the prophyllus.

Primary leaves are essentially oval in shape having petiole of about 1-2 cm length. All the leaves have pinnate venation. Simple primary leaves and seed leaves are arranged opposite while trifoliates are alternatively arranged on the stem. Each of the leaves has a pair of stipules at its base. The leaflets of trifoliate leave have glabrous and pubescent, though the extent of pubescence varies according to varieties. The fourth types of leaves are very tiny paired prophylls that are present at the base of each lateral branch. Inflorescence:

Two types of flowering have been observed in case of soybean - first type in case of indeterminate stems, in which the terminal bud continues to grow and produce axillary raceme type of inflorescence.in this case the pods are evenly distributed on the branches with a diminishing frequency towards the tops of the stems. The second type is in the determinate stems in which the growth of terminal bud ceases when it becomes an inflorescence. This type of stems have both axillary and terminal racemes and pods are found in dense clusters along the stems.

Flowers

Soybean flower is a typical papilionaceous flower with a tubular calyx of five unequal lobes, a five parted corolla that has a large posterior banner petal, two lateral wing petals andtwo anterior keel petals that are in contact but are not fused. The stamens compose a typical diadelphous androecium in qwhich the filaments of nine of the stamens are fused and elevated as a single structure with a posterior stamen remaning separate. By the time of pollination the diadelphous stamens have been elevated to a position so that the anthers form a ring around the stigma. Pollen thus is shed directly on the stigma, resulting in a high percentage of self fertilization. Natural crossing varies from less than 0.5 to about one per cent. Pollination may occur the day before full opening of the flower i.e it takes place within the bud.

Pods

Soybean pods are straight or slightly curved and vary in length from less than 2 cm up to 7 cm or more in some varieties. The pod colour at maturity varies from light yellow to yellow-grey, brown or black depending upon extent of carotene and xanthophylls pigments present on them. The number of pods varies from two to more than 20 on a single inflorescence and up to 400 on a single plant.

Seeds

The seeds are matured ovules development in pods. The fully developed seeds are formed after 35 to 45 days of blooming. The seeds continue to lose moisture, they change elongate rainform shape to more oval or spherical shape.

Soybeans as Food

Soybeans are primarily consumed by humans after being fermented and turned into a curd. Tofu, a bland, cheese-like substance made from the whey of fermented soybeans, is the most common example of this type of soybean application. Once known as the "Cow of the Orient," the soybean is about 40 per cent protein, 35 per cent carbohydrate, 20 per cent fatty oil and 5 per cent ash. It is one of the few plants that provide a complete protein, and is therefore often used as a substitute for meat and dairy products. Some food companies such as Morningstar Farms produce simulated bacon, sausage and hamburger from soy with taste and texture that is remarkably similar to the real thing. Because soy protein is quite stable at high temperatures, it is particularly suited to *wok* cooking and is a staple of many Chinese, Korean, Japanese and Southeast Asian dishes. Another common food use is in milk substitutes, such as soy milk. It was once thought that these applications were primarily modern, but words such as "soy milk" are at least 2000 years old and it is likely that such uses are in fact quite ancient.

Soybeans are highly versatile, and the beans can be processed into oil, flour, and meal. Each of these forms has many dietary uses, and soy is one of the more dietarily versatile legumes.

Soybean Controversies

In the U.S., soybeans are a chief source of vegetable oil. Because the oil is extracted with the use of the hydrocarbon chemical *hexane* and is usually hydrogenated in order to create semi-solid shortening, several sources have raised health concerns. Another concern, although one with less scientific grounding, is the production of genetically-modified soy. These GMO beans have been created in order to allow farmers to use certain pesticides, such as *Roundup®*, without causing harm to the plant itself. This advantage is such a enormous incentive to farmers that the proportion of genetically-modified soybeans has jumped from about 8 per cent in 1997 to 89 per cent by 2006. Some concern has been raised about preserving the diversity of the soybean genome, but Roundup modification has been added to nearly all strains, leading to a relatively steady level of genetic diversity in the species.

There are many claims about the health benefits of soy consumption; some scientists say that the *isoflavones* in soy help to prevent cancer, and the U.S. Food and Drug Administration recently approved health claims that soy consumption can lower cholesterol levels. However, another study showed that raw soybean flour induced pancreatic cancer in laboratory rats, although these rats were fed amounts far in excess of that which normal humans would normally ingest. Additionally, there have been no studies linking soy consumption and pancreatic cancer in humans, who do not normally eat uncooked flour in any event.

Some owners of diesel-powered vehicles have been fueling their cars with used, filtered soybean oil. However, in order to do this, modifications must be made to the fuel system so that the oil does not congeal under cold temperatures. Soybean oil when applied to the skin as also been shown to be effective at repelling mosquitoes and other insect pests.

Soybean Production

The U.S. has been the largest producer of soybeans, followed by Brazil. However, soybean production has been falling in the U.S. recently, a trend which may continue in spite of the increasing demand for soybeans, owing to competing demands for arable lands as pressure on food crops increases. In 2005, there was a total of 214.3 metric tons of soybeans harvested, over a third of which came from the U.S. This is expected to reach 280 metric tons in the next decade as the demand for biofuels increases. Most US soybeans are actually raised for export.

Soybeans: World Supply and Distribution (000' metric tons)

	2004/05	2005/06	2006/07	2007/08	2008/09
Production					
US	85,019	83,507	87,001	72,859	80,536
Brazil	53,000	57,000	59,000	61,000	59,000
Argentina	39,000	40,500	48,800	46,200	49,500
China	17,400	16,350	15,967	14,000	16,800
India	5,850	7,000	7,690	9,300	9,700
Paraguay	4,040	3,640	6,200	6,800	5,600
Canada	3,042	3,161	3,460	2,700	3,300
Other	8,422	9,513	9,428	8,028	8,765
Total	215,773	220,671	237,546	220,887	233,201
Imports					
China	25,802	28,317	28,726	37,816	36,000
EU-27	14,539	13,937	15,291	15,148	14,150
Japan	4,295	3,962	4,094	4,014	4,000
Mexico	3,640	3,667	3,844	3,650	3,585
Argentina	692	584	1,986	2,954	2,535
Taiwan	2,256	2,498	2,436	2,149	2,350
Thailand	1,517	1,473	1,532	1,733	1,650
Indonesia	1,112	1,187	1,309	1,200	1,300
Korea	1,240	1,190	1,231	1,231	1,260
Egypt	762	776	1,325	1,100	1,200
Other	7,629	6,489	7,280	7,640	7,907
Total	63,484	64,080	69,054	78,635	75,937
Exports					
United States	29,860	25,579	30,386	31,598	29,937
Brazil	20,137	25,911	23,485	25,364	25,250
Argentina	9,568	7,249	9,559	13,830	14,400
Paraguay	2,888	2,315	4,500	5,080	4,000
Canada	1,124	1,318	1,683	1,775	1,830
Other	1,210	1,408	1,889	1,830	1,771
Total	64,787	63,780	71,502	79,477	77,188

Soybeans grow best in temperatures between 68 and 86° F, and can grow in a wide range of soil types. The plant is susceptible to a number of bacterial diseases, including blight and wilt. Modern plants reach a height of about 1 meter, and take between 80 and 120 days from planting to harvest.

Nutritional Value of Edible Soybean

Components	Percentage
Proteins	40
Carbohydrates	30
Fibre	05
Lecithins	0.5
Saponins	04
Oil	18-20

Season

Soybean grows well in warm and moist climate. The climatic requirements for soybean are almost the same as for maize. A temperature of 26.5 to 30° C appears to be the optimum for most of the varieties. Soil temperatures of 15.5° C or above favour rapid germination and vigorous seedling growth. The minimum temperature for effective growth is about 10° C. A lower temperature tends to delay the flowering. Day length is the key factor in most of the soybean varieties as they are short day plant and are sensitive to photo-periods. Most of the varieties will flower and mature quickly if grown under condition where the day length is less than 14 hours provided that temperatures are also favourable. The time of planting is a very important consideration in soybean. In northern India soybean can be planted from third week of June to first fortnight of July.

Latest research results from the Department of Agricultural Research and Education, ICAR, Government of India, have shown that planting soybean in the last week of June results in maximum yield and after 7 July causes reduction in seed yield @ 40 kg/ha/day.

Soil

Well-drained and fertile loam soils with a pH between 6.0 and 7.5 are most suitable for the cultivation of soybean. Sodic and saline soils inhibit germination of seeds. In acidic soils, liming has to be done to raise the pH to about seven. Water logging is injurious to the crop.

Rotation

Mixed cropping of soybean with maize, mandua and sesamum has been found feasible and more remunerative. In mixed stand of maize and soybean, the yield of maize is not affected at the same time 10-12 quintals of soybean per hectare can be obtained. In mixed cropping of maize and soybean, plant maize at 100 cm row spacing keeping plant to plant distance 10 cm and three rows of soybean in between maize rows. Soybean has tremendous scope as an intercrop in arhar, cotton, and upland rice in northern India. In southern part of the country, soybean has a good scope as intercrop in sorghum, cotton, sugarcane, arhar and groundnut. In central India, soybean has been found very remunerative on the fallow lands in Kharif. In low rainfall areas of Madhya Pradesh it has been a common practice to keep the land fallow in Kharif to conserve moisture for a rainfed Rabi crop. It has been found that rainfed Rabi crops after Kharif fallow are generally low return crops. However, when soybean is grown in Kharif instead of keeping the land fallow, about 8-10 quintals of soybean per hectare can be obtained. This is more remunerative than the rainfed Rabi crops on Kharif fallow. And if the Kharif rains were substantial, a profitable Rabi crop could also be raised after Kharif soybean to yield a bonus. Some of the common rotations followed in north India are as given below:

- Soybean-wheat
- Soybean-potato
- Soybean-gram
- Soybean-tobacco
- Soybean-potato-wheat.

Cultivation

In general the preparation of the land for soybean should be the same as it is for maize. It requires a good seedbed with a reasonable fine texture and not too many clods. Land should be well leveled and be free from crop stubble. One deep ploughing with mould board plough followed by two harrowing or two ploughing with local plough are sufficient. There should be optimum moisture in the field at the time of sowing.

Sowing

The sowing should be done in lines 45 to 60 cm apart with the help of seed drill or behind the plough. Plant to plant distance should be 4-5 cm. The depth of sowing should not be more than 3-4 cm under optimum moisture conditions. If seed is placed deeper or there is crust formation just after sowing, the seed germination may be delayed and may result in a poor crop stand. Seed rate of soybean depends upon germination percentage, seed size and sowing time. If seed is of 80 per cent germination, 70-80 kg seed per hectare is required. For late planting and for spring crop, seed rate should be 100-120 kg per hectare.

Fertilizer and Nutrient Management

For obtaining good yields of soybean apply 15-20 tonnes of farm yard manure or compost per hectare. A good crop of soybean yielding about 30 quintals per hectare will remove about 300 kg nitrogen per hectare from the soil. But soybean being a legume crop has the ability to supply their own nitrogen needs provided they have been inoculated and there it efficient nodulation in the plant. An application of 20-30 kg nitrogen per hectare as a starter dose will be sufficient to meet the nitrogen requirement of the crop in the initial stage in low fertility soils having poor organic matter. Soybean requires relatively large amounts of phosphorus than other crops. Phosphorus is taken up by soybean plant throughout the growing season. The period of great demand starts just before the pods begin to form and continues until about ten days before the seeds are fully developed. The soil should be tested for the availability status of phosphorus to meet the requirement of the crop. With the application of phosphorus the number and density of nodules are stimulated and the bacteria becomes more mobile. Soybean also requires a relatively large amount of potassium than other crops. A crop of soybean yielding 30 quintals per hectare will remove about 100 kg potassium from the soil. The rate of potassium uptake climbs to a peak during the period of rapid vegetative growth then slows down about the time the bean begins to form. Soil test is the best guide for the application of potash in the soil. In the absence of soil test, 50-60 kg K_2O per hectare should be applied. The fertilizers should preferably be placed, at sowing time, about 5-7 cm away from the seed at a depth of 5-7 cm from seed level.

Water Management

The soybean crop generally does not require any irrigation during *Kharif* season. However, if there were a long spell of drought at the time of pod filling, one irrigation would be desirable. During excessive rains proper drainage is also equally important. Spring crop would require about five to six irrigation.

Zone-wise Major Commercial Varieties

Zone	State	Name of Variety
North zone	**Uttar Pradesh and Rajasthan**	Alankar, Ankur, Clark – 63, PK-1042, PK-262, PK-308, PK-327, PK-416, PK-564, Shilajeeth
Central zone	**Madhya Pradesh and Maharashtra**	Bragg, Calitur, Durga, Gaurav, Indira Soya -9, JS-2, JS-71-05, JS-75-46, JS-76-205, JS-79-81, JS-80-21, JS-90-41, JS-335, MACS-13, MACS-58, MAUS-47 (Parbhani Sona), MS-335, NRC-12(Ahilya-2), NRC-2(Ahilya-1), NRC-7(Ahilya-3), PK-472, PUSA-16, PUSA-22, PUSA-37, TYPE-49, MACS-57, MACS-450, MAUS-2, MAUS-1, MAUS-32(Prasad)
Southern zone	**Karnataka**	KB-79(Sneha), MACS-124, PUSA-40

Climatic Requirement

Soybean grows well at 15 to 32° C temperatures. But for rapid growth it needs slightly higher temperature. The crop does not grow if the temperature falls below 10° C but at the same time if it goes above 40° C the crop gets a greater setback in its growth, flowering, seed formation or even in the seed quality. It is reported that cold temperature lowers the oil content and requires about 60-65 cm annual rainfall. It needs irrigation if the rainfall is less than 65 cm; however higher rainfall is equally or more harmful than lower one because higher moisture at germination causes rotting of seeds and seedlings and at later stages of growth, excess water causes anaerobic conditions, poor nodulation and poor growth and yield of the crop. Drought at flowering or just before flowering results in flower and pod drops while rain during maturity impairs the grain quality of soybean.

Soil Requirement

It can be cultivated in all types of soil. Well-drained, fertile loam soil rich in organic matter is ideal for the cultivation of soybean. The soil should have pH ranges above 6. For acidic soil, liming is essential.

Cropping System

Soybean is grown as a sole crop or it may be intercropped with other suitable crops. With inter-cropping, the stability in production can be ensured and the control of pests and diseases can be done conveniently. Inter-cropping of maize and soybean, traditionally prevalent in Sikkim, is a good practice. Inter-crops like orange-soybean, tapioca-soybean, etc. can also be practised.

Field Preparation and Sowing

The land should be prepared properly by 3-4 ploughings during summer months to expose the harbouring insects and harmful micro-organisms to direct sunlight. This will help to minimize the pest population to some extent. The soil should be friable and free from weed growth. Before sowing it is better to level the land. Farm Yard Manure (FYM) or compost should be incorporated with the soil during final land preparation. The clods should be broken down into pieces to make the soil friable, porous and contour. Before sowing the soil moisture is to be ensured for better germination.

Seed Rate

About 70-80 kg seed per hectare is required for maintaining proper plant population.

Seed Germination Testing

Raising of a successful soybean crop mainly depends on the use of healthy seeds of suitable varieties considering the aspect of maturity group, the kind of soil and the possibility of virus and fungal diseases. It is always advisable to test seed germination by the farmer himself using common techniques like germination in beds, jute bags, towel paper, broken pitcher, pots, leaf cups, etc.

Seed Treatments

The available seeds are to be graded and treated with:

- ***Rhizobium japonicum***, the specific strain for soybean crop, *Azotobacter* and *Azospirillum*. The amount of culture should be 200 gm each per 10 kilogram of seed. It will help to fix atmospheric nitrogen in the nodules. The Rhizobium not only supplement nitrogen to plant in its growing phase but also provides residual nitrogen to successive crop after harvest of the previous crop and enables the crop to tolerate drought condition.

- **Phosphorus Solubilizing Microorganism (PSM).** In the soil the crop can absorb only 20 per cent of phosphorus and rest amount (80%) of phosphorus remains in soil in immobilizing form. Hence the seeds should be inoculated with PSM or Phosphatica which may have any bacteria/microorganism such as *Azospirillum awamorii, Pseudomonas striata, Bacillus polymixa, Penicillium* sp. etc. That breakdowns insolubale phosphorus in the soil so the plant can absorb soluble phosphorus and maintain plant growth/vigour.

There are three methods by which soybean seeds can be treated. The methods are as follows:

- **Seed treatment**: Depending on seed rate, the required amount of jaggery is boiled in water and cooled. Rhizobium inoculation is sprinkled, mixed in jaggery solution and dried in shade.
- **Soil treatment**: The Rhizobium inoculum is mixed with required amount soil and spread over the field.
- **Soil application**: If *Rhizobium inoculum* is not avalable, 200 kg of soil (2-10 cm surface soil) can be collected from a particular area, where Rhizobium had been applied before or leguminous crop had been cultivated luxuriantly, and this soil can be broadcasted over the field.

Spacing and Depth

Soybean can be sown by broadcasting or by line sowing methods. But it is always advisable to sow the seeds in line sowing method to get better plant stand. A distance of plant to plant =10 cm and row to row = 45 to 60 cm is maintained. The depth should be 3 cm. after sowing the seeds should be covered by a thin layer of soil by laddering.

Sowing

In Sikkim, soybean is a Kharif season crop and its sowing is done with the onset of monsoon.

- For obtaining desirable number of plants, sowing should be done in sufficiently moist field, at the depth of three cm.
- The seed rate for yellow/white/light brown four lakh plants per hectare can be obtained (i.e. 35-40 plants/sq. m) or in one meter long line there will be some 12 plants.
- Black soybean seeds are sown at the rate of 40-50 kg per hectare so that 2.00-2.50 lakh plants are obtained per hectare (i.e. 20-25 plants/sq. metre) or in one metre long row some 15 plants are obtained. If sowing is delayed due to any reason the seed rate should be increased by 25 per cent and row spacing should be reduced.

To increase production distance between lines is kept at 30-35 cm, then in sq. meter 40-45 plants (i.e. 4.50 lakh plants per hectare) can be obtained. Accordingly 10 per cent increase in yield can also be obtained.

Application of Culture in Standing Crop

Each of one kg Rhizobium two kg P.S.B. and one kg Azotobactor should be mixed separately with two basket full of dried F.Y.M. Then all the three heaps are to be mixed together. This is to be drilled in the standing crop or broadcast and thoroughly mixed with soil in between the rows of the crop at the age of 15-25 days. Application of bio-cultures by this technique in the standing crop not only enhances aeration in the soil, but enables bio-culture to reach roots/rhizosphore, whereby use-efficiency increases.

Nutrient Management

Soybean is a leguminous crop. Hence the nutrient requirement is lesser than any other crops. The FYM (Farm Yard Manure) @ 5-10 tonnes per hectare should be applied and incorporated with soil during final land preparation. The additional nutrient of crop should be met from green manuring, use of bio-fertilizers, vermicompost, etc.

Water and Irrigation

Soybean is a Kharif crop grown under rainfed condition in Sikkim. In heavy rainfall; it is necessary to provide proper drainage around the field to drain away the excess rain water to Jhoras or main drainage system. Water stagnation in the field should be avoided.

In the drier areas of the State, water harvesting should be followed to manage water for crop in time. Rain water is the nature's precious gift; collect it and conserve. For this purpose, channels or furrows are prepared around the field. A water harvesting structure should be constructed in each field for conserving drainage water and using it at the time of need. The field should be free from weeds. The channels prepared through up of the crop in lines should be obstructed at certain for impounding rain water in furrows.

Soybean plants indicate requirement of water if leaf drooping starts even in the early hours (9.00 am). In that case, it is necessary to the crop.

- Irrigation channels are to be prepared after sowing the crop. If there is no rain during flowering or grain filling stage, irrigation must be given. The irrigation during these stages increases yield by one and half times. If irrigation is not given then the yield reduces drastically.
- By sprinkler irrigation more area can be covered with lesser amount of water in a short time. By this method water can be used proficiently. About 70 per cent water can be saved by this method and this can be utilized for other crop too.

Weed Management

The field should be free from weed to optimize the efficient use of nutrient, sunlight, water and space. Manual weeding is generally followed to keep the weed population below economic threshold level. Bullock driven small blade harrow should be used time to time for loosening the soil and for removal of weeds. The soybean seeds before sowing should be free from weed seeds as far as possible. Mulching the field with dry grasses protects soil borne microbes, at the same time they increase the organic carbon content of the soil and conserve the soil moisture. Precaution needs to be taken so that prescribed dose is used with proper method in the following manner.

Disease Management

Soybean crop is vulnerable to different insect pests and diseases, which results into considerable loss in yield. It is, therefore, necessary to adopt integrated plant protection measures as follows:

Cultural Measures

1. Cultivation should be done in time.
2. The stubbles and other plant residues should be collected and are to be used in compost making.
3. Varieties should be selected that they are early maturing and are resistant to pests and diseases.
4. Sowing should be done in the whole area within a short span of time.
5. Adopt inter-cropping method of sowing /planting.
6. During inspection and survey, light traps, pheromone trap, etc. are to be used.
7. For perching/sitting of birds, 4-5 perching places should be provided.
8. Maize and the millet plants provide place for predators and parasites.

Biological Control of Insects Diseases

There are some 20 different kinds of parasites, predator insects and birds which control the insect pests and diseases in soybean. In controlling Girdle beetle, predators like Crysopa and pentamoid bug are found to be quite successful. Required predators should be obtained from the production centres and released in the field. By using Trichogramma and N.P.V. (Nuclear Polyhedrosis Virus), Spodoptera and Heliothis can be controlled. By using the bacteria *Bacillus thuringiensis* (*Bt*) the control of the larvae of Lepidopterran insects are possible.

HARVESTING AND POST-HARVEST CARE

Harvesting Care

The following harvesting care should be taken:

1. Soybean should be harvested, when leaves start falling and pods look dry, but before getting dried completely.
2. The moisture in the seeds at the time of harvesting should not be more than 14 per cent.
3. Harvesting before maturity means a low yield and also a higher proportion of immature seeds, poor quality and more chances of disease attack during storage of grain.

4. Delay in harvesting results in grain shattering and cracking of grains in the pods and exposure to insects, rodents, birds and pests attack.
5. Avoid harvesting during wet weather conditions.
6. Harvesting should be done by adopting proper method.
7. Protect the harvested grains from rain and excessive dew by covering.
8. Keep the harvested grains separately for each variety, to get true to type variety seed.
9. Dry harvested crop for 8-10 days at the threshing floor.
10. Avoid direct sun drying and excessive drying, which leads to an increase in breakage of the grains.
11. During delayed Threshing, keep the harvested Soybean in a dry and shady place, which facilitates the air circulation and prevents excessive heating.
12. Transport the grain in bags, which minimises the grain losses.
13. Avoid too much post harvest handling to minimise the grain losses.
14. Pack the Soybean in sound B-Twill jute bags totally free from any contamination.

Post-harvest Care

To following measures should be followed to minimise the post-harvest losses.

1. Timely harvest at optimum moisture percentage (not more than 14%).
2. Use of proper method of harvesting.
3. Avoid the losses in threshing and winnowing by adopting better mechanical methods.
4. Precaution must be taken to avoid severe beating in threshing operation, as it may decrease the germination of the seeds.
5. Avoid excessive drying, fast drying and rewetting of grains.
6. Ensure uniform drying to avoid hot and wet spots on grain and mechanical damage in handling.
7 Adopt the grading practices to get more profit.
8. Use efficient and good packaging for storage and transportation.
9. Use proper scientific technique in storage for maintaining optimum moisture content i.e. less than 9 per cent.
10. Use pest control measures (fumigation) before storage.
11. Provide aeration to stored grain and stir bulk grain occasionally.
12. Move stocks in sacks to discourage pest incidence and their multiplication.
13. Proper handling (loading and unloading) of Soybean with good transportation facilitates helps in reduction in losses at farm and market levels.

GRADING

Grading is an important facilitating service in the marketing process of an agricultural commodity. It has been observed that uniform variety having bold grains fetch higher price in the market. Soybean price depends on the basis of following quality parameter:

(a) Cleanliness
(b) Boldness
(c) Colour
(d) Moisture
(e) Shrinkage
(f) Admixture
(g) Oil content, etc.

Importance

1. To get higher price of the produce and facilitates marketing.
2. It widens the marketing process because buying and selling take place between two parties at distant places.
3. It reduces the cost of marketing and minimises storage losses.
4. It facilitates the keeping quality of the produce.
5. It promotes easy finance.
6. It facilitates to settle the claims in dispute.
7. It facilitates the future trading.

Steps for Grading

1. **Cleaning and sorting**: After arrival, entire produce should be cleaned and sorted manually/mechanically to separate the foreign matter, dust, dirt and stone particles, admixture of other seeds, husks, immature, split, shriveled, damaged and diseased grains.
2. **Packing and sealing**: The cleaned and sorted homogeneous produce is to be filled in gunny bags and then packed and sealed.
3. **Sampling**: For grading of a lot, the drawing of truly representative sample is essential and is done in such a way so that it represent the exact composition of the commodity. The sample is then packed, coded and sealed.
4. **Analysis**: The analysis of the sample should be done as per prescribed grade specifications.
5. **Grading and certification**: Grade is confirmed by analytical method and certificate is given on the basis of result of the analysis.

Salient Features of Sampling

1. **Primary sample:** Each sample drawn from the heap or bag by parkhi or tube sampler from a single position of the lot.
2. **Composite sample:** Primary samples drawn from the same lot shall be thoroughly mixed and blended to form homogeneous composite sample in a sample divider.
3. **Test sample:** One portion of composite sample weighing 500 gms is packed in cloth bag.
4. **Sample for moisture:** Part of the composite sample weighing about 150gms. packed in polythene bag and heat sealed kept in airtight container.

5. **Labelling of sample:** Appropriate labels are affixed with cloth bags and polythene bags samples showing the following particulars:
   (a) Name of the commodity and variety
   (b) Lot number
   (c) Quantity, whether in bags or in bulk
   (d) Place and date of sampling
   (e) Details of wagon/truck/warehouse in the case of bulk samples
   (f) Name of sampling officer
   (g) Signature

Sampling Procedure

The Soybean falls under the medium oilseed. The sample of Soybean consignment may be taken from bulk and bags. The consignment broken in lots and sub-lots to get representative sample of the same species, variety, type, grade source and the year of production. Depending on the size and uniformity of the lot, the number of sub-lots may be two or more as indicated for consignments in bags and in bulk.

One representative gross sample shall be obtained from each sub-lot. Thus there will be as many gross samples as the number of sub-lots in a lot. The samples for tests shall be prepared from the gross sample. In order to achieve randomness in selection of bags, the following procedure may be adopted:

Starting from any bag count them in one order as 1,2,3….. up to r, r being the integral part of N/n, where N is the total number of bags and n the number of bags to be selected. Every rth bag thus counted is withdrawn to constitute the sample.

In India, soybean cultivation has increased tremendously. It is grown in an area of 8.32 m ha with a production of 8.85 mt and productivity of 1063 kg/ha. Among the different States, Madhya Pradesh ranks first both in area (4.76 m ha) and production (4.78 mt) where as Andhra Pradesh ranks first in productivity (1,515 kg/ha) followed by Rajasthan (1,203 kg/ha). In Karnataka, soybean is grown over an area of 0.13 million ha with a production of 0.09 mt and productivity of 718 kg/ha. Karnataka contributes 1.56 per cent of area to the total area in India and 1.02 per cent of production to the total production in India. As the soybean area has expanded with the introduction of high yielding varieties with wide adaptability, there has been a considerable change in agronomic and cultural practices.

One consequence is a sudden and drastic alteration of the plant micro-environment favouring the development of more and new diseases with increased incidence. There are hundreds of non-viral pathogens (NVP) known to attack soybean, of which 35 are economically important. Soybean is also prone to be attacked by viruses or viral strains. Among the viral diseases, six viral diseases are believed to have some economic significance in India. These are Soybean mosaic potyvirus (SMV), Mungbean yellow mosaic geminivirus (MVMV), Cowpea mild mottle carlavirus (CPMMV), Chlorotic mottle bromovirus (CMV), Peanut bud Necrosis tospo Virus (PBNV) & *Tobacco ring spot* nepovirus (TRSV). Currently the emerging viral disease is bud blight of soybean.

Bud blight of soybean was first described in the United States in 1941. In India it was observed for the first time in Kangra (Himachal Pradesh) in 1972. It was then sporadically reported from Maharashtra, Rajasthan, Uttar Pradesh and Madhya Pradesh. It was severe in most of the soybean growing areas of Madhya Pradesh during monsoon, 1987. Later the disease has occurred with an increasing regularity in various parts of the country such as New Delhi, Karnataka, Maharashtra, Madhya Pradesh etc.

The incidence ranged from 25-40 per cent in Sehore district of Madhya Pradesh and at Delhi, the incidence varied from 50 to 100 per cent. Due to this incidence the yield was reduced to 92 per cent in India. In-general, the losses were greatest when young plants were infected. Soybean plants infected at pre-bloom stage did not produce any seeds. However, post-blooming infection may allow the production of some seeds. Yield was lowered by reduced plant height and reduced pod set. Seed formation on infected plants reduced 1,000 grain weight and increased number and empty pods.

In India, the virus causing bud blight of soybean was identified as *Tobacco ring spot virus*. Researchers from Maharashtra also reported as *Tobacco ring spot virus*. But in the upcoming years there have been a lot of controversial statements and arguments regarding the exact etiology of bud blight disease of soybean.

Researchers reported Peanut bud Necrosis tospo Virus (PBNV) as the cause of bud blight of soybean from Chhattisgarh. Researchers reported that the bud blight of soybean is caused by *Groundnut Bud Necrosis Virus* (GBNV) based on nucleo capsid protein (N) gene sequencing.

Uses

Soybean can be used for various purposes. The following are uses of soybean:

(a) Broken grain:

- The broken grain of soybean is used as food material for cattle, birds, fish, honey bees etc.
- It is used for the preparation of different items like noodles, food drinks, candy, etc.
- For the preparation of alcohol.

(b) Soybean oil:

- IT is used for culinary purposes. It is also used for margarine, pharmaceuticals, sandwich spreads, and coffee whitener's purposes.
- Soybean oil is used for the preparation of soap, pesticides, fungicides, weedicides, cement etc.

(c) Soybean grain:

- As seed,
- As food for birds, cattle etc.
- For bakery items, candy etc.

(d) Soybean plant:

- Soybean plant is sometimes used as cattle feed.

2

Major Groups of Plant Pathogens

Plant Disease

A plant disease is any abnormal condition that alters the appearance or function of a plant. It is a physiological process that affects some or all plant functions and may reduce the quality and/or quantity of the harvested product.

Disease is a process or a change that occurs over time. It does not occur instantly like many noninfectious disorders (e.g., herbicide injury or lightning strike).

Visible effects of disease on plants are called symptoms. Any detectable change in colour, shape and/or function of the plant in response to a pathogen or disease-causing agent is a symptom. Leaf spots or blights, discolouration of plant tissue, stunting and wilting are symptoms that may be evidence of disease.

Symptoms can occur throughout the plant or be confined to localized tissues. Although certain symptoms can be used to identify a particular disease, a number of pathogens may cause the same or similar symptoms. Furthermore, symptoms often change over time and are influenced by environmental conditions and can vary among soybean varieties. Signs of plant disease are physical evidence of the pathogen, for example, fungal fruiting bodies, bacterial ooze or nematode females. Signs also can help with plant disease identification.

What causes Plant Disease?

Infectious plant diseases are caused by organisms that obtain their nutrition from the plants they infect. The parasitic organism that causes a disease is called a pathogen. Plants infected by a pathogen and serving as its food source are referred to as hosts – in this case the host is the soybean plant. Fungi, bacteria, viruses and nematodes are pathogens of soybeans in Iowa. Plants may be simultaneously infected by more than one pathogen.

A favourable environment is critically important for disease development. Even the most susceptible plants exposed to large amounts of a pathogen will not develop disease unless environmental conditions are favourable. Environmental conditions can affect disease development in two ways: directly affecting plant pathogens and/or causing soybeans to be more prone to attack by some pathogens. Temperature and moisture are the most important environmental factors; relative humidity, soil pH, soil texture, light and nutrient status also may affect disease development. Soil compaction, tillage practices, planting depth, seed bed preparation and residue management affect how soybean plants respond to particular environmental conditions.

Plant Disease Triangle

A susceptible host plant, a pathogen and a favourable environment are the three factors composing the plant disease triangle (Fig. 2.1). All three factors are necessary for development of a plant disease; thus, disease can be affected by altering any of these three factors.

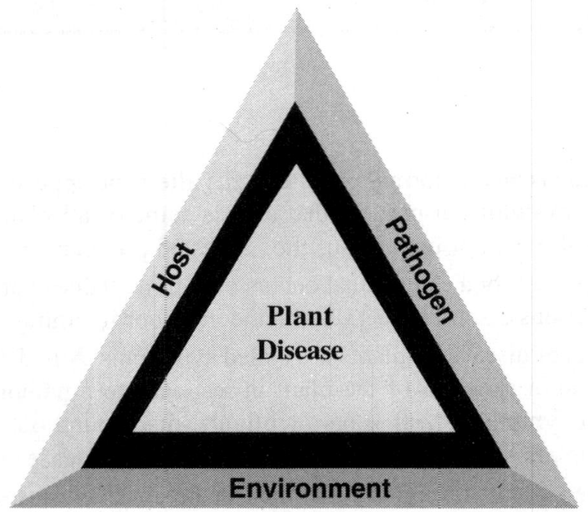

Fig. 2.1: **Plant Disease Triangle**

Fungi

Fungi are the largest and perhaps most well-known group of plant pathogens. The vast majority of fungi, however, do not cause disease. Many help decompose organic matter, releasing nutrients for plants and other organisms to use. However, numerous fungi can cause plant disease, and a relatively small number of them cause disease in humans and livestock. Most plant pathogenic fungi are extremely small and, except for possible extensive growth on the surface of a plant, normally cannot be seen without a microscope.

Most fungi are composed of delicate, thread-like filaments called hyphae. Hyphae absorb water and nutrients needed for growth and reproduction of the fungi. Hyphae may also secrete enzymes, toxins and other chemical substances that may be important factors in disease development and symptom expression. A mass of hyphae is referred to as mycelium. The "fuzzy" fungal growth that is sometimes visible on plant surfaces is this mycelium. Oftentimes, however, mycelium develops completely or primarily inside the host and is not visible on the plant's surface.

Most fungi reproduce by producing spores, which can be seen with a microscope. Spores are carried to plants primarily by wind and water. Some types of spores are produced inside structures called fruiting bodies, that may be seen on or in plant tissues. Spores and fruiting bodies are often used to identify a fungus. Some spores and fruiting bodies are resistant to adverse environmental conditions and can survive in soil or decaying plant material for a long time. Some fungi produce specialized resting structures known as sclerotia or microsclerotia. These structures are compacted masses of hyphae and stored foods that can endure long periods of unfavourable conditions.

Fungi can cause a variety of symptoms including leaf spots and blights, root rots, seedling blights, seed discolouration, wilts and stem rots.

Bacteria

Bacteria are perhaps more familiar to us as the cause of important human and animal diseases, such as tuberculosis and pneumonia. However, most bacteria are harmless and many are even beneficial, such as the nitrogen-fixing bacteria that form nodules on soybean roots. Nonetheless, some bacteria can also be destructive plant pathogens.

Bacteria are extremely small microorganisms, much smaller than fungal spores. They reproduce by individual cells splitting into nearly equal halves, each becoming a fully developed bacterium. A bacterial population may increase to very high numbers within a short period of time. For example, if a bacterium divided every 30 minutes, a single cell would produce more than 250 trillion descendants in 24 hours.

As bacteria divide, the cells tend to clump together in masses called colonies. Bacterial cells and colonies vary in size, shape, colour and growth habit. These characteristics are used to identify specific bacteria.

Bacteria cannot make their own food; they must obtain it either from dead or decaying organic matter, or living tissue. Nearly all bacteria have the ability to grow and develop on dead tissue. Most plant pathogenic bacteria do not compete well with other organisms in the soil in the absence of their host plant, so their populations may decline rapidly when the host plant is not grown. Bacteria are primarily spread from plant to plant by wind-driven rain and gain entrance into host tissues through natural plant openings. Wounds in plant tissues from insects, hail, wind or other causes also provide entry points for bacteria.

Typical symptoms of bacterial diseases include leaf spots, water soaking and soft rots of plant tissues.

Viruses

Like bacteria, viruses are probably most familiar to us as the cause of human and animal diseases, such as influenza, polio, rabies, smallpox and warts. Viruses, however, also cause several plant diseases.

Viruses are infectious, disease-producing particles that can only be seen with a very high magnification electron microscope. Virus particles are very small, measuring only about one-millionth of an inch. Viruses multiply by causing host cells to form more viruses instead of performing normal cell processes.

Almost all viruses can survive only in living cells. Therefore, their spread from diseased to healthy plants depends on some means of direct movement from host to host. Many viruses are transmitted by insects, called vectors, particularly aphids and leafhoppers. Some viruses are transmitted when equipment or people spread sap or juice from diseased plants to healthy plants. This type of mechanical transmission may happen by simple leaf contact between healthy and diseased plants.

Typical viral symptoms include mosaic patterns on leaves, deformation of plant tissues, stunting, seed discolouration and reduced yield.

Nematodes

Nematodes are microscopic, non-segmented, round, slender worms. Several thousand species of nematodes are found in soil, in fresh and salt water, in animals and within or on plants throughout the world.

Nematodes are aerobic animals that require oxygen, which they absorb from water through their body wall. Most nematodes feed on dead or decaying organic material. Some are parasites on animals, plants, insects, fungi or other nematodes.

A single acre of cultivated soil may contain hundreds of millions of nematodes, but due to their small size, they are seldom, if ever, seen. Most adult parasitic nematodes of plants cannot be seen unless magnified. They rarely exceed 1/8 inch and may be smaller than 1/64 inch.

Plant-parasitic nematodes have a hollow, needle-like feeding structure called a stylet that is used to puncture plant cells. Nematodes inject substances into host plant cells through their stylets and then withdraw nutrition from the plant cells through their stylets.

The life cycle of a nematode includes an egg, four juvenile stages and an adult. Females lay eggs that hatch into juveniles. Juveniles molt between stages and become adults, and the egg-laying process is repeated. The life cycle of a plant-parasitic nematode can take 20 to 60 days to complete.

Nematodes survive winters mainly in the egg stage. Most plant-parasitic nematodes live in the soil and feed in or on plant roots. Some nematodes live part or all of their lives inside plant roots.

Most important, plant-parasitic nematodes feed on plant roots and directly interfere with water and nutrient uptake by the plant. Root injury from nematodes causes aboveground symptoms similar to those produced by other conditions that damage root systems. Plants frequently appear to be suffering from lack of moisture or nutrient deficiency, even when water and minerals are adequate. When nematodes occur in high population densities, stunting, yellowing, loss of vigor, general decline and eventual death of plants are typical aboveground symptoms.

Non-infectious Disorders

Non-infectious disorders are caused by nonliving agents or factors. A noninfectious disorder can be caused by any physical or chemical component of the environment that is harmful to the plant's growth and development. Examples of noninfectious disorders are temperature and moisture extremes, hail, wind, lightning, unfavourable light, improper soil nutrient levels, toxic chemicals and mechanical damage.

Differences between Non-infectious Disorders and Plant Diseases

Noninfectious disorders cannot reproduce or spread from plant to plant. Symptoms of noninfectious disorders may appear suddenly and often occur in patterns across a field. Although symptoms on individual plants may change by becoming progressively better or worse, the area of a field that is affected will not increase over time. These points help differentiate noninfectious disorders from plant diseases.

A common example of a noninfectious disorder is herbicide injury. Herbicide injury can occur from drift onto soybeans from a neighboring field or if a sprayer used to treat the field was contaminated. If the symptoms appear in a drift pattern, then herbicide injury is a logical explanation.

Noninfectious disorders may produce symptoms such as wilting, stunting, yellowing, deformation or death of plant tissues. Symptoms of some types of non-infectious disorders are similar to those of certain fungal and viral diseases (Fig. 2.2).

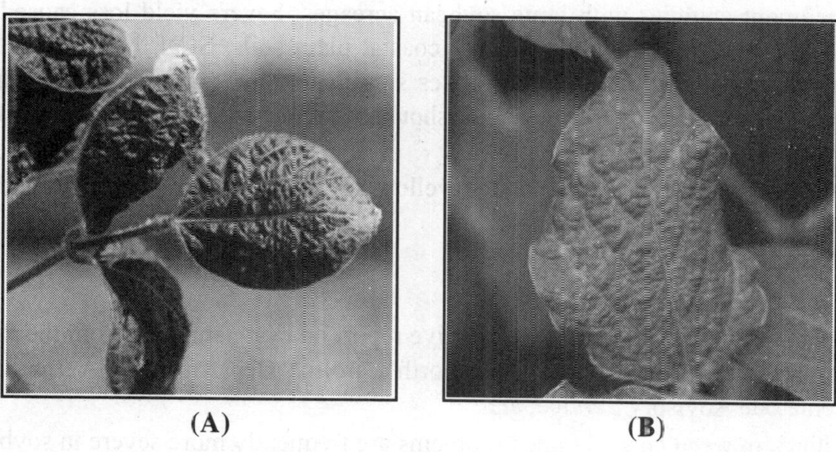

(A) (B)

Fig. 2.2: **Herbicide injury (A) can appear similar to virus symptoms (B)**

Plants stressed by non-infectious disorders may be more prone to attack by infectious diseases. For example, soybean plants stressed by herbicide injury may be more prone to root rot diseases. Problems on field crops frequently occur in combination, so when diagnosing a problem, all possible causes or combinations of causes must be carefully considered.

3

Soybean Cyst Nematode

Introduction

Soybean cyst nematode (SCN) (*Heterodera glycines*) is the most serious soybean disease problem in North Carolina. Since its discovery in North Carolina (and the United States) in 1954, it has spread to all counties in the Coastal Plain, Tidewater, and some Piedmont counties with large soybean acreages. Severe yield loss caused by this pest is especially common in sandy coastal plain soils. SCN, however, is not restricted to any soil type and often causes significant soybean yield losses which may go unnoticed. Soybean cyst nematode should be suspected as a possible production problem if any of the following apply:

1. irregular patches of stunted and/or yellow soybeans - an up-and-down pattern of soybean growth is common;
2. soybeans grown without rotation;
3. yields declining over several years;
4. detection of cysts on roots or a positive report on cyst nematode from the Plant Disease and Insect Clinic or the North Carolina Department of Agriculture, Nematode Advisory Service; and
5. failures in weed control (weed problems are frequently more severe in soybean cyst nematode infested fields).

The second-stage juvenile, or J2, nematode is the only life stage that can penetrate roots. (The first-stage juvenile occurs in the egg, and third- and fourth-stages occur in the roots). The J2 enters the root moving through the plant cells to the vascular tissue where it feeds. The J2 induces cell division in the root to form specialized feeding sites. As the nematode feeds, it swells. The female swells so much that her posterior end bursts out of the root and she becomes visible to the naked eye. In contrast, the adult male regains a wormlike shape, and he leaves the root in order to find and fertilize the large females. The female continues to feed as she lays 200 to

400 eggs in a yellow gelatinous matrix, forming an egg sac which remains inside her. She then dies and her cuticle hardens forming a cyst. The eggs may hatch when conditions in the soil are favourable, the larvae developing inside the cyst and the biological cycle repeating itself. There are usually three generations in the year. In the autumn or in unfavourable conditions, the cysts containing dormant larvae may remain intact in the soil for several years. Although soybean is the primary host of SCN, other legumes can also serve as hosts.

Microscopic worms burrowing through cells, injecting foreign compounds through hypodermic-needle-like structures, altering the basic biology of the cells being fed upon. Worms that grow so large in just a few weeks that they rupture out of the tissue they are feeding upon. Sound like a science fiction movie plot? Believe it or not, it is the basic biology of a widespread, serious pathogen of soybeans - the soybean cyst nematode.

Symptoms and Signs

High population densities of the soybean cyst nematode (SCN) can result in large portions of soybean fields with plants that are severely stunted and yellow. More frequently, however, few aboveground symptoms of SCN can be observed - yet soybean yield losses of 10-20 per cent or more can be attributed to SCN damage in these fields. This hidden cause of yield loss has presented a major problem for growers who must learn to recognize when their fields are infested with SCN. Reduced yields in SCN-infested fields often are attributed to adverse cultural or environmental conditions rather than to SCN - a tragic mistake that leads to increased SCN infestation and damage in subsequent years. Also, the age and vigor of the soybean plants, the nematode population density in the soil, soil fertility and moisture levels, and other environmental conditions influence the intensity of the symptoms. Soybean cyst nematode damage usually is more severe in light, sandy soils, but will occur readily in all types of soil.

The whitish-yellow adult females of SCN on the outside of roots dug from the field are a telltale sign of SCN infestation that can be easily seen. The SCN females are lemon-shaped, slightly less than 1 mm in diameter, and considerably smaller than *Bradyrhizobium* root nodules. Reduced nodulation was associated with infection of soybean roots by populations of SCN identified as race 1. Analysis of soil and root samples by a diagnostic lab, however, is the only reliable means to confirm SCN diagnosis. The vermiform (worm-shaped) juvenile and adult males can be extracted from soil samples, as well as the brown cysts (dead female body containing eggs) and freed eggs in the soil. Developing SCN juveniles and females can be observed in stained soybean root samples. Diagnostic labs also can estimate the population density of SCN in a field to provide recommendations of SCN management options. Determination of the race of SCN in a field is a laborious task, and it may or may not be helpful in choosing a soybean cultivar for that site.

Pathogen Biology

Early reports of the cyst-forming nematodes on soybeans from Asia classified them as variants of the sugar beet cyst nematode, *Heterodera schachtii*, and occasionally as the pea cyst nematode, *Heterodera goettingiana*. Ichinohe described the soybean cyst nematode (SCN) as a distinct species, *H. glycines*, in 1952. Morphological features of the adults of SCN are used for species identification. SCN adults are sexually dimorphic, meaning that they are dissimilar in appearance. The females are swollen and sedentary, and the males are vermiform (worm-shaped) and motile. Only the swollen female stage on the surface of soybean roots can be seen with the naked eye – the male and juvenile stages must be extracted from soil or plant roots and viewed under a microscope.

The second-stage juveniles (J2) of SCN are worm-shaped, 375-520 µm long, and about 18 µm in diameter. The overall body shape of the nematode is determined by the pressure of its internal body fluids pushing against its strong, but flexible, outer "cuticle" (like a water balloon). The outside of the cuticle has a series of fine rings (annulations), like an accordion, that allows the cuticle to bend at any point along the nematode's body. The cuticle is composed mainly of the structural protein collagen, and the cuticle is molted four times to allow growth and maturation of the nematode. The "head" of the nematode can be recognized by the presence of a short, dark spear with basal knobs (the "stylet") just inside the tip of the head. The stylet is hollow (like a hypodermic needle) and protrudes from the head when used by the nematode for feeding from plant cells and penetrating plant tissues. The very outer tip of the nematode head above the stylet (called the "lip" region) is slightly elevated, rounded, and darkened in J2 of SCN. In a relatively clear area just below the stylet, a round, muscular pumping organ called the metacorpus can be seen - the metacorpus pumps substances (i.e., food and secretions) up and down the esophagus of the nematode. Just below the metacorpus is another relatively translucent area that contains three esophageal glands that overlap the nematode's intestine on the ventral (stomach) side of its body. The intestine can be recognized as a fairly long, dark area extending from the esophageal glands to the tail of the nematode. The tail of SCN J2 tapers uniformly to a fine, rounded tip that is hyaline (clear).

Adult females of SCN are the most easily diagnosed stage for this species. The females are lemon-shaped, ranging from 500 to 900 µm long and 200 to 700 µm wide. The female's stylet is slender with knobs that project slightly backward. The vulva and anus collectively form a cone-shaped projection from the rear of the female's body, giving them a characteristic "lemon" shape. The SCN females swell and molt through the juvenile life stages until they protrude from the plant roots. The adult females of SCN are initially white (on the root surface), and their heads are buried within the root for feeding. As the female ages, she turns yellow and eventually brown as she dies. Her body becomes a protective cyst encasing the eggs.

Adult males of SCN are worm-shaped and relatively long, compared to second-stage juveniles. They are 1,200 to 1,400 µm long and 26 to 30 µm wide. Although the head, stylet, and esophagus are similar to second-stage juveniles, the tail is short with a blunt, rounded terminus. An easy, defining characteristic of males is the presence of two dark hooks (called "spicules") that are always present at the opening of the testis near the tail.

Diagnosis

Diagnosis of cyst-nematode problems on soybean can be accomplished by several means. Generally, a soil sample must be processed in order to positively identify the nematode problem. If you suspect a nematode problem, take systematic (stratified) soil samples in the fall when nematode numbers are high. Pull 20 to 30 soil cores 6 to 8 inches deep from 4 to 5 acres. Send soil in a plastic bag and appropriate box (obtained from county Extension agent) along with the appropriate form and payment to the North Carolina Department of Agriculture, Agronomic Services, Nematode Advisory and Diagnostic Lab, 4300 Reedy Creek Road, Raleigh, NC 27607. If you know you have soybean cyst nematode, you may request an egg assay from the NCDA. Numbers of SCN eggs are more indicative of the severity of the problem, but egg assays may overlook other nematode problems. If you detect a problem during the growing season, plant and soil samples should be taken. Infected plants (stunted, but not dead) should be carefully dug from the soil. Small, white to yellow cysts (about the size of the head of a pin) on the root system indicate that cyst nematode is a problem. If you cannot identify cysts on roots, your county extension agent can assist you in identification, or forward the samples (soil and roots) to the Plant Disease & Insect Clinic or to the NCDA Nematode Advisory Service for diagnosis. Analysis of the soil and/or root sample for nematodes has the advantage that it may reveal other nematode or disease problems. Include an accurate crop history (including soybean varieties planted previously). Information about fertility, herbicides and cultural practices can also aid in diagnosis.

Disease Cycle and Epidemiology

Like all nematodes, the soybean cyst nematode (SCN) has six life stages - egg, four juvenile stages (J1-J4), and the adult stage. The duration of the SCN life cycle runs from 3-4 weeks, but this may be influenced by environmental conditions (mainly adequate temperature and moisture). Depending upon the environment, several generations of SCN can be completed in a typical soybean growing season. After embryonic development within the egg to the first-stage juvenile, the nematode goes through four molts to the adult stage. The molt to second-stage juvenile (J2) occurs within the eggshell, and it is the J2 that emerges from the egg. Egg hatch seems to have evolved as a survival strategy in SCN. A low percentage of SCN eggs appear to hatch spontaneously - it has been suggested that these eggs are the ones that are laid in a gelatinous matrix outside the female body. A significant proportion of eggs that are retained within cysts are in a dormant state - they do not hatch until soybeans are planted for the next growing season. It is hypothesized that exudates from soybean roots provide the hatching signals for dormant SCN. Another proportion of eggs within cysts do not hatch, even when conditions are favourable - they are in a state termed diapause. Diapause appears to be a time-mediated hatching process, the basis of which is not presently understood.

The J2 is the infective stage of SCN. The J2 migrates in soil and penetrates plant roots completely, usually just behind the root tip. The J2 moves intracellularly to the root vascular tissue, often leaving a zone of visible root necrosis along their migratory path within the root. The J2 uses thrusts of its stylet and secretes cell-wall-degrading enzymes (cellulases) to migrate directly through plant cells. When the J2 reaches the root vascular tissue, nematode stylet secretions modify selected plant cells into an elaborate feeding site called a syncytium. The J2 will not continue development unless a syncytium is formed for feeding. The syncytium is a large, metabolically active feeding site that becomes multinucleate as neighboring plant cells are incorporated into the syncytium by cell wall dissolution and cell fusion. The J2 feeds from the syncytium and begins to swell and become immobile.

The subsequent juvenile stages molt and continue to enlarge as the nematode feeds. Approximately half of the juveniles will become swollen females, and the majority of the female body (except for the head) breaks through the root surface and becomes visible on the surface of the root. Males develop coiled within the swollen J4 cuticle, and they emerge from the cuticle and root as motile, vermiform adult nematodes.

It has been documented that a higher percentage of males is produced when the nematodes or host plants are under stress. Males do not feed, but they are required for sexual reproduction (copulation) with females that are exposed on the root surface. After fertilization, the majority of the 200-600 eggs produced by the female are retained within its body, but some eggs may be laid in a gelatinous matrix extruded from the posterior (vulva) of the female. As the gravid female dies, its cuticle becomes a brown, hardened structure (the cyst) that encases and protects hundreds of viable eggs. Cysts often fall from roots and remain free in the soil.

Epidemiology

As with many plant-parasitic nematodes in soil, soybean cyst nematodes do not move far from the root zone that they currently infest. In most cases, the natural migration of SCN within a field is defined as "contagious" – small patches of infested areas that gradually enlarge to encompass significant areas of disease. Diseased areas become much more pronounced in sections of soybean fields that are under environmental stress (i.e., insufficient fertilization or water, extreme temperatures). The spread of these nematodes within fields usually is accelerated by cultural practices of the grower (i.e., dissemination of nematodes by soil cultivation). SCN can be introduced to uninfested sites via poorly sanitized farm equipment and within soil peds (small, seed-size clumps of dried soil) within contaminated seed stocks. SCN is not transmitted inside individual seeds nor on the seed surface (SCN is not "seed borne"). The cysts of SCN are lightweight and can survive desiccation. They can be transmitted in surface water, by wind, and also by the movement of animals. It can take from 5-9 years from the time of introduction of SCN into a field until the SCN populations reach detectable levels. By that time, infestation with SCN has become a permanent problem in that site.

Races of Soybean Cyst Nematode

Field populations of SCN are characterized as races 1 through 16. A race of cyst nematode is an indication of a field populations' ability to reproduce on selected soybean host differentials (a set of varieties or breeding lines). Knowing the race of cyst nematode in a given field can assist the grower in making decisions about which resistant varieties should be utilized. For example, if a field has race 1 or 3, then selection of a variety resistant to these races would be the appropriate choice. Centennial and Forrest are two examples of soybean varieties that are resistant to races 1 and 3. Centennial or Forrest, however, are susceptible to races 2 and 4.

Unfortunately, many growers have relied on resistant varieties as a sole means of controlling this pest. Continued use of one resistant variety generally results in a change in the nematode population's ability to attack "resistant varieties", referred to as a race shift. If the grower starts with race 1 and grows the variety Forrest for 3 to 5 years, the population may shift from race 1 to race 2 or 4. Thus, the grower needs to know the race of cyst nematode present in addition to the population density.

The Nematode Advisory Service (NCDA) will perform race determinations on a limited number of samples. Samples for race determinations should include soil and roots taken from several locations in a field. Assays to ascertain the race of cyst nematode need to be taken during late summer before the nematodes enter a dormant state. The Nematode Advisory Service may not designate the race, but will tell you which resistant varieties are appropriate to your situation. A new soybean variety, Delsoy 5710, is apparently resistant to all races of SCN. Delsoy 5710, however, does not have the yield potential of the older resistant varieties, so the variety resistant to the specific race present is still a desirable option for many growers. Currently, about 60 per cent of the populations of SCN in North Carolina can be categorized as races 2 or 4. Only a very few varieties such as Delsoy 5710 or Fowler have useable levels of resistance to these races.

Disease Management

Once established in a field, SCN cannot be eradicated. However, there are various practices that can be implemented in an integrated pest management (IPM) programme to minimize SCN reproduction and maximize soybean yields in infested fields.

Scout for early detection (look for symptoms and signs in the field). Aboveground symptoms can range from nonexistent to severe, and they are influenced by many factors. (One cannot rely solely upon aboveground symptoms, however, for definitive identification of SCN infestations). If the soybean yield obtained in a particular field has leveled-off or decreased for no apparent reason, or if SCN has been confirmed on nearby land, it is recommended that soil samples be taken from the plant root zone. A professional diagnostic lab should examine the samples for the presence of SCN. Soybean roots should also be examined directly for the presence of SCN females on the root surface.

Genetic Resistance

Grow SCN-resistant soybean cultivars. Resistant soybean cultivars are an effective management tool. Planting resistant soybeans in SCN-infested fields will usually reduce reproduction of the nematode. Most SCN juveniles do not feed and hence are unable to complete their life cycle on the roots of resistant cultivars; a few, however, will survive and reproduce. Some resistant soybean cultivars may yield slightly less than susceptible cultivars in non-infested fields, but they will yield significantly better than susceptible cultivars in fields infested with SCN. If the same resistant cultivar is grown in the same field year after year, SCN has the ability to adapt to the cultivar, or "break resistance." To reduce the possibility of this happening, some university researchers recommend that growers alternate use of the soybean cultivars with different sources of SCN resistance, and also that a susceptible cultivar be grown once after all types of available resistance have been rotated. The "HG-Type" system that has replaced the race system indicates which genetic sources of soybean resistance any given population of SCN can infect.

Cultural Practices

Grow SCN nonhost crops. SCN is an obligate parasite; the nematode is unable to mature and reproduce in the absence of host roots. Consequently, SCN population densities decline during any year that nonhost crops are grown. For example, a 1-2 year rotation with corn (nonhost) has proven effective for many growers. The magnitude of decline of SCN population densities during a year that a nonhost crop is grown is somewhat unpredictable, however, because the change in population density varies from year to year and is greatly influenced by environmental conditions. SCN-resistant soybean cultivars often are incorporated into a multi-year cycle of rotations with nonhosts crops - this combination of practices is an excellent integrated management strategy.

Maintain a healthy crop. Plants that have adequate moisture and nutrients are better able to withstand infection by SCN. In land infested with SCN, maintaining proper soil fertility and pH levels and minimizing other plant diseases, insect, and weed pests that weaken the plants is more critical to maximizing soybean yield than when land is noninfested.

Manage the movement of soil. If only certain fields on a farm are infested, planting and cultivating of infested land should be done only after noninfested fields have been worked. Soil on equipment should be thoroughly removed with high-pressure water or steam, if available, after working in infested fields. Also, seed grown on infested land should not be planted in noninfested fields unless the seed has been properly cleaned; SCN may be spread in the seed-size soil peds (clumps) mixed in with the seed.

Chemical Control

Use nematicides. No nematicide will kill all SCN in the soil. There are a few nematicides that are labeled for use against SCN, including the fumigant 1, 3-dichloro-propene (Telone) and the nonfumigants aldicarb (Temik or Bolster) and oxamyl (Vydate). Different products may be labeled in different states. When applied at planting, the effect of the nematicides may last long enough to provide an economic yield benefit. By the end of the growing season, however, SCN numbers may be as high or higher than they were at planting. The performance of the nematicide will depend on soil conditions, temperatures, and rainfall. Yield and economic benefits are not guaranteed, and nematicides are expensive. All nematicides are extremely toxic, especially the nonfumigants like Temik and Vydate that are nerve poisons. Only licensed applicators may use these pesticides.

Population Changes

The population density of soybean cyst nematode is relatively static during winter and early spring, but is changing constantly through the soybean growing season. Eggs are dormant until March or April when juveniles start to hatch. Hatching accelerates in May and June. Juveniles must penetrate soybean root systems within a few weeks in order to survive. If soybean planting is delayed to mid- to late-June the preplant nematode density may be cut in half. Once soybeans are planted, the population starts to build up again until soil temperatures become very high in July or August. Reproduction resumes in September through October with the onset of cooler weather.

The soybean maturity group largely determines the amount of reproduction in the fall. Group IV or V soybean varieties mature in September and October, whereas a group VII or VIII will not mature until late October or November. Late maturing soybean varieties allow for an extra generation of cyst nematode to develop, which generally doubles or triples the population density of this nematode. The early infection of soybean root systems by SCN causes the most serious damage to the root system. In the first 2-4 weeks after planting, 30 to 50% of the soybean plant's yield potential is determined. Thus, the primary determinant of soybean yield is the initial population density (or preplant population density) of this pest at planting. Later infections may cause additional yield loss and provide a reservoir for this pest to survive to infest the next soybean crop. These aspects of life cycle determine the tactics we use to manage this pest. The key to management of this plant parasite consists of limiting reproduction of SCN such that the cyst nematode population density (the number of eggs present at the beginning of the season) is minimized. This goal is accomplished by a long term (2-4 years) strategy aimed at minimizing reproduction of this pest.

Rotation

Crop rotation is an effective means of managing SCN. Planting a nonhost crop such as corn, tobacco, peanut, cotton or grain sorghum for one year can significantly reduce the SCN population. Two years of a nonhost may be necessary to reduce the SCN densities to levels which will cause no damage, especially in sandy soils. Soybean is more tolerant of SCN in heavier soils than in sandy soils, thus growing soybeans every third year may be the best option on light land; whereas, growing soybeans every other year on heavier land may be an economical solution. Some damage from SCN will generally occur in rotations of less than 3 years (soybean grown every third year), but it may be at tolerable levels.

Soybean double cropped with wheat is usually not severly damaged. A switch from a corn-wheat-soybean rotation to a corn-wheat-soybean-soybean rotation can result in severe damage to the second soybean crop. Rotation is recommended even if resistant varieties are used. Table 3.1 shows rotations of resistant and susceptible varieties that have proved useful if followed rigorously. The rationale behind this scheme is that resistant varieties will suppress or hold the population density of cyst nematodes at low levels so that the susceptible variety can be grown every third or fourth year. The inclusion of a nonhost as frequently as possible will reduce the nematode population density and delay the shift to a race which cannot be controlled by a resistant variety, thus prolonging the use of the resistant variety.

Table 3.1: Suggested Rotations for Managing Soybean Cyst Nematodes with Resistant Varieties

	Year 1	Year 2	Year 3	Year 4	Year 5
Preferred	Non-host Crop	Resistant Variety	Non-host Crop	Susceptible Variety	Repeat Cycle
Optional	Non-host crop	Resistant variety	Susceptible variety	Repeat cycle	

In situations where resistant varieties are not available, rotations in Table 3.2 should be considered. In general, the longer the interval between soybean crops, the higher the soybean yield. If a rotation shorter than 3 years (soybean grown every third year) is used, growers should use a maturity group V or earlier soybean variety. Early maturing varieties will not affect yield loss in the current year, but will result in lower population densities in subsequent years, and thus higher soybean yields.

Table 3.2: Suggested Rotations for Managing Soybean Cyste Nematode Without Resistant Varieties

	Year 1	Year 2	Year 3	Year 4	Year 5	Year 6
Preferred	Non-host crop	Non-host crop	Soybean	—Repeat cycle—		
Optional	Non-host crop	Soybean Group V or earlier	Non-host crop	Soybean Group V or earlier	Non-host crop	Repeat cycle

Resistant Varieties

When available, resistant varieties are an economical means of managing SCN. Resistant varieties, however, are not a cure-all. The resistant variety must be matched to the race of SCN to which it is resistant and then used judiciously. Seed companies and the North Carolina Cooperative Extension Service publish information on soybean varieties and relative resistance or tolerance to various nematode species and races. Currently, SCN resistant varieties fall into several categories: resistant to races 1 and 3, resistant to race 3, resistant to races 3 and 4 (3, 9, and 14 by the new scheme), or resistant to all races. Many of the cultivars resistant to race 3 may also be resistant to race 1, and some cultivars resistant to races 3 and 4 may also be resistant to race 1 and partially resistant to race 2. When practical, resistant varieties should still be grown in a rotation with non-hosts and/or susceptible varieties.

Resistant varieties that limit reproduction of SCN are still attacked by SCN. A resistant variety may still be damaged by SCN if it follows a susceptible crop, but will still out-perform a susceptible variety. The more frequently a resistant variety is grown, the sooner a race shift will occur to end the usefulness of this resistant variety (this may or may not be the case with Delsoy 5710). Although many of the new resistant varieties have good yield potential, frequently a susceptible cultivar will outyield a resistant cultivar provided the nematode preplant population density has been reduced. A highly resistant soybean variety will suppress the nematode population density such that a susceptible cultivar could be grown in rotation with it. Varieties resistant or tolerant to SCN are available. There is a distinction between a resistant variety and a tolerant variety. Resistant varieties "resist reproduction by SCN" and thereby limit damage caused by this pathogen. Tolerant varieties "do not resist SCN reproduction". Nematode reproduction is unrestricted on most tolerant varieties, and yields of tolerant varieties are less affected by the nematodes than are susceptible varieties. Tolerant varieties may be an option if the race of SCN present cannot be controlled by a resistant variety. Tolerance of some soybean varieties has been noted, but has not been adequately evaluated in North Carolina.

4

Soybean Seed and Seedling Diseases

General Information

Seedling diseases in soybean are a minor, yet chronic problem in North Carolina. Our mild coastal climate usually results in warmer soil temperatures earlier in the spring than occurs in states further inland. As a result, seedling diseases are generally of minor importance in this state. Nevertheless, because of the wide range of planting dates and soil types encountered, seedling diseases cause problems for some growers on a yearly basis. Seedling diseases can cause reduced stands and limit crop growth, thus getting the crop off to a slow start. These factors may lower yields and make management of other pest problems more difficult.

Environmental Factors

Seedling diseases tend to be more severe in poorly drained soils. They can, however, present problems in any soil type, especially when high rainfall or cold weather follow planting. Any factor that delays germination and seedling emergence such as poor seed quality, inadequate seedbed preparation, compaction, planting too deep, nematode infestations, and high rates of some herbicides can contribute to the incidence and severity of seedling diseases.

Distinguishing between Diseases and Herbicide Injury

Most soybean fields receive one or more herbicides, and most of the available soybean herbicides have the potential to injure soybeans. Some can generate visual symptoms that are similar to disease symptoms. Soybean tends to be more seriously injured by broadleaf herbicides than grass herbicides. Pre-emergence herbicides whose label suggests planting soybean below a certain depth probably have the greatest potential to injure soybeans if the herbicide gets into the soybean root zone.

Distinguishing between herbicide injury and seedling diseases is frequently difficult. The pattern of where symptoms do and do not appear may give the best indication of whether it is a disease problem or herbicide injury. Symptoms of seedling diseases usually occur in irregular patterns which may correspond to changes in soil type. A disease is more likely to be severe on one plant and show no symptoms on adjacent plants than is herbicide injury. The pattern of herbicide injury symptoms typically appear to be equipment related, although they may be modified by differences in soil type. Weed control is often excellent in the affected areas, and seldom will one plant be seriously affected and the adjacent plants appear unaffected. Finding an area in the field the sprayer may have missed, or overlapped in a previous pass, can be very useful in diagnosing herbicide injury.

Soilborne Diseases

Soybean seedling diseases are caused by fungi that reside in the seed or the soil. *Pythium* spp., *Phytophthora sojae*, and *Rhizoctonia solani* are the soil fungi most commonly associated with seedling diseases. *Pythium* and *Rhizoctonia* are found in all agricultural soils. These fungi will commonly cause a root rot and either lesions on the stem or soft watery stem tissue.

Sore shin (a red-to-brown lesion at or above the soil line), damping off and root rot can be caused by *Rhizoctonia solani*. Plants frequently recover from the root rot phase if optimal conditions for soybean growth occur soon after emergence. This fungus affects many plant species and is found in all soils. Other common soil inhabitants are various species of *Pythium*. Pythium rot can occur at any stage of plant development, but is primarily a seedling disease favoured by high moisture. A variety of symptoms are associated with this disease: a seed rot, a wet rot (soft watery stem tissue), baldhead (retarded development of the growing point), swelling of the stem below the cotyledons (which can be confused with herbicide injury), a root rot and/or wilt and death of seedlings. Diseases caused by *Pythium* spp. and *Rhizoctonia* may be suppressed, but not eliminated by rotation with grass crops such as corn or sorghum. Although rotation is not an especially effective tactic for managing these diseases, the reduction in other soybean pests which occurs with rotation generally results in a lower incidence of these seedling diseases. Seed-treatment fungicides containing thiram or PCNB are reasonably effective against *Rhizoctonia solani*, whereas seed-treatments containing mefanoxam (Ridomil Gold, Apron) are necessary if *Pythium* is the problem.

The soil fungus responsible for Phytophthora rot of soybean, *Phytophthora sojae*, is similar to *Pythium* spp. It is most commonly a problem in heavy, poorly drained soils or in low spots in the field. Diseases caused by this organism range from seed rot to stem and root rot, which may result in plant death. Rotation with non-leguminous crops (two or more years may be required), resistant or tolerant varieties and fungicide (mefanoxam) treatments can be used to manage this pest.

Seedborne Diseases

Several fungi that cause seed decay and seedling diseases are seedborne. Phomopsis seed decay, frogeye leaf spot (SOY003), anthracnose, purple seed stain, and downy mildew can cause seed rots, reduce emergence and prevent adequate stand establishment. These problems are usually more severe in cool wet soils. The best tactic for avoiding these diseases is the use of high quality disease-free seed.

The most common of these seedborne diseases is phomopsis seed decay. Seed infected with *Phomopsis* spp. typically have greatly reduced seed germination in a cold test compared to a standard germination test. This seed decay, like most other seedborne diseases, is a result of delayed soybean harvest and humid conditions during seed development. Pod and stem blight caused by *Phomopsis* spp. is present in nearly all fields at soybean maturity. If soybean harvest is late and warm humid conditions persist, infection of the seed will occur. Seed from these plants may not germinate and may produce seedlings lower in vigor. The other seedborne fungi mentioned cause similar problems, but are less common. Late-season scouting of soybean fields should include identification of foliar, pod, and stem diseases if soybeans are grown for seed. Seed should not be saved if anthracnose or frogeye leaf spot are present in the field. If seed of dubious quality must be planted, the use of a fungicide-seed treatment may prove beneficial. Seed treatments containing carboxin and/or captan are most effective against these fungi with the exception of downey mildew, which can be controlled with metalaxyl.

When to Replant

Soybean can yield well over a relatively wide range of plant population densities. Unless populations are so high that lodging becomes a problem or so low that the canopy does not close, yields will not be affected markedly. Target population densities are 6-8 plants per foot of row with 36-inch row spacing and 2 per foot of row in 7-inch rows for May-planted soybean. A higher population is desirable in June with 9-11 plants per foot of row and 2.5-3 plants per foot of row with 36- and 7-inch rows, respectively.

If the remaining plants are healthy, and fairly uniformly distributed, stands of half the levels in the previous paragraph are probably adequate. The added productivity of the replanted crop would have to be enough to cover the additional twenty to thirty dollars per acre cost of replanting. The later planting date lessens the likelihood that this will happen. The greatest uncertainty comes in guessing the current and future health of the remaining plants. When evaluating an uneven stand of very young soybean plants, it is difficult not to view the remaining stand pessimistically. Probably more fields are replanted which did not need to be than fields not replanted which should have been.

The herbicides used on the field must be considered when a decision to replant is made. Do not apply more pre-emergence herbicide with the second planting. Scout the field periodically to determine if a post-emergence treatment is necessary. Tillage can be used to dilute the concentration of the broadcast herbicide if it is labeled for preplant incorporation and is suspected of being part of the problem. If the broadcast herbicide is not labelled for preplant incorporation (e.g., linuron and linuron tank mixes), or does not appear to have been leached deep enough into the seedbed to be causing injury to the first crop, additional tillage should not be performed before replanting. If a soil-applied herbicide was banded over the original planting, and the decision is made to replant between the original rows (and thus away from the banded herbicide) a banded herbicide could also be used over the replanted rows as well, provided the sum of the two banded applications do not exceed the labelled per-acre rates for that herbicide.

Management of Seed and Seedling Diseases

1. Plant high quality disease-free seed. Professionally grown seed is worth the added cost.
2. Rotations with a grass crop such as corn or grain sorghum are generally beneficial in reducing population densities of soilborne pathogens.
3. Soils which tend to be poorly drained and/or cool should be planted later in the season when conditions for soybean germination and growth are optimal.
4. Consider resistant or tolerant varieties for fields where *Phytophthora* rot is frequently a problem.
5. Seed treatments may be beneficial when planting in cool, wet soils or when seed is of marginal quality.
6. In-furrow fungicide treatments may be considered when a persistent problem with *Phytophthora sojae* or *Pythium* spp. occurs and other options are unacceptable.
7. When soybean are grown for seed, inspect the crop for diseases and harvest in a timely manner.

5

Frogeye Leaf Spot of Soybean

General Information

Frogeye leaf spot of soybean has been detected in the Piedmont and the northeastern counties of North Carolina. This potentially destructive disease of soybean has not been common in North Carolina in the past 25 years, because the majority of varieties grown were resistant. Frogeye leaf spot caused severe soybean yield losses in the mid-South and Mississippi Delta regions in 1989. While it is still too early to assess the current importance of this disease in North Carolina, many varieties released in the past 5-10 years are susceptible. Frogeye leaf spot, as the name indicates, is primarily a foliar disease of soybean. The fungus, *Cercospora sojina*, which causes this disease, however, can be seedborne. Frogeye leaf spot is most likely to become a problem if infected seed is planted or if the disease occurred in the previous year's soybean crop and the land is not rotated. Extended periods of wet weather during the growing season will favour disease development.

Symptoms

Lesions on leaves are circular to angular spots which vary in size from less than 1 mm to 5 mm in diametre. Lesions are first visible on the upper surface of the leaf. These lesions are distinctive in that the brown spots are surrounded by a narrow red or dark reddish-brown margin. As lesions age, the central area becomes ash-grey to light brown. Older lesions are light to dark brown and frequently are translucent, having a grey to white centre which may contain minute dark spots. Smaller lesions may coalesce to form larger, irregular spots on leaves. During a wet year, symptoms of Frogeye leaf spot may appear uniformly over the foliage. In years with intermittent wet periods, the symptoms may appear layered within the plant canopy since only young leaflets are susceptible to infection. When plants are heavily infected, leaves may die and fall prematurely. This can result in early defoliation of soybean plants. If high rainfall and humidity persist, stems and seeds also may become infected. Lesions on pods are reddish brown, may appear sunken, and are circular or elongate in shape. Older lesions on pods become brown to gray, usually with a narrow, dark-brown border.

Leaf symptoms of frogeye leaf spot

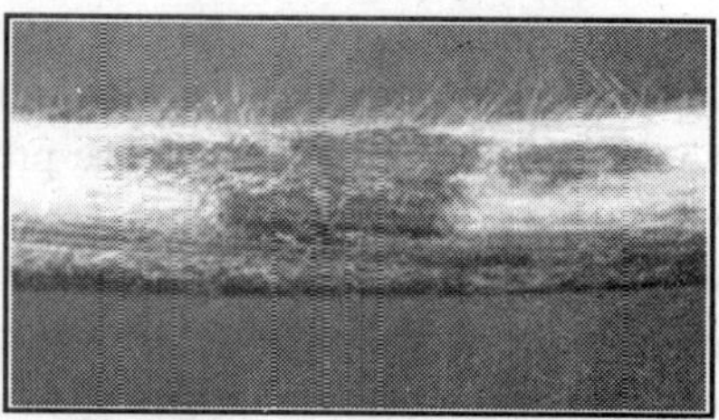

Soybean stem lesions caused by the frogeye leaf spot pathogen

Disease Cycle

Cercospora sojina survives in infected seed and plant debris from an infected crop. Infected seed may germinate poorly, and plants that do emerge from infected seed are often stunted and may have lesions on the cotyledons. These lesions produce spores that can be inoculum for leaf infections.

The fungus car also produce spores on the residue of a previous soybean crop. Although most soybean is grown in rotation with corn (meaning there is little soybean residue in newly planted soybean fields), enough soybean residue can remain to supply spores to begin an epidemic. Wind readily transports the spores of *Cercospora sojina* (whether these have been produced on residue or new lesions) from one field to another.

Spore production and infection requires warm, humid weather. Leaves are most susceptible to infection when they are just emerging and become less susceptible as they mature. This range of susceptibility can lead to a layered occurrence of disease in the plant canopy, depending on how conducive conditions were as each leaf layer emerged.

Frogeye leaf spot is a polycyclic disease, meaning that the number of lesions on the plant will continue to increase as long as the weather is favourable for infection. The greater the number of lesions, the greater the reduction of green leaf area, and the greater the reduction in yield. If favourable conditions for infection persist until late in the season, the fungus will infect pods and seeds.

Management

The most important means for managing this disease in soybean is avoidance. Planting resistant varieties or high quality seed of certified varieties free of this pest are the best packages for management. If you detected or think you detected frogeye leaf spot in your soybean crop last year, there are several actions you should take. The first step would be selection of a resistant variety. If you cannot plant a resistant variety (SOY006), fields which had frogeye leaf spot last year should not be planted to soybean for at least one year and preferably two. The fungus which causes this disease will survive in crop residue. By all means, avoid planting seed from fields which may have been infected with frogeye leaf spot the previous year. The seed-borne aspect of this disease is probably the most important form of spread over long distances. Soybean varieties differ in their resistance to this pathogen. Some public varieties and many varieties developed by private companies appear to be immune while many other varieties possess resistance to certain races of the pathogen. Since we don't know which races are prevalent in North Carolina, selection of a variety with a high level of resistance or immunity is preferable. If this disease was not present last year, it is not necessary to select a variety solely on the basis of frogeye leaf spot resistance. However, if the disease was detected in your crop last year a resistant variety (SOY006) would be an appropriate choice.

Planting

Plant clean, pathogen-free seed. The relative contribution of primary inoculum (the spores that initiate disease in the crop) in infected seed versus crop residue is not known. It is believed that residue may be a more significant source of inoculum than infected seed, but infected seed may establish the fungus in new areas.

Tillage

Burying infected soybean residue will help reduce the inoculum in a field. Many growers use fairly clean tillage prior to planting corn, which destroys and buries soybean residue in the soybean-corn rotation, which may explain why frogeye leaf spot has not been a serious problem in Indiana for many years. However, severe frogeye leaf spot outbreaks in several Indiana areas in 2005 indicate that the disease is capable of establishing itself here under current tillage practices.

Rotation

Rotating out of infected soybean for at least two years will help reduce the frogeye leaf spot risk.

Resistant Varieties

Several different genes for frogeye leaf spot resistance have been discovered and described in soybean. Because the disease is a more chronic problem in the southern United States, resistance is more commonly available in varieties of maturity group V and higher. Resistance is available in some, perhaps many, varieties adapted to Indiana. However, some varieties were clearly very susceptible to frogeye leaf spot during 2005. *Rcs1*, *Rcs2*, and *Rcs3* are three named genes for frogeye leaf spot resistance, and additional sources of resistance have been reported. There are several races of the pathogen, which are distinguished by their ability to infect soybean varieties with different genes for resistance. A soybean variety with one particular gene for resistance will be resistant to some races of the pathogen, but not others. Apparently, the *Rcs3* gene confers resistance to all races that occur in Indiana, but the information about the races here is very limited.

Chemical Control

Fungicide seed treatments can reduce the risk of infection. Spray applications of fungicides after growth stage R1 can reduce disease severity. But applications made at stage R3 are considered most effective in southern states. Frogeye leaf spot has caused only limited problems in Indiana in recent years. But with the arrival of Asian soybean rust and the increased awareness of leaf diseases in soybean, frogeye leaf spot will probably be given more attention than in the past. When scouting soybean fields for weeds and insects, take notes on the severity and prevalence of foliar diseases. If you suspect frogeye leaf spot in your crop, contact your County Extension Agent and have symptomatic plants sent to the Plant Disease and Insect Clinic, North Carolina State University, at the first opportunity. Should you encounter this disease or if you have fields that were suspect last year, control methods are:

1. plant-resistant varieties,
2. rotate fields to corn or cotton (1-2 years),
3. treat seed which may be infected with a fungicide labeled for seed treatment,
4. plow under any crop residues on the soil surface, and
5. the use of a foliar fungicide (Table 5.1) at the R2 and R5 soybean growth stage may be beneficial if the disease is present and environmental conditions that favour disease development occur. Fungicides, however, are not generally recommended in North Carolina since we rarely encounter disease pressures sufficient to reduce soybean yield below the cost of treatment.

Table 5.1: Foliar Fungicides for Control of Frogeye Leaf Spot on Soybean

Fungicide	Rates & Remarks*
Benomyl	0.5 - 1.0 lb/acre
Chlorothalonil	2.0 - 3.5 pts/acre

* Make two applications, one at R2-3 growth stage and a second application 14-21 days later. Do not graze treated fields or feed hay or vines to livestock.

6

Columbia Lance Nematode on Soybean

General Information

Columbia lance nematode, *Hoplolaimus columbus* Sher, was first reported by Q.L. Holdeman in a field of declining soybean [*Glycine max* (L.) Merr.] and cotton (*Gossypium hirsutum* L.) near Eastover, South Carolina. The nematodes grew poorly in monoxenic and greenhouse cultures. Experiments requiring large numbers of monospecific nematodes have been limited, but success in culturing the nematode offers great opportunities to conduct research on this species. The growth of the nematode on petri plate culture allows for the observation of individual nematodes and their development over time. The present study used *in vitro* observations on the biology of the nematode to determine the time associated with different nematode stages, the nematode activity at different stages, and specific sequence of events that occur during the nematode's development.

The Columbia lance nematode, *Hoplolaimus columbus*, has become established in much of the southern portion of the North Carolina coastal plain. The distribution of this nematode seems to be restricted to the sandier soils found in these areas. This pest can severely damage cotton and soybean. It may occur with other nematodes such as soybean cyst, reniform, lesion, root-knot and sting. A related species, *Hoplolaimus galeatus*, is common to the Northeastern portion of the state, but has not been associated with damage to soybean. Nematodes should be suspected as a possible production problem if any of the following apply:

1. irregular patches of stunted and/or yellow soybeans - an up-and-down pattern of soybean growth is common;
2. yields declining over several years or yields lower than expected;
3. a positive report on lance nematode from the Plant Disease and Insect Clinic or the North Carolina Department of Agriculture Nematode Advisory Service; and

4. failures in weed control (weed problems are frequently more severe in nematode-infested fields.

Morphology and Anatomy

Adults are 0.75-1.0 mm long.

Female

- Stylet knobs have two anteriorly projecting processes.
- Esophogeal glands overlap intestine dorsally.
- Excretory pore behind level of esophago-intestinal valve.
- Ovaries are outstretched and spermatheca is absent.
- Intestine overlaps rectum, extending partly into the tail.
- Tail is rounded, with 16-22 annules.
- Lateral field, represented by only 1 indistinct incisure.
- Cephalic region offset, usually with 3 annules, but a fourth annule is often seen on one side of the cephalic region due to subdivision of one annule. The basal annule of the lip region has 10-15 longitudinal lines. Basal plate with 6 arms.
- Hemizonid 2-5 annules posterior to excretory pore.
- Hemizonian not seen.
- Anterior phasmid is 38 per cent from the anterior end on the right side; posterior phasmid at 81 per cent from the anterior end on the left side.
- The diovarial reproductive system is fully developed after the fourth molt, and occupies about 61 per cent of the body length.
- Eggs are laid individually and have a stalk up to 15¼ m long which can be used as a diagnostic character.

Male:

- Extremely rare.
- Body shape and general morphology similar to female except for sexual dimorphism and the following differences:
- Cephalic region with 3 or 4 annules with 7-8 longitudinal lines on basal annule.
- Excretory pore anterior or posterior to esophago-intestinal valve.
- Hemizonid 2-8 annules posterior to excretory pore and hemizonion 10 annules posterior to hemizonid.
- No longitudinal incisure on body
- Gubernaculum trough like, with distinct titillae
- Spicules 37-53¼ m long, slightly arcuate with a very thin velum observed only when spicules are extended. Telamon distinct, lying between spicules. Bursa begins at about anterior end of the spicules and extends around the tip of the tail.

Diagnosis

Accurate diagnosis of nematode problems on soybean can be accomplished by several means. A soil sample must be processed in order to positively identify a lance nematode problem. If you suspect a nematode problem, take systematic (stratified) soil samples preferably in the fall when nematode numbers are high. Samples should be taken from the plant row.

Life Cycle, Host Range and Pathology

The Columbia lance nematode feeds both externally and internally on soybean roots. Lesions may develop on the roots which can coalesce and give the appearance of a root rot. This nematode remains wormlike throughout its life cycle and can only be identified microscopically. The population densities of this nematode fluctuate only slightly during the course of a year. Columbia lance nematode can usually be detected in soil samples regardless of time of year, but fall assays still are best for predictive purposes. The amount of damage to soybean and subsequent yield loss will be directly proportional to the density of this nematode at soybean planting. Corn, cotton, and soybean are good hosts for this nematode. Nematode densities are generally in the moderate-to-high range following these crops. Peanut, tobacco and small grains are poor or nonhosts for Columbia lance nematode.

Management Tactics

Management of this nematode is difficult because of the limited acreage of rotational crops available (peanut, tobacco and small grains). Several tactics to restrict soybean yield suppression caused by this pest can be utilized however. Soils in the affected part of the state tend to have hard pans. Sub-soiling has often been as effective as a nematicide treatment in increasing soybean yield. Hard-pan management should thus be a primary concern if this nematode is present in a field. Soybean varieties with moderate levels of tolerance to this nematode have been identified (Table 6.1).

Table 6.1: Soybean Varieties Moderately Tolerant to Columbia Lance Nematode

AG6101	DP5644RR	Mott
Centennial	DP6880RR	Musen
Benning	Hagood	Northrup King S83-30
Bogge	Maxcy	Pritchard
Dillon		

The tolerance of these varieties are based on a limited number of tests. Other varieties not listed may also be tolerant.

Tolerant varieties are not resistant, but these varieties will suffer only about a 10 per cent yield loss if this nematode is at damaging levels. Growers should use tolerant soybean varieties with caution, since a cotton crop grown in rotation with a tolerant soybean variety can still be damaged. Planting early has been recommended as a tactic to manage this nematode because it does not become active until soil temperatures become warm. Research on planting date and damage caused by Columbia lance nematode on soybean has not been conclusive. There are indications that damage may be just as great or greater in early planted soybean.

7

Mid-to-Late Season Soybean Stem and Root Rots

Introduction

Several soil-borne fungi cause lower stem and root rot of soybean. These diseases usually result in the occurrence of dead or dying soybean plants in mid-to-late summer. Certain diseases are especially prevalent after periods of drought stress. Frequently, two or more pathogenic fungi can be found associated with these dead plants. Steps can be taken to reduce these diseases in future soybean crops if the disease is properly diagnosed.

The most common soybean root and stem rots in North Carolina are Phytophthora Rot, Pythium Root Rot, Red Crown Rot, Southern Blight, and Charcoal Rot. Each of these diseases may occur singly or in combination with the others. Damaging levels of plant-parasitic nematodes will generally cause these diseases to be more severe. In many instances, disease severity may be a symptom of other problems such as inadequate fertility, soil compaction, poor drainage, herbicide injury, high levels of nematode infestation, or low pH. Correcting these yield limiting problems is the first step toward disease management in soybean.

Obtaining Proper Diagnosis

Proper identification 'diagnosis' of the disease causing fungus is essential to formulating a management strategy. Growers should provide as much information about the problem as possible on the forms sent to the clinic. Symptoms, patterns and distribution of disease, variety, crop history, as well as rates and methods of application of herbicides and fertilizers can aid in proper diagnosis. Soil pH, soluble salts, and nematode numbers, may be determined if a soil sample is provided with the plants. Plants which show all stages of decline and which are representative of the problem should be included. Dead plants may provide clues as to the exact nature of the disease, but are often inadequate to make an accurate diagnosis.

COMMON ROOT AND STEM ROTS OF SOYBEAN

Phytophthora Rot

This disease is caused by the soil-borne fungus *Phytophthora sojae*. This fungus is widely distributed in North Carolina, but is most important in heavy, poorly drained soils. It may cause a seedling disease or pre- and post-emergence damping off. This disease is most common after soil temperature increases and high rainfall results in soils waterlogged for long periods.

It is especially prevalent in low-lying areas of the field. Soybean varieties differ in their tolerance and/or resistance to Phytophthora Rot. Therefore, symptoms may vary in their severity depending on the relative susceptibility of the variety planted. Symptoms on older plants are root rot, wilting, and death of plants.

The stem of highly susceptible cultivars is usually dark brown, and this discolouration may extend from the base of the plant to more than 10 inches above the soil line. Leaves remain attached to wilted plants. The vascular and cortex tissue of the plant has a brown-to-black discolouration and "pith discing" may be visible in dead plants. The disease may appear to be restricted to low-lying areas of the field, portions of the field with heavier soils, or the entire field may be affected if poorly drained.

Management

Improve drainage, if possible. Varieties possessing high levels of resistance should be used in fields where Phytophthora Rot is identified as a problem. Rotations of two-to-three years with grain crops, tobacco, cotton, or non-leguminous crops are necessary if resistant varieties are not used. A seed treatment with a mefonoxam (Ridomil Gold, Apron) containing fungicide is effective against the damping-off phase of the disease, but an in-furrow application may be required if resistant varieties are not used.

Pythium Root Rot

Various species of *Pythium* cause root rots of soybean. *Pythium* spp. may cause disease at any time of the season, but seed rots and damping off diseases are most common. Symptoms caused by *Pythium* spp. are very similar to those caused by *Phytophthora sojae*. The determination of which fungus is the causal organism must generally be done in the laboratory. Diagnostic kits are available and can accurately distinguish between these organisms but are fairly expensive. Pythium Root Rot at mid-season may affect scattered plants, but economic losses in North Carolina are rare.

Management

This disease is difficult to manage because of the wide host range of the pathogen and its persistence in soil. If the problem occurs on a yearly basis, changing varieties and improving drainage may be effective. A seed treatment with a mefonoxam (Apron) containing fungicide is effective against the seed rot and damping off phase of disease. Root rots caused by *Pythium* spp., however, must be controlled by an in-furrow treatment (Ridomil Gold).

Red Crown Rot (CBR)

The fungus *Cylindrocladium parasiticum*, which causes CBR or Black Root Rot of peanut (PDIN-002) also causes a root rot of soybean Symptoms usually appear late in the season, during or after pod set. Foliar symptoms are generally noticed with the onset of cool weather in the fall. Upper leaves may turn yellow and leaves will later become brown between the veins. Plants will defoliate early and petioles will drop with the leaves. The roots of affected plants will have a black root rot and stalk tissue will be grayish or reddish brown above the soil line for two-to-four inches. The presence of bright-red fungal structures (about the size of the head of a pin) near the soil line are a positive indication for this disease though they are not always present. Affected plants may be scattered throughout the field or confined to one area of the field. Infestations of cyst (SOY-001) and root-knot nematodes result in more severe disease in conjunction with *C. parasiticum*.

Management

Two or more years of non-host crops such as corn or cotton may be necessary to reduce the density of *C. parasiticum* microsclerotia to non-damaging levels. Do not include peanuts in a rotation with soybean if this disease is present in a field! Soybean is generally more tolerant of *C. parasiticum* than is peanut. Differences in soybean varietal responses to this fungus have been noted, but are not adequately documented. Nematode management through the use of appropriate soybean cyst nematode or root-knot nematode resistant varieties (SOY-006) may aid in suppression of Red Crown Rot.

Southern Blight

The soil fungus, *Sclerotium rolfsii* causes southern blight and is present in nearly all North Carolina fields. Disease is most common in sandy soils, however. Plants suddenly wilt and die during hot, humid weather. Leaves remain attached to the dead stem. A white mat of fungal tissue may appear on soil and the base of the stem. Fungal structures called sclerotia frequently cover the fungal mat Sclerotia are spherical, tan or brown in colour, and about the size of a mustard seed. Diseased plants are usually scattered throughout a field, although it is common for the disease to spread from plant-to-plant within a row during hot, humid weather.

Management

Soybean is generally tolerant to this disease and economic losses are rare in North Carolina. Growers should check for other soil-related factors such as nematode infestation, fertility or pH-related problems if disease is severe. Rotations with non-hosts (corn or grain sorghum) and deep plowing to bury crop residue are reasonably effective tactics for managing this disease.

Charcoal Rot

Macrophomina phaseolina is a fungus which is widely distributed in soils and may be either seedborne or soilborne. This fungus attacks a wide variety of plants, including cornsoybean, cotton, grain sorghum, and numerous weeds. It can attack soybean plants at any stage of development, but is most evident following periods of hot, dry weather. Infected plants have smaller leaves and grow slowly. Leaves of older plants turn yellow and wilt, but remain attached to the plant. A grayish or silvery discolouration of tissue under the bark of the upper tap root and lower stem are symptomatic on older plants. A reddish, brown-to-black discolouration of the vascular tissue may extend from the tap root up the stem. The distribution of infected plants may be scattered or uniform. This disease should be suspected if previous corn crops were also poor.

Management

The key to managing this disease is alleviation of plant stress. Charcoal rot is most common when soil pH and fertility are low and/or plants are under moisture stress. Correcting nutrient deficiencies and subsoiling, if a hardpan is present, will reduce disease severity. Corn and cotton are somewhat less susceptible to this fungus, so rotations of two to three years with these crops may prove beneficial.

8

Phytophthora Root and Stem Rot

General Introduction

Phytophthora sojae is an oomycete and a soil-borne plant pathogen that causes stem and root rot of soybean. This is a prevalent disease in most soybean growing regions, and a major cause of crop loss. In wet conditions the pathogen produces zoospores that move in water and are attracted to soybean roots. Zoospores can attach to roots, germinate and infect the plant tissues. Diseased roots develop lesions that may spread up the stem and eventually kill the entire plant. *Phytophthora sojae* also produces oospores that can remain dormant in the soil over the winter, or longer, and germinate when conditions are favourable. Oospores may also be spread by animals or machinery.

Phytophthora sojae is a diploid organism with a genome size of 95 Mbp (Millions of base pairs).

Natural chemical farinomalein (a metabolite from entomo-pathogenic fungus *Paecilomyces farinosus*) has shown potent and selective inhibition (0.15-5¼g/disk) against eight isolates of plant pathogenic *Phytophthora sojae*. These results suggest that farinomalein might be useful as a candidate pesticide for the treatment of *Phytophthora* stem rot in soybean.

Phytophthora sojae is also very similar to *Phytophthora megasperma* in many ways that they're often mistaken for each other. In the early years of research, *Phytophthora sojae* and *Phytophthora medicaginis* were respectively known as *Phytophthora megasperma* f. sp. *glycines* and *Phytophthora megasperma* f. sp. *medicaginis*. Recent discoveries about their molecular structure, however, proved that they were indeed unambiguous species.

Phytophthora sojae is a soil borne pathogen that in the past has caused very large economic losses. During the late 1970s, 300,000 soybean acres were lost due to *P. sojae*. This disease has since been effectively managed predominately through the incorporation of single-gene mediated resistance but quantitative or partial resistance has been used as well. In fact, today, we can repeat 100 per cent loss by planting soybean cultivars that were popular during earlier epidemics. Without high levels of resistance to this pathogen, many soybean acres would be lost each year to this disease. *Phytophthora* doesn't forget and it doesn't go away!

Symptoms and Signs

Phytophthora root and stem rot is caused by the oomycete plant pathogen *Phytophthora sojae*. This water mold can infect seeds, seedlings, and plants in all reproductive stages of growth when soil conditions favour pathogen development. Symptoms usually become apparent one to two weeks after heavy rains and are most common on soils that are poorly drained.

Seed rot and damping-off. *Phytophthora sojae* causes seed decay, and pre- and post-emergence damping-off of soybeans under wet and warm soil conditions. The optimum temperature for disease development is 25 to 30°C (77 to 86°F). Fields with extensive seed rot and pre-emergence damping-off often require replanting. A light brown soft rot may develop on roots or the hypocotyl as seedlings emerge from the soil. As the roots and or hypocotyls become colonized, the seedlings may die.

Root and stem rot. The severity of the infection on soybean plants in the vegetative and reproductive stages of growth is directly related to the level of resistance in the plant. In highly susceptible cultivars, *P. sojae* colonization begins in the roots, then spreads several nodes up the stem. The roots and stem turn a chocolate brown colour, the leaves of the plant turn yellow, and the whole plant turns a reddish-orange to orange-brown colour. Occasionally a lesion will only occur on one side of the plant, but it is continuous from below the soil line up the plant. The yellowed, wilted leaves cling to the plant as it dies. In highly susceptible cultivars, virtually every plant in the field may be killed during the course of the production season; cultivars with moderate to low levels of partial resistance may suffer between 20 and 50 per cent stand loss. For cultivars with higher levels of partial resistance, the stem rot phase does not develop. Roots are still colonized and are light brown in colour, and in some cases the plants may be stunted. There are usually no visible symptoms, other than reduced yields, under field conditions for cultivars with high levels of partial resistance.

Pathogen Biology

Phytophthora sojae is an oomycete, a close relative of the golden brown algae, in the Kingdom Stramenopila (or Straminipila). This group of organisms produces swimming spores (zoospores) which have tubular flagella. While oomycetes have little taxonomic affinity to fungi, they are "fungus-like" in their growth since they also produce mycelium. The mycelium is coenocytic (aseptate – lacking cross walls) but as a laboratory culture ages, false septae will form. Lima bean agar is one of the most common media used to culture *P. sojae*; on it, the mycelium grows close to the agar surface and has no colour. Interestingly, *P. sojae* does not grow on full strength potato dextrose agar, a commonly used medium for many fungi and oomycetes. Reducing the concentration of potato dextrose agar and supplementing with water agar improves the growth. On V8 juice agar medium, the hyphae are white and branch mostly at right angles. The optimum temperature for growth of most isolates on any medium is 25 to 28°C (77 to 82°F).

On lima bean agar, oospores (thick-walled, sexual spores) form readily, often within 3 to 4 days. *Phytophthora sojae* is homothallic (self-fertile). Antheridia (male structures) are predominantly paragynous (attach to the side of the oogonial stalk), but some will be amphigynous (encircle the oogonial stalk). Oospore walls are smooth and the oogonia are 40μm in diameter, sometimes as large as 45μm.

Sporangia (thin-walled lemon-shaped spores) do not form in agar culture but can be induced with repeated flooding and washing of cultures. Once formed, a sporangium has an inconspicuous papilla (a small rounded process on the tip) so it appears nonpapillate. Sporangia have long pedicels and are non-caducous (do not shed or break off from main mycelium). Sporangia are approximately 40 μm long by 28 μm wide. Germination is either direct by production of hyphae or indirect by the production of large numbers of zoospores (>20). From the empty sporangium, another sporangium will develop in an extended and nested pattern.

Zoospores swim toward the root and encyst on the root surface. A single germ tube emerges and penetrates the root cell wall.

Nomenclature

Phytophthora sojae can readily be mistaken for *Phytophthora megasperma*. In fact, at one time, *P. sojae* and *P. medicaginis* were known as *Phytophthora megasperma* f. sp. *glycines* and *P. megasperma* f. sp. *medicaginis*, respectively. Molecular analysis of the mitochondrial region and isozyme analysis provided evidence that these were in fact distinct species.

P. sojae has a gene-for-gene relationship with its host, soybean. Fourteen different single resistance genes, designated Rps genes, have been described. A number of sets of differential cultivars are available to characterize pathotypes (races) of *P. sojae*. These sets were developed by backcrossing different sources of resistance into common genetic backgrounds to develop isolines, i.e., varieties that are almost identical to each other, except that they differ in one resistance gene. There are 55 coded races, but many more virulence combinations have been described in the US. Many publications today refer to the pathotype, the exact listing of virulence reactions that each isolate has on the isolines of the differential set rather than a race code number, as the number of races and diversity has become too great. A pathotype is determined by inoculating an isolate on the series of differentials. If a spreading brown lesion forms following an inoculation (compatible or susceptible interaction) on a differential carrying a specific R-gene, then that response becomes part of the pathotype. For example, isolates that are designated Race 30 cause susceptible responses on differentials with *Rps*1a, *Rps*1b, *Rps*1k, *Rps*3a, *Rps*6 and *Rps*7.

Disease Cycle and Epidemiology

Phytophthora sojae is a soilborne plant pathogen that survives as oospores in soil and plant debris. Oospores can survive for a number of years in a dormant state, and can withstand freezing and long periods of cold temperatures. Oospores of *P. sojae* have endogenous dormancy and not all will germinate at the same time even when conditions are highly favourable. Oospores germinate to form mycelia under high soil moisture conditions, and this mycelium then produces sporangia and zoospores under continued or subsequent saturated soil conditions. Zoospores are attracted to soybean roots, specifically to the soybean specific root exudates daedzein and genestein. Once they reach a root, the zoospores lose their flagella, produce a cell wall (encyst), germinate, and subsequently infect root tissues. *P sojae* colonizes the root and stem tissues where it produces oospores.

Phytophthora sojae is readily baited from soils collected at any time of year. To bait, soils are planted with susceptible soybean lines and flooded for 24 hours. Seedlings with characteristic symptoms can be collected and the pathogen isolated from infected tissues. Alternatively, soils can be submerged and leaf discs floated on the surface to capture zoospores, then leaf discs can be plated on selective medium. However, soils which are dry or have been frozen require saturation followed by an incubation period of 1 to 2 weeks of continuous moist conditions and temperatures of 60-65°F. This incubation period helps "break" dormancy of the oospores.

Soybean root and stem infections can occur throughout the season and are thought to arise directly from oospores. In most fields, inoculum of the pathogen survives as oospores, often in high numbers. The diseases caused by *P. sojae* are considered monocyclic, i.e., having only one effective infection cycle per growing season, primarily due to the nature of oospores which do not all germinate at one time. The role of secondary (root-to-root) inoculum in enhancing disease severity is largely unknown. Infection often appears random; in the field it is common to see one symptomatic plant, then 10 healthy plants followed by another symptomatic plant. Conversely, large areas of damping-off can occur in low areas of a field or areas with reduced drainage.

Disease Management

Phytophthora sojae is prevalent in many soybean production regions of the world and is managed primarily with host resistance. *P. sojae* consists of many races but the occurrence of these races or virulence pathotypes is quite variable across the north central region of the United States both within fields and between fields. This diversity of pathotypes can make soybean cultivar selection challenging for producers.

Host Resistance

Several types of resistance have been described in the *P. sojae*-soybean pathosystem: R-gene mediated resistance, root resistance, and partial resistance. R-gene mediated resistance has been described for 14 *Rps* genes and most have been mapped on the soybean genome. Commercially, only six genes, *Rps*1a, *Rps*1b, *Rps*1c, *Rps*1k, *Rps*3a and *Rps*6, have been deployed and one more, *Rps*8, is in commercial development. This type of resistance is expressed as a hypersensitive response and is most often measured in laboratory and greenhouse assays through inoculation of the hypocotyl region on young seedlings. However, it is only effective against some races.

Root resistance and partial resistance are both expressed in the roots. Root resistance is almost a complete resistance that is expressed in the roots but is quantitatively (several genes that each contribute to the level of resistance) inherited. Partial resistance is also quantitatively inherited and is primarily expressed as reduced colonization of the roots.

Partial resistance is expressed in plants after the cotyledons and first true leaves are visible, but *Rps* gene resistance is expressed in the seed and therefore is effective from germination onwards. Partial resistance is expressed as reduced colonization and slower lesion expansion, and is inherited as a multi-genic trait. Since more genes are involved in the expression of this resistance and the assays take longer, partially resistant cultivars are more difficult to breed. A combination of *Rps* gene and partial resistance has provided the best protection, especially in regions where individual fields may harbor a large number of races.

Chemical Control

Fungicide seed treatments are the only chemical control practiced to manage *P. sojae* and they are used for managing early season seed decay and damping-off. Mefenoxam and metalaxyl, two very similar compounds, can both be used as seed treatments. For adequate management of *P. sojae*, higher rates of seed treatment product have higher efficacy than low rates. Many oomycete species have been identified that have adapted to these fungicides and are no longer sensitive. However, the north central region of the United States was surveyed from 2001 to 2005 for the presence of metalaxyl/mefenoxam-insensitive isolates of *P. sojae*, but none were found.

Cultural Practices

Phytophthora root rot is more severe in poorly drained or flooded areas of the field. Any cultural practice that improves soil drainage ultimately reduces the time that soils are saturated, and thus reduces the infection period. Soil tillage and placing drain tiles in fields either in combination or alone may reduce the incidence and severity of Phytophthora root and stem rot. Rotation and tillage are not effective management options since the oospores of *P. sojae* are capable of surviving for long periods of time in soil.

9

Pythium Root Rot

While root rot can be caused by several different species of the fungus-like organism *Pythium*, the three most commonly encountered species are *Pythium irregulare*, *Pythium aphanidermatum*, and *Pythium ultimum*. *P. ultimum* and *P. irregulare* are often found in field soil, sand, pond and stream water and their sediments, and dead roots of previous crops. *P irregulare* has been isolated from almost every type of greenhouse crop grown but *P. aphanidermatum* seems to be associated primarily with poinsettia and very few other crops. *Pythium* can be in commercially available soilless potting mixes. It is easily introduced into pasteurized soil or soilless mixes by using dirty tools, dirty pots or flats, walking on or allowing pets to walk on the mixes and by dumping the mixes on benches or potting shed floors that have not been thoroughly cleaned. Fungus gnat and shorefly activity may also be involved in moving *Pythium* from place to place in greenhouses. When introduced into a soil mix that has been heat-treated for too long or at too high a temperature, *Pythium* can cause severe root rot because it has few competitors to check its activity. *P. aphanidermatum* and *P. irregulare* pose a threat to crops grown in ebb and flow systems because they form a swimming spore stage that can move in water. This is likely to occur only if irrigation times are long (45 min. or longer) or if pots sit in puddles of water because the bench or floor does not drain completely. If *Pythium* infests a cutting bed or if contaminated water is used in propagation, large losses occur. *Pythium ultimum* is primarily associated with soil and sand. As growers switched to soilless mixes, this species became less important than when growers used field soil in the potting mix. P. ultimum does not form the swimming spore stage but can be a problem in ebb and flow systems if the reservoir becomes fouled with potting mix and plant debris particles harboring it. Almost all plants are susceptible to *Pythium* root rot. Root tips, very important in taking up nutrients and water, are attacked and killed first. *Pythium* also can rot the base of cuttings.

Symptoms

- Plants are stunted.
- Root tips are brown and dead.
- Plants wilt at mid-day and may recover at night.
- Plants yellow and die.
- Brown tissue on the outer portion of the root easily pulls off leaving a strand of vascular tissue exposed.
- The cells of roots contain round, microscopic, thick-walled spores.

Management

Pythium root rot is difficult to control once rot has begun. Every effort should be directed toward preventing the disease before it begins by using heat-pasteurized potting mix (entire pile heated to 180°F and held at that temperature for 30 min. Longer times and higher temperatures will kill beneficial organism in the soil.). Cover the treated soil and store it or commercial soilless mixes in an area that will not be contaminated through the introduction of non-treated soil.

If pond or stream water is used for irrigation, be certain the intake pipe is well above the bottom so that sediment is not drawn in. If the water supply is suspected of being a source of *Pythium*, it may be necessary to treat the water before use. First, contact the author (see address above) to arrange to have the water tested for *Pythium*. Slow sand filtration has been shown to be an effective, simple, and inexpensive method for removing *Pythium* from water. Heat, ultraviolet light, ozone, and chlorination can be effective but are expensive and require some training to be used properly.

Cover ebb and flow system reservoirs to prevent contaminated debris from entering the system. Pass return water over a coarse screen to remove potting soil and plant debris in order to help keep *Pythium* out of the reservoir.

Disinfect all bench surfaces, potting benches, tools, and equipment that will contact the potting mix. Periodically, thoroughly clean and disinfect ebb and flow reservoirs, benches, and flood and drain floors.

In a greenhouse operation with a history of *Pythium* root rot, apply a fungicide or a biological control agent as early in the cropping cycle as possible. Biological agents should be applied to the potting mix before, during or immediately after transplant. They can even be applied to plants in plug trays before transplanting. Do not apply ANY chemical pesticides to the potting mix 10 days before or for 10 days after applying the biological control agent. Biological control agents and fungicides may have to be applied more than once in order to maintain adequate protection.

Some populations of *Pythium* have resistance to metalaxyl, mefenoxam and/or propamocarb. If these chemicals do not appear to be protecting your plants, switch to another product and contact the author of this fact sheet for assistance in assessing the cause of the problem.

The following biological agents and chemicals are registered for controlling *Pythium*. Be certain the crop to be treated is listed on the product label before treating the crop.

Active Ingredients and Trade Names of the Chemicals

FRAC Group No.	Risk Level	Class	Active Ingredient	REI Restricted Entry Interval	Trade Names (EPA Reg. No.)
4	3	Acylanine	Mefenoxam	0	Subdue MAXX (100-796)
14	1	Thiadiazole	etridiazole	12	Truban (58185-7), Terrazole (400-416)
28	1	Carbamate	propamocarb	12	Banol (432-942)
40		Cinnamic acid derivative	dimethomorph	12	Stature (241-419-67690)
U	1	Phosphonate	fosetyl-A1	12	Aliette (432-890)
		Phosphite	phosphorus acid salts	4	Alude (71962-1-1001)
			potassium phosphate	4	Vital (42519-24)
Combined 1 products					
1+M			thiophanate methyl + etridiazole		Banrot (58185-10)

Fungicides and Fungicide Resistance Management

Certain fungicides, usually systemic fungicides, are said to be 'at risk' to the development of resistance if they are used repeatedly. A numbering system in which chemicals with the same FRAC Group number have the same mode of action has developed . It is recommended that chemicals at high risk be used sparingly and in rotation or mixed with chemicals with different modes of actions (different FRAC number).

Biological Control Agent (Type of Organism)	Trade Name (EPA Reg. No.)
Bacillus subtilis (bacterium)	Companion (GB03 strain) (71065-1), Serenade (69592-4), Rhapsody (QST 713 strain) (69592-10)
Candida oleophila (yeast)	Aspire (55638-29)
Gliocladium catenulatum (fungus)	
Streptomyces griseoviridis	Mycostop ((64137-5)
Trichoderma harziamum (fungus)	PlantShield, (68539-4)
Trichoderma virens	SoilGard (70051-3)

10

Cylindrocladium Black Rot (CBR)

Introduction

The fungal disease Cylindrocladium black rot (CBR) was first found in 1965 in peanut in southwest Georgia. It was not until 1975 and 1976 that CBR was first found in peanut in Florida, in Alachua and Columbia counties. In the mid 1980s CBR was found in peanut in the panhandle section of Florida. Since 1975, CBR has been found in alfalfa, clovers, and soybean.

Also, CBR has been found in hairy indigo, coffeeweed, and beggarweed in Florida. Among the weed species in the central Florida area, hairy indigo is the weed that is most commonly seen with CBR. In soybean, this disease is sometimes called red crown rot. Other crops reported to be susceptible to CBR are cowpea, bean, blueberry, and tobacco but in Florida CBR has not been found in these four crops. However, in blueberry, a related fungus has caused disease in Florida.

Yield losses from CBR in some infested fields of peanut in Florida have exceeded 50%. Cylindrocladium black rot has become a limiting factor for the production of peanut in some fields in the panhandle area, particularly in Santa Rosa County. In general, CBR appears to be gradually increasing in severity in peanut throughout the peanut-producing areas of Florida. Additionally in Florida, Cylindrocladium black rot has caused significant damage to plantings of alfalfa but levels of damage from CBR in soybean have been minimal. However, in Louisiana severe damage to soybean from CBR has been reported.

The fungus that causes CBR is *Cylindrocladium parasiticum* (*Cylindrocladium crotalariae)*. The sexual stage, *Calonectria ilicicola* (*Calonectria crotalari*ae), produces spores called ascospores. They are produced within bright red spherical structures called perithecia which sometimes can be seen on lower stems or peanut pods. The asexual stage produces spores known as conidia, which are formed externally on infected tissue. Neither spore type is considered to be important in the causation of this disease. However, ascospores are likely to function as sources of genetic variation within the species. Other species of *Cylindrocladium* have been reported to infect soybean.

Temperatures near 77° F are optimal for fungal growth, formation of ascospores and perithecia, and development of symptoms. The severity of CBR is reduced as soil temperatures deviate from 68° F to 86° F. Fungal growth and production of ascospores and perithecia can occur from 58° F to 91° F.

Ascospores can be produced more than one time within the same perithecium. Ascospores are discharged within a mucilaginous ooze from the perithecium during periods of reduced humidity. However, ascospores lose their germinability rapidly after discharge into reduced humidities. Spread of ascospores is primarily by physical contact with rain drops or other mechanical means. High soil moisture and abundant rainfall are favourable for infection and development of CBR.

The fungus, *C. parasiticum,* produces microsclerotia. (small aggregates of hyphae with a hardened exterior) within infected tissue, particularly in roots. Microsclerotia serve as inoculum for CBR by germinating to form fungal strands (hyphae) in the soil. These hyphae penetrate root, pod (for peanut), or lower stem tissue. Roots of peanut are commonly infected via hyphae through nitrification nodules.

Microsclerotia are distributed for long distances by wind which blows crop debris and infested soil, and by equipment and livestock which moves soil from field to field. Additional spread of the fungus within a field occurs with tillage of soil and harvest operations.

Microsclerotia in soil and infected weeds during rotation periods provide mechanisms for long term survival of *C. parasiticum*. A five-year interval of bahiagrass between peanut plantings was inadequate to reduce CBR in one situation. Soils that remain at 40° F or less for four weeks or longer during the winter have fewer sclerotia than warmer soils. Thus, winters in Florida are not cold enough to reduce inoculum (microsclerotia) for CBR. Microsclerotia survive better when buried with tillage operations than when left on the surface of the soil after harvest.

Some additional factors can influence the severity of CBR. For example, nematode damage can increase levels of CBR in some peanut varieties. Damage to root systems from cultivation is also likely to enhance CBR.

Symptoms

In peanuts, symptoms generally appear during July or August in Florida. However, in forage legumes, symptoms have been observed in May to June in Florida. Cylindrocladium black rot tends to be more severe during seasons with excessive rains, particularly on heavier (less sandy) soils. The greater severity of CBR in Santa Rosa County and a few other areas in the panhandle area, when compared to the central peanut-producing area from Ocala to Live Oak, is likely caused by the presence of heavier soil in the panhandle area. Sandier soils allow better drainage of excess moisture. Like many other soilborne diseases, CBR does not occur in a random pattern in fields.

Rather, CBR occurs in non-random patches. After the disease becomes distributed within a field across many years, the patchy occurrence becomes less obvious. Often the more severely affected areas in the field are in the wetter sites. Symptoms include wilting and eventually death of entire vines or plants.

When the fungus invades plant tissues, discoloured plant tissues result. Initially, infected tissue may be brown, but usually such infected tissue becomes black. Such discolouration is common in lower stems, pegs, and pods. Additionally, red perithecia can often be seen on lower stems or pods. The presence of perithecia is useful in distinguishing CBR from other soilborne diseases, such as white mold (caused by *Sclerotium rolfsii*), Rhizoctonia-induced diseases, nematode damage, or other diseases. The soilborne disease white mold and other soilborne problems can occur at the same time as CBR in the same field. Occasionally in Florida, a related fungus, *Nectria* spp., produces red perithecia seen on lower stems of peanut. The importance of *Nectria* spp. in relation to causation of disease in peanut has not been determined. Another fungus that produces reddish perithecia on peanut is *Neocosmospora sp.* Its causal relationship to disease in peanut is imperfectly understood at this time, but it can be pathogenic.

Symptoms and signs of CBR in other legume crops, such as soybean and alfalfa, are similar to those in peanut. Infected hairy indigo generally produces an abundance of perithecia on the lower blackened stem. The initial wilting associated with CBR in peanut, soybean, alfalfa, or clovers from CBR tends to be associated with bright yellow to red leaf discolouration. Browning of leaves occurs later. Initial leaf discolouration associated with white mold tends to be dull green to silvery. Confirmation of field diagnoses with laboratory tests is recommended if any doubt exists.

Ecology and Life Cycle

The fungus overwinters as microsclerotia. Intercellular penetration of the root cortex and *Rhizobium* nodules occurs within 24 hours of germination, and hyphae begin producing microsclerotia within several days. Peanut can produce protective periderms (dermal tissues typical of secondary growth) to wall off invaded and injured areas, and differences between susceptible and resistant varieties of peanut may be mainly due to the speed with which these periderms can be produced. Epidermal weaknesses may occur as a result of injury or the emergence of secondary roots, providing the pathogen additional entrance points.

The decay of dead tissue releases microsclerotia into the soil. Microsclerotia can be dispersed in wind-blown plant debris and by equipment. These propagules are not effective saprophytic competitors.

Perithecial initials can be found on peanut stems within a week after inoculation, and perithecia will form in large quantities on stems if adequate moisture is available. In North Carolina, perithecia have been observed as early as mid-June. Mature ascospores can be present within two to three weeks after inoculation. Conidia are rarely observed under field conditions, but ascospores appear to play a significant role in secondary disease spread within a growing season. Ascospores are discharged both by ejection and in viscous droplets that presumably can be dispersed by rain splash and runoff. Ascospore formation and discharge appear to be controlled by day-night relative humidity fluctuations. Ascospores mature under 100 per cent night-time humidity conditions. The drop in humidity that occurs at dawn triggers a widespread ascospore discharge coinciding with dew precipitation. Both ascospores and conidia are extremely sensitive to desiccation, and survival of either under normal day-time field levels of temperature and humidity is under 10 per cent after two minutes. Ascospore ejection occurs between 20 - 30° C, and maximally at 25° C, more or less coinciding with vegetative growth temperature optima

Control

At this time, tactics that are likely to elicit total control for CBR are not available for any susceptible crop. The best control available is to utilize as many of the control tactics as possible for each field. If possible, avoid planting susceptible crops in infested fields. Crop rotations of peanut with four to five years of bahiagrass have not been adequate for suppression of CBR in some situations. However, because higher levels of CBR are directly related to higher levels of microsclerotia in soil, crop rotation with non-susceptible crops is likely to be useful to some degree. Susceptible weeds such as hairy indigo, beggarweed, and coffeeweed should be reduced or eliminated.

Such weed control should be done when the susceptible crop is being grown and during rotational years when the susceptible crop is not being grown.

Plantings should be in fields that are well drained. Soil and plant debris should be removed from tractor tires and implements before moving from an infested to a non-infested field. Later planting of peanut has resulted in reduced levels of CBR. Because peanut is typically planted earlier than soybean in Florida, the later planting of soybean may be why CBR typically occurs less frequently in soybeans when compared to peanut.

Resistance to CBR in alfalfa has been pursued in Florida and elsewhere, but resistant varieties are not currently available. Some varieties of peanut (e.g., NC 10C) have low levels of resistance to CBR for use in Virginia and North Carolina. Comparisons of varieties in Florida and elsewhere have resulted in less CBR in Florunner, a commonly grown variety, when compared to NC 10C, Florigiant, and some other varieties. However, severe cases of CBR in Florunner in commercial plantings in Florida override any consideration that Florunner possesses any useful level of resistance to this disease. Some Spanish-type varieties possess slight resistance to CBR. The peanut varieties NC 12C, Georgia Green, Florida MDR 98, and Southern Runner incur less damage than Florunner and other susceptible varieties.

Chemical control for CBR in peanut has provided some control. In Virginia, North Carolina, and to a limited extent in Georgia, preplant fumigation with metam-sodium has been used successfully, particularly if fumigation is coupled with use of a resistant variety. The fumigant must be applied two to three weeks prior to planting. Typically, the fumigant is applied behind a chisel set 10 to 12" deep along the intended center of the row followed by hilling with coulters (ripping & bedding, ripping & hipping).

In Florida, CBR has been suppressed in peanut by means of post-plant sprays of select sprayable fungicides (e.g. Folicur) at mid-season. Control from sprays has been slightly erratic, but usually wilt and black pods have been reduced and higher yields occurred. In some situations the initial yellowing of leaves, is not dramatically reduced but pod blemish is reduced dramatically. More than two tons of peanut have been harvested per acre in some situations after midseason sprays were employed, even though widespread yellowing of plants occurred. However, if plants turn brown in the latter stage of discolouration, i.e., turn brown after the initial yellowing, yield losses increase drastically.

Some studies show that applications of nitrogen reduce CBR in peanut. This tactic should be avoided because applications of nitrogen to peanut have reduced yields. Reduced nodulation and delayed pod formation occur with increases in applied nitrogen.

11

Southern Blight of Soybeans

Southern blight is a minor disease of soybeans in the United States. Although the disease can occur in plants anytime from emergence through pod fill, it most commonly occurs in isolated plants in the latter stages of reproductive development. Occasionally, southern blight develops when plants are in the early to mid-vegetative stages. When this occurs, the disease may spread rapidly down rows, resulting in serious stand losses in patches. However, even in the worst case scenario, it would be extremely rare for southern blight to cause measurable yield losses in a commercial soybean field.

Symptoms and Signs

Plants affected by this disease wilt suddenly and die. Leaves of affected plants turn brown, dry up, and usually remain attached to the plant. Examination of diseased plants will reveal a light brown girdling lesicn at just above or just below the soil line. The most characteristic sign of this disease is the white fungal mat of mycelium which fans out over and about the lesion area. Fungal mats may also be present on plant debris and on the soil surface in the vicinity of an affected plant.

However, hot, humid weather favours the development of this fungal growth and it may not form, or may disappear altogether during dry weather. Affected plants usually develop numerous tan to brown fungal structures (sclerotia) which appear embedded in the fungal growth (Fig. 11.1). Sclerotia, which are about the size of a mustard seed, are the means by which the fungus survives from

Fig. 11.1

season to season. Sclerotia are not especially long-lived and rarely survive more than 3 to 4 years in the absence of a host crop.

Cause and Disease Development

Southern blight is caused by a soil-borne fungus, *Sclerotium rolfsii*. The conditions that favour this disease include high moisture levels, both in the soil and under the plant canopy, and relatively high temperatures. Drought conditions frequently precede severe disease outbreaks by predisposing plants to infection. The disease tends to be most prevalent in sandy or sandy loam soils, or soils with high levels of undecomposed organic matter.

Disease Management

In most situations, it is unnecessary to implement specific measures to control southern blight in soybean. However, where necessary, certain production practices may help to limit the impact of the disease. There are no resistant varieties.

Crop Rotation

When high populations of the southern blight fungus exist in a field, the only practical management option is to rotate the field to a non-host or least-favoured host crop, such as corn, milo, or pasture grasses, for a period of 3 to 4 years. The fungus can infect over 500 greatly diversified plant species. Thus, selection of a rotational crop should be done with great care. Where southern blight is a concern, but has not caused serious losses, rotating to a non-host, such as corn, for 2 years should be adequate for disease control in subsequent soybean crops.

Sanitation

If practical, burying infected soybean stubble, by deep plowing the first year out of soybeans, followed by less tillage in subsequent offsoybean years, will help reduce levels of the fungus in soil. If deep tillage is not an option, any tillage operation that encourages decomposition of infested soybean stubble and may help to reduce populations of the fungus in soil.

Cultural Practices

Disease incidence may also be moderated by application of calcium and nitrogen fertilizers.

12

Reniform Nematode (*Rotylenchulus reniformis*)

The reniform nematode (*Rotylenchulus reniformis*) like lesion and Columbia lance nematode is largely restricted to the southeastern portion of the state. Unlike these other species, however, it may be found in any soil type. Cotton, many vegetables, tobacco and soybean are good hosts for this nematode Corn and the certain soybean varieties are moderately to highly resistant to this parasite and resistant varieties should be considered as options, or in rotation, where reniform nematode is a problem.

Reniform nematodes in the genus *Rotylenchulus* are semiendoparasitic (partially inside roots) species in which the females penetrate the root cortex, establish a permanent-feeding site in the stele region of the root and become sedentary or immobile. The anterior portion (head region) of the body remains embedded in the root whereas the posterior portion (tail region) protrudes from the root surface and swells during maturation. The term 'reniform' refers to the kidney-shaped body of the mature female.

There are ten species in the genus *Rotylenchulus*. *Rotylenchulus reniformis* is the most economically important species and is called the reniform nematode.

Distribution and Host Range

Rotylenchulus reniformis is largely distributed in tropical, subtropical and in warm temperate zones in South America, North America, the Caribbean Basin, Africa, southern Europe, the Middle East, Asia, Australia, and the Pacific. It was first found on cowpea roots in Hawaii, and first reported as a parasite of cotton in Georgia and of tomato in Florida. Today, it is found throughout the southern United States.

In Florida, reniform nematodes are especially common in southern counties, Dade and Monroe, where Rockdale soils in this area favour the reniform nematode population development. Reniform nematodes are also common in the northwestern counties of Florida (Panhandle region), from Jefferson to Santa Rosa, especially in the cotton production area with heavier soils such as sandy loam, sandy clay and clay loam.

At least 314 plant species are host to reniform nematodes. Among them, cotton, cowpea, soybean, pineapple, tea and various vegetables are the most common hosts. Many weed and ornamental hosts to reniform nematode in Florida have been reported by the researchers. In south Florida, sweet potato, papaya, and several edible aroids are excellent host to reniform nematodes, and the reniform nematode was associated with several kinds of tropical fruit trees.

Life Cycle

Eggs hatch one to two weeks after being laid. The first-stage juvenile molts within the egg, producing the second-stage juvenile (J2) that emerges from the egg. The infective stage is reached one to two weeks after hatch. Once root penetration occurs, one or two more weeks are required for females to reach maturity. The male, which remains outside of the root, can inseminate prior to the female gonad maturation, and sperms are stored in the spermatheca. Numbers of females and males in a population are usually equal. Some populations of reniform nematodes reproduce parthenogenetically, i.e., egg production without fertilization. Soon after female gonad maturation, the eggs are fertilized with sperm, and eggs are then deposited into a gelatinous matrix with about 60 to 200 eggs. The life cycle of this nematode is usually shorter than three weeks depends on soil temperature. However, it can survive at least two years in the absence of a host in dry soil through anhydrobiosis, a survival mechanism without water.

Technical Description

The average body length is about 0.34 to 0.42 mm for juveniles and males, and 0.38 to 0.52 for mature female nematodes. Rest in a C shape when killed by heat. The lip region of the young female is not offset, and the cephalic framework is conspicuous. The stylet, 16 to 21 μm long, is of moderate strength with small rounded knob. The dorsal gland orifice is more than one-half the stylet length posterior to the base of stylet knobs. The basal glands overlap the intestine laterally, or less often ventrally. The vulva is post-median (V>63%). The female reproductive system is amphidelphic with two flexures in immature females and highly convoluted in mature females. The female tail is usually more than twice the anal body diameter. The juvenile tail tapers to a narrow, rounded terminus with about 20 to 24 annules. Phasmids are porelike, about the body width or less behind anus. Males have weak stylets and stylet knobs, a reduced esophagus, and an indistinct median bulb and valve. Caudal alae are adanal. The lateral field of males, young females, and juveniles has four incisures which are not areolated.

Economic Impact

Only females infect plant roots. After infection, a feeding site composed of syncytial-cells is formed. A syncytial cell is a multinucleated cell resulting from cell wall dissolution of several surrounding cells.

Among the crops most severely affected by reniform nematode are upland cotton, pineapple and many vegetable crops including tomato, okra, squash, and lettuce. The university extension services in Mississppi and Alabama recommend nematicide treatment for cotton fields if population density exceeds two nematodes/cm^3 soil in the spring and 10 nematodes/cm^3 in fall or winter. Economic threshold for reniform nematode on pineapple is 310 nematodes/250 cm^3 soil. Reniform nematode population densities reduced snap bean yield by 10 per cent in south Florida. Besides the direct damage, reniform is also an important factor in the incidence of *Fusarium* and *Verticillium* wilts of cotton, causing the *Fusarium*-wilt resistant varieties of cotton to become susceptible.

Management

No cotton and pineapple cultivars are resistant to reniform nematodes. Tolerant cotton breeding lines to reniform nematode had been developed. Soybean cultivars 'Peking', 'Dyer', 'Custer', and 'Pickett' are highly resistant to reniform nematode. Certain tomato cultivars are resistant to this nematode.

Crop rotation with resistant or immune plant species is recommended. These include mustard (*Brassica nigra*), oats, rhodesgrass (*Chloris gayana*), onion, sugarcane, and sun hemp (*Crotalaria juncea*). Pineapple is rotated with sugarcane or pagolagrass in Puerto Rico. Sorghum, maize and reniform nematode resistant soybeans are recommended as rotation crops for cotton.

Currently, Hawaiian pineapple plantations manage plant-parasitic nematodes by fallowing after pineapple for six to 12 months, then fumigating before planting, and applying postplant non-fumigant nematicides. However, dry fallow may be ineffective as a means of control since this nematode can enter into anhydrobiosis in slowly drying soils and revives when environmental conditions are favourable. Apt suggested that moist fallow would be more effective as a means of control. Fallow with weeds is also unfavourable because many weeds could be host to reniform nematode.

Areas free of reniform nematode impose regulation against this nematode. Chile and Switzerland are among the countries that have quarantine against reniform nematode. In the United States, Arizona, California and New Mexico restrict reniform nematode to protect their cotton industries. The ornamental industries of southern Florida and Hawaii are adversely affected by this regulation when the plant shipments are contaminated with reniform nematode. Therefore, expensive sanitation practices and the use of clean materials are required for ornamental plant nurseries.

Cultural Control

Crop rotation.Non-host crops or resistant crops can be planted when nematode population is high.

Use of Organic Amendments

Use of trap and antagonistic crops. Planting Tagetes erecta and Crotolaria spectabilis in nematode infested soil has been found effective against the nematode.

Biological Control

Paecilomyces lilacinus, a fungal egg parasite was found effective against the reniform nematode.

13

Soybean Sudden Death Syndrome

General Information

Sudden death syndrome (SDS) is the common name for a root-rot of soybean caused by the fungus *Fusarium solani* f.sp. glycine. The disease was first found in North Carolina in 2001, although it may have been present earlier. Yield loss in 2001 was negligible. The likelihood that major yield loses from SDS will occur in North Carolina is unclear, but SDS is a potentially serious disease. Periodically this disease has been a problem in the mid-south and mid-west since the 1980's. Most years the disease is of minor importance. In years when disease symptoms are widespread and apparently severe, soybean yields are generally excellent. The name "sudden death" refers to the early defoliation and death of the soybean plant. The common name stems from the fact that in wet years, foliar symptoms seem to spread rapidly through a field at or after the pod filling stage. Disease is usually more severe in high yield environments. Sudden death syndrome is often associated with the soybean cyst nematode, *Heterodera glycines*.

Phytophthora root and stem rot symptoms were first observed in Indiana in 1948 and in Ohio in 1951. The causal agent was identified in Ohio and North Carolina in 1954. Since that time, Phytophthora rot has been reported in Argentina, Australia, Brazil, Canada, the People's Republic of China, Hungary, Italy, Japan, the former Soviet Union, and throughout the soybean-growing regions of the United States.

The disease may cause plant stand losses and complete yield reductions in very susceptible soybean cultivars. The estimated reduction in yield in 1994 was 560,300 metric tons. The severity of losses depends on cultivar susceptibility, rainfall, soil type, tillage, and compaction. Phytophthora rot is most severe in poorly drained clay soils that are readily flooded. Plant loss can occur in lighter soils and on well-drained soils if they are saturated for an extended period of time when plants are young.

Soybean is the only important host of the causal fungus. It has been isolated from *Lupinus* spp. native to the United States. In greenhouse inoculation tests but not in the field, it has been found to be pathogenic to alfalfa, sweet clover, snap bean, and crane's-bill. For several years, Phytophthora isolates from alfalfa soybean, and other hosts were considered to be the same species, leading to confusing reports on the host range of the species that infects soybean. There is one report of *P. parasitica*, a pathogen with a large host range, causing soybean stem rot.

Symptoms

Foliar symptoms of soybean sudden death syndrome resemble those caused by several other plant pathogens and or damage from certain insects. Red crown rot (black root rot), phytophthora root rot, charcoal rot, stem canker, brown stem rot, southern blight, and occasionally, damage from dectes stem borer (an insect) may also cause leaf symptoms that resemble SDS. The symptoms associated with red crown rot, caused by *Cylindrocladium parasiticum* (the same fungus causes CBR in peanut), are virtually identical to those found with sudden death syndrome caused by *F. solani*.

Foliar symptoms of sudden death syndrome typically do not appear prior to soybean flowering. Early symptoms at the R3 and later growth stages, if present, are only chlorotic (yellow) spots on the leaves between veins. As the soybean plant progresses to the pod forming stage these yellow spots may coalesce, becoming yellow between the veins which remain green. Leaves may become crinkled, resembling virus infection. As disease progresses further, the yellow between the veins will become brown (necrotic) as the tissue dies. Roots will exhibit an obvious root rot and plants can be easily pulled from the soil. Splitting the stem with a sharp knife will reveal a brown to reddish-brown discoloration of the lower stem and root. The discoloration of the vascular elements, usually will not extend more than an inch or two above the soil line.The pith will remain white, unless other diseases such as phytophthora root rot or charcoal rot are also present. Pods may be aborted and plants may defoliate early. Often, defoliated plants will retain their petioles. Retention of the petioles is a symptom frequently associated with SDS, but less commonly with red crown rot of soybean). Symptoms on the root system are difficult to distinguish from other soybean root rots. Typically the causal fungus must be isolated in a lab and the pathogen identified under a microscope. Occasionally the fungus will form masses of white spores on the roots that may become blue to blue-green as they mature. Correct identification of disease is important in formulating a management strategy.

In older plants of highly tolerant cultivars, the only symptoms are generally rot of the secondary roots and discoloration of the taproot. These plants are not killed by the fungus but may be stunted and slightly chlorotic, and symptoms may resemble those of mild nitrogen deficiency or flooding. Occasionally, a one-sided stem lesion may occur in such cultivars. These mild symptoms, referred to as hidden damage, may reduce yield by as much as 40 per cent. Hidden damage can be seen and measured by comparing nontreated plants with those treated with a fungicide such as metalaxyl or by comparing near-isogenic lines with and without race-specific resistance.

Foliar blight has been reported after heavy rains and can be produced in a growth chamber on young leaves. Symptoms consist of progressive, light brown lesions with yellow margins that can form on young leaflets under continuous misting. Older leaves are resistant to foliar blight, a phenomenon referred to as age-related resistance.

Causal Organism

P. sojae produces simple, indeterminate sporangiophores. Typically, terminal sporangia (conidia) are obpyriform (32–53 × 42–65 µm) and nonpapillate. Sporangia germinate indirectly by extruding fully formed zoospores into a thin, delicate, membranous, evanescent vesicle, which quickly expands and ruptures. Zoospores are sometimes trapped within sporangia and germinate there. The resulting germ tubes penetrate the sporangium wall. Empty sporangia commonly proliferate internally, forming new sporangia terminally or within the old sporangia. Sporangia may also germinate directly, functioning as conidia. Hyphal swellings are commonly formed.

The optimum temperature for direct germination is 25ºC, for indirect germination 14ºC, and for zoospore production 20ºC. Zoospores are ovoid, bluntly pointed at one or both ends, and flattened on the sides. They have two flagella, a short one directed anteriorly and the other, four to five times as long, directed posteriorly. At the end of the motile period, which may last up to several days, zoospore movement becomes sluggish and jerky and encystment occurs. Encystment may be triggered prematurely by agitation or by bivalent or trivalent cations. The cysts frequently germinate immediately and directly, producing germ tubes, which generally swell to form appressoria when they contact a solid surface. After a short time, normal growth of mycelia is resumed from the appressoria. Cysts sometimes germinate by producing secondary zoospores, leaving the cyst membrane behind. Rarely, a miniature sporangium is formed at the tip of the germ tube. Cysts germinate more vigorously in nutrient solutions than in distilled water.

P. sojae is homothallic. Antheridia and oogonia develop in abundance on corn meal, lima bean, V8, or potato dextrose agar. The antheridia are diclinous and generally paragynous, although amphigynous antheridia may be found. The oogonia (29-58 µm) are thin walled and spherical or subspherical. An oospore develops after an antheridium fertilizes an oogonium. Dormant oospores have thick, smooth inner and outer walls, fine-grained cytoplasm, a spherical, refractive body in the centre, a well-developed reserve granule, and a pair of pellucid bodies at the outer edge of the cytoplasm. Germination may occur after the pellucid bodies merge and fuse. At germination, the pellucid bodies are no longer detectable, the smooth inner wall erodes, the central refractive body is absorbed, and the spore has the appearance of a sporangium. When the oospore germinates, the inner wall is absorbed and the germ tube produces either a sporangium or mycelium.

Oospores may germinate about 30 days after formation. Germination occurs in distilled water and is increased by low levels of nutrients and root exudates. Light increases the percentage of germination but inhibits subsequent formation of sporangia. This inhibition of sporangial formation is reversed by root exudates. Oospore germination is initiated within 2 days of separation from mycelium but is nonsynchronous and may continue for 30 days or more. The optimum temperature for formation and germination of oospores is 24°C.

Diagnosis

As mentioned earlier, a number of pathogens cause symptoms that resemble SDS. Red crown rot, in particular, has symptoms that are virtually identical to SDS. Often it will be necessary to have the fungus isolated to be certain of the cause. Plant and soil samples can be sent to the plant disease and insect clinic through your North Carolina Cooperative Extension Service County Agent.

Disease Cycle and Epidemiology

Sudden death syndrome is caused by the soil-inhabiting fungus *Fusarium solani* f.sp. glycine The fungus survives in the soil for numerous years and may be able to increase on other hosts. Crop rotation does not seem to affect disease severity, and sudden death syndrome has occurred following corn or cotton crops. Suppression of soybean cyst nematode through crop rotation or the use of cyst resistant soybean varieties may result in less disease. Infection of soybean roots by *F. solani* probably takes place shortly after soybean emergence. Wounds or changes in plant physiology caused by infection by plant-parasitic nematodes may increase the severity of SDS. Disease development is favoured by high soil moisture. Symptom development may progress rapidly following cool weather. The fungus survives in decayed plant tissue and soil after the plant dies.

Because of the foliar symptoms, researchers have suggested that a toxin produced by the fungus induces these symptoms. The similarity of the SDS foliar symptoms to several other soybean diseases that affect the vascular system, however, suggests that symptom expression is probably a response of the plant to stress at pod filling.

Management

Recommendations for management of SDS is based on data developed in other states. Soybean varieties with moderate-to-high levels of resistance to SDS are available. Growers are advised to check literature provided by their seed supplier for information on disease resistance. Varieties resistant to SDS should be considered in fields known to be affected by this disease. In choosing a variety, however, be certain that it has resistance to pathogens known to be present such as *Phytophthora sojae*, cyst or root-knot nematodes. Many new varieties and especially varieties in later maturity groups have not been evaluated for resistance to this disease.

Crop rotation does not seem to affect disease severity. Sudden death`syndrome has occurred following corn or cotton crops. Nonetheless, growers should continue with rotations and or cropping systems that suppress population densities of plant-parasitic nematodes. Suppression of soybean cyst and (or) root-knot nematode through crop rotation or the use of soybean varieties resistant to the species and races of plant-parasitic nematode present may limit yield loss from SDS.

Sudden death syndrome tends to be more severe in fields under reduced tillage regimes. Late planting, as occurs with double cropping small grains and soybean or the use of early maturing varieties may also suppress disease development.

14

Diseases of Leaf

Soybean Rust

An important new disease threat to soybean is currently the cause of much concern in the agricultural community. Asiatic soybean rust, caused by *Phakospora pachyrizi*, has emerged as a major constraint to soybean production in South America since 2001. Another species of rust *Phakospora meibomiae* has been endemic to portions of South America for many years but is considered less of a threat because it is not as aggressive as the Asiatic soybean rust. During the 2003-2004 growing season in Brazil, Asiatic rust was severe in many areas and required sprays of fungicides in order to control this disease. Many industry leaders and some scientists predict that its introduction to North America is eminent and that it will impact US soybean production. Asiatic soybean rust is present in Hawaii, but has not yet been reported in the Continental US. Some plant pathologists, however, suspect that it would be a minor problem if and when it does arrive in the US. Predictive models suggest that conditions in Georgia, South Carolina, Virginia, and North Carolina are favourable for development of an epidemic of soybean rust. The soybean rust pathogen is primarily tropical in distribution and would be able to survive over winter in only the most southern portions of the US (Southern Florida and Texas). Alternate hosts for Asiatic soybean rust in the US include kudzu, winter vetch, and lupines. Should this disease be introduced to the US an emergency registration of additional fungicides for use on soybean will take effect for three years.

Symptoms

Asiatic soybean rust causes superficial, tan to reddish brown, lesions that will be observed on plant tissues. Lesions will contain one to three rust pustules which are raised on the leaf surface. The lesions may have an angular appearance and be limited by leaf veins. Rust pustules may appear on cotyledons, leaves, petioles, stems, or pods, but are most likely to be observed as raised pustules on the under side of the leaf. The pustules are quite small (about the size of a pin head) and can be confused with another disease, bacterial pustule. Bacterial pustule, however, is rare in commercial soybean varieties, since most if not all are resistant to this disease. A hand lens may aid in seeing the raised nature of the pustule. Also, placing leaves in a plastic bag with a moist paper towel for twenty four hours may cause the pustules to erupt, thus making identification easier. Each pustule contains hundreds of spores. Spores are elliptical to obovoid in shape, colourless to yellowish or yellowish brown and minutely and densely spiny. Infected plants will senesce early and have smaller seed with reduced yield.

Disease Cycle and Epidemiology

Windblown spores infect susceptible tissue at temperatures of 45 to 83 degrees. Leaves must be wet for infection to occur. Pustules will develop within a week to ten days after infection, and spores are produced after about three weeks. The spores are the only survival structures for this fungus and they will not survive freezing weather. The role other hosts (kudzu, winter vetch, lima beans, dry beans, and lupines) might play is not known, but fields with kudzu along borders might be a good place to start scouting.

Soybean rust may be able to survive in southern Florida and Texas, but the soybean acreage in these states is limited at this time. Several species of common bean are also hosts for this fungus, but fungicide sprays to control other diseases on these vegetable crops may limit rust development. For states on the Atlantic Coast, windblown spores will have to move northward from southern Florida. A second possibility is for spores to come from the Mississippi Valley. In 2003, Soybean acreage in Florida was less than 10,000 and only about 150,000 in Georgia. Thus the potential for windblown inoculum coming from these sources is not terribly high. For rust to be damaging first infections will probably have to occur before the R3 stage of soybean development.

Management

There are no commercial soybean varieties with resistance to soybean rust at this time. Management of soybean rust will be with fungicides. Currently, the only fungicides labeled for soybean that are effective in managing soybean rust are chlorothalonil (various brands) and azoxystrobin (Quadris). Although Topsin M is also labeled for soybean, it is not effective against rusts. If soybean rust is identified in the Continental US an emergency registration of eight additional fungicides will go into effect for three years (Table 14.1).

In general the recommendation will be to make one application at the R3 stage of development and a second one 10-14 days later. Late season sprays (after R5 to R6) have not been effective in South America unless they follow an earlier spray. Because soybean rust may develop resistance to the triazole and strobilurin class of fungicides, it may be best to rotate the use of materials. Preliminary reports indicate that the triazole type fungicides have more curative activity than the strobilurin class fungicides, the first spray should be a triazole fungicide and the second spray should be made with a strobilurin. If a third spray is required chlorothalonil might be the best option since it may control some other late season diseases that the other materials do not.

Table 14.1: Fungicides for Management of Soybean Rust

Brand Name	Common Name	Fungicide Class	Currently Labelled	Will be Labelled
Bravo	Chlorothalonil		Yes	
Quadris	Azoxystrobin	Strobiurin	Yes	
Headline	Pyraclostrobin	Strobilurin	No	Yes
Tilt, PropiMax, Bumper	Propiconazole	Triazole	No	Yes
Folicur	Tebuconazole	Triazole	No	Yes
Laredo	Myclobutanil	Triazole	No	Yes
Domark	Tetraconazole	Triazole	No	Yes
Stratego	Propiconazole + Trifloxystrobin	Triazole/ Strobilurin	No	Yes
Pristine	Pyraclostrobin + Boscalid	Strobilurin/ Anilide	No	Yes

Cercospora Leaf Blight and Purple Seed Stain

Cercospora leaf blight most often occurs in southern areas of the U.S, but also occurs in the northern Midwest. The disease can cause severe defoliation of plants and reduce yields, especially in the southern U.S. Symptoms usually become apparent during seed set. Seeds on infected plants can develop purple seed stain.

Symptoms

The first symptom of Cercospora leaf blight is the development of light purple spots and areas on the top surface of leaves exposed to light. The discoloured areas expand and deepen in colour to a reddish-purple or bronze. The infected leaves appear leathery and 'sunburned'. Red-brown spots may develop on both leaf surfaces. The spots may coalesce to form large necrotic areas on leaves, which eventually results in defoliation of infected leaves in the upper canopy. Reddish-purple lesions may also occur on petioles, stems, and pods. Infected seeds have pink to purple discolouration on the seed coats.

Conditions and Timing that Favour Disease

Infection and disease development is favoured by high humidity and warm temperatures. Plants are susceptible from flowering to maturity.

Causal Pathogen

Cercospora leaf blight is caused by the fungus *Cercospora kikuchii*. The pathogen overwinters on infested debris or seed. The same pathogen causes purple seed stain.

Disease Management

Use pathogen-free seed and varieties with low susceptibility to Cercospora leaf blight. Rotation out of soybeans may be helpful, and foliar and seed treatment fungicides may be useful for managing this disease.

Bacterial Blight

- **Pathogen:** Bacterium. *Pseudomonas syringae pv. glycinea*
- **Symptoms:** Initial symptoms are small angular watersoaked spots on leaves. Lesion centres dry out and turn brown to black with watersoaked margins and yellow halos. Lesions may coalesce resulting in large blighted areas. Affected tissue often drops out, giving a tattered appearance to the leaves. Rarely a serious disease in Indiana soybeans.
- **Conditions:** Cool, rainy weather. Outbreaks often follow thunderstorms.
- **Inoculum Survival:** Seed, infected crop residue.
- **Inoculum Dispersal:** Airborne bacteria from rainsplash, mechanical (cultivators).
- **Management:** Resistant cultivars, plant pathogen-free seed, crop rotation, avoid cultivation when foliage is wet.

Bacterial blight can be found in most soybean fields every year in the Midwest, but at low levels that do not limit yield. Leaf spots caused by the bacterial blight pathogen, *Pseudomonas syringae* pv. *glycinea*can occur at any time, but are most common during rainy, humid periods in July and August. The bacteria can also infect snap bean and lima bean.

Bacterial blight can be confused with brown spot (Septoria leaf spot) and with bacterial pustule. Bacterial blight and brown spot are especially common. Both diseases often occur in the same fields and even the same plant, and symptoms can be diffilcult to separate.

Disease Cycle

The bacteria that cause bacterial blight overwinter in crop residue and on seed. Initial infections can occur during seedling emergence, especially if infected seed is planted. The bacteria are spread by wind and rain, and outbreaks that occur later in the season often follow wiindy rainstorms. Bacterial blight is favoured in continuous soybean fields, no-till soybean fields, or fields planted with seeds from infected soybeans.

Agronomic Impact

Bacterial blight occurs every year in the Midwest without causing significant yield losses except in unusually rainy growing seasons. However, bacterial diseases should be monitored carefully in seed production fields because they are seedborne and can affect seed quality.

In severe cases, bacterial foliar disease may cause some early defoliation, but it will not kill whole plants. Severely affected plants may have smaller seeds. Soybean varieties differ in their susceptibility.

Symptoms and Scouting

Outbreaks typically develop several days after a rainstorm or hailstorm. Symptoms are most evident on new growth that is expanding at the time of the rain event. New lesions of bacterial blight are small, angular, water-soaked, yellow to brown spots on leaves.

The angular lesions enlarge in cool (70-80° F), rainy weather and merge to produce large, irregular patches of dead tissue. The centres of these patches often drop out, giving infected leaves a ragged appearance. The bacteria can also infect stems, petioles, and pods.

Brown spot lesions caused by *Septoria* develop a more generalized yellowing where brown spots are present.

Look-alikes

Bacterial blight is often confused with brown spot, a leaf spot disease caused by the fungus *Septoria glycines*. Bacterial blight occurs on upper new leaves and brown spot infection begins on older leaves, or leaves on the lower part of the plant. A characteristic yellow halo forms around lesions caused by bacterial blight, whereas leaves infected by brown spot show a more generalized leaf yellowing when numerous brown spots are present.

Management

Control measures are generallly not needed. However, if bacterial blight was severe this season, the following agronomic practices will reduce the disease next season:

- rotate soybean with a non-legume
- cover soybean residues after harvest by tillage, if possible, or shred residue for quick decomposition.
- plant pathogen-free seed. Do not use seed from plants infected with bacterial blight.

Foliar fungicides will not affect bacterial blight because it is a caused by a bacterial pathogen, not a fungus.

Bacterial Pustule

Bacterial pustule is most common in areas prone to frequent warm and wet weather. The disease rarely causes defoliation and reduced yields. Early symptoms of bacterial pustule look similar to bacterial blight. Bacterial pustule can be differentiated by a lack of water soaking at the initial site of infection, less chlorosis around lesions, and by the formation of tiny tan bumps on the undersides of leaves. The pustules can be mistaken for those of soybean rust, however, bacterial pustule does not have an opening in the pustules or masses of spores like those of soybean rust.

Symptoms

Symptoms begin as small, light green spots (not water-soaked) with raised centres on the upper and lower surfaces of leaves. Light-coloured pustules (blisters) often develop in the centre of lesions, especially on the undersides of leaves. The lesions can grow together into large irregular brown areas. The infected areas may tear away from the leaf. Small raised spots may also develop on pods.

Conditions and Timing that Favour Disease

The disease can occur at any time during the growing season and is favoured by warm, wet weather conditions.

Causal Pathogen

Bacterial pustule is caused by the bacterium *Xanthomonas axonopodis* pv. *glycines*. This pathogen overwinters in unburied crop residue and on seeds. The pathogen can be transmitted by seed, and can be spread by windblown rain, rain splash, and by machinery during wet conditions. Bacterial pustule can also infect snap beans.

Disease Management

Plant resistant varieties and use pathogen-free seed to help manage bacterial pustule. Rotate soybeans with non-host crops. Plowing may be beneficial in fields where bacterial pustule is common. Avoid field cultivation when the foliage is wet.

Bean Pod Mottle Virus

Bean pod mottle virus (BPMV) is widespread viral disease in the U.S soybean growing areas that is transmitted by leaf-feeding beetles. BPVM can affect seed quality and cause yield loss, especially when plants are infected as seedlings. In addition, plants infected with bean pod mottle virus may be predisposed to seed infection by Phomopsis fungi that also reduce seed quality.

Symptoms

Bean pod mottle virus causes green to yellow mottling of young leaves. In severe infections, leaves may become distorted. Seeds from infected plants may be mottled or discoloured, but other factors can also cause mottled seed. Symptoms may not be apparent at high temperatures or after pod set. Pod formation may be reduced when infected plants are under moisture stress. BPMV can interact with the soybean mosaic virus to create severe symptoms in plants infected by both viruses. BPMV may also be related to the development of green stem syndrome, in which plants retain green stems and leaves after pods and most nearby plants have matured.

Conditions and Timing that Favour Disease

Plants can be infected at any time during the growing season, but infection generally seems to occur early in the season. Cool temperatures favour development of BPMV symptoms. Infection is also favoured by high populations of bean leaf or other beetles that transmit the virus. The rate of infection is reduced following severe winters that result in poor survival of beetles.

Causal Pathogen

The causal agent of BPMV is a virus. The disease is transmitted by leaf-feeding beetles, such as the bean leaf beetle and the western corn rootworm adults. The virus can also be transmitted sap and by infected seed, but seed transmission rates are very low and have been estimated to be 0.1 per cent. The host range of BPMV includes common bean and some clovers. Overwintering beetles and some perennial weeds near the edges of fields may be sources of the virus in the spring and early summer.

Disease Management

At this point, effective management tactics are not available. Resistant varieties are in development and not available commercially. The value of insecticides for controlling transmission via the bean leaf beetle is uncertain.

Brown Spot - Septoria Leaf Blight

- **Disease Name:** Brown Spot
- **Pathogen:** Fungus. *Septoria glycines*
- **Symptoms:** Irregular light-brown lesions, ranging in size from small specks to a few mm in diameter. Lesions eventually darken to brownish black. Lesions are primarily found on leaves, but can also occur on stems, petioles and pods. Early season infection is restricted to unifoliate and first trifoliate leaves.
- **Conditions:** Extended warm, wet weather.
- **Inoculum Survival:** Seed, infected crop residue.
- **Inoculum Dispersal:** Airborne spores.
- **Management:** Plant pathogen-free seed, crop rotation, foliar fungicide at R-3 stage, plow under crop residue.

The brown spot pathogen, the fungus *Septoria glycines*, is common in soybean residue and spreads from the soil to young soybean plants by splashing rain. Infection occurs as early as the V2 growth stage on lower leaves, causing small, irregularly shaped brown spots or lesions.

In warm, wet weather, the disease may move up through the plant. Late in the growing season, infected leaves may turn rusty brown or yellow and drop prematurely. The spread of the fungus usually stops during hot, dry weather.

Sometimes, brown spot can be mistaken as bacterial blight but the two diseases are easy to distinguish because bacterial blight occurs on upper new leaves and brown spot infects the older leaves on the lower parts of plants.

Brown spot does not usually affect soybean productivity unless more than 25-50 per cent of the canopy defoliates prematurely. Disease severity at the R6 growth stage is predictive of yield. Severe brown spot results in smaller seed size.

Symptoms

Symptoms of brown spot appear first on the cotyle-dons and unifoliate leaves early in the growing season. Angular, red to brown spots that vary in size from tiny specks to 1/4 inch diameter can be seen on the upper and lower leaf surfaces. Leaves with numer-ous spots rapidly turn yellow and fall to the ground. Defoliation proceeds from the bottom of the plant toward the top of the plant. Irregular brown lesions with indefinite borders may also develop on infected pods, stems, and petioles.

Management of Brown Spot

- **Soybean Variety**: Symptoms of brown spot appear earlier in the season on early-maturing soybeans. Complete resistance has not been identified in soybean varieties or lines, but varieties do differ in partial or rate-reducing resistance which can be used effectively.
- **Crop Rotation and Tillage**: *Septoria* leaf blight is more severe in continuously cropped soybean fields. The host range includes most species of *Glycine*, other legume species, and common weeds such as velvetleaf. For fields with very high levels of *Septoria* leaf blight, plow under soybean straw to promote decay.

- **Fungicide**: Although rarely needed, fungicides applied at growth stages R3 and R6 effectively slow the rate of disease development. Thiophanate-methyl is registered in the USA as a fungicide to control *Septoria* leaf blight of soybean.

Downy Mildew

Downy mildew is a widespread disease that occurs during periods of high humidity and moderate temperatures. The disease is typically superficial and causes no yield loss, but can cause defoliation of plants and reduced yields under rare conditions. Downy mildew can be distinguished from other foliar soybean diseases by the tufts of tan-coloured fungal growth on the underside of infected leaves.

Symptoms

The initial symptoms of downy mildew are small, light green spots (not water-soaked) on upper leaf surfaces. The spots enlarge and turn pale to bright yellow. They may coalesce into large irregular brown areas. Tan to gray tufts of fungal growth often develop on lower leaf surfaces, especially under wet and humid conditions. Infection of pods and seed can also occur. Seeds may become covered with a whitish coating of fungal hyphae and spores.

Conditions and Timing that Favour Disease

Downy mildew can occur on plants of all ages, although the disease is most common after flowering begins. Young leaves are most susceptible and infected leaves are often seen on the tops of plants. Dew and high humidity favour disease development, as well as mild temperatures.

Causal Pathogen

Downy mildew is caused by the fungal-like organism *Peronospora manshurica*. Common snap bean is also a host. The fungus overwinters on infected leaves and seeds, and can be transmitted by seed.

Disease Cycle

The downy mildew pathogen, Peronospora manshurica, survives in crop residue and on the surface of seed. Spores carried onto plants by wind and rain infect soybean leaves and can spread quickly through a field during periods of cool, wet or humid weather. The fungus can also infect seedlings systemically if mildew-infected seeds are planted.

Agronomic Impact

Although common, downy mildew rarely causes yield loss from leaf infection. Epidemics have occasionally occurred in the Midwest, causing yield losses of 9 to 18 per cent, depending on the soybean variety.

Downy mildew is carefully monitored during the development of new soybean varieties, especially when new sources of soybean germplasm or transgenic technology is used. This is because the downy mildew fungus is a biotrophic organism, which means it can grow and reproduce only in association with the soybean plant. Because of this very close relationship with the soybean plant, it is capable of rapid genetic change in response to genetic changes in soybean, and many different races of the downy mildew pathogen exist.

Symptoms and Scouting

Downy mildew is very weather-dependent and is most likely to occur during periods of cool, wet weather. Younger leaves are more susceptible to downy mildew than older leaves, so the disease will generally appear first on the upper surface of young leaves.

Look for pale green to light yellow spots which enlarge into pale to bright yellow spots. The centre of the spots eventually turns brown, bordered by yellow margins. Check the leaves for signs of grayish to pale-purplish spores on the lower leaf surface during humid weather. The presence of this sporulation is diagnostic for downy mildew. Some soybean varieties express mild leaf distortion that may resemble symptoms caused by common soybean viruses.

Pods can also be infected without obvious external symptoms. Infected seed has a dull white appearance and is partially or completely covered with a pale coating of fungal spores which can be confused with white mold.

Management

- Fungicides are not recommended for control of downy mildew because it rarely reduces yield. Implementing cultural controls to reduce the risk of downy mildew is generally all that is needed.
- Plant clean seed. Plant certified, disease-free seed. Do not plant seed from infected fields.
- Rotate crops and manage crop residue. The downy mildew fungus survives in crop residue and on the surface of seed. Longer crop rotations, tilling crop residues after harvest, or shredding soybean straw with a combine-mounted shredder will reduce disease risk.
- Consider variety resistance. Soybean varieties grown in the Midwest are rarely characterized for downy mildew resistance because the disease is considered to be a minor one. However, numerous sources of resistance to *P. manshurica* are present in soybean germplasm, and soybean variety reaction to downy mildew ranges from susceptible to resistant to specific races of the pathogen. No variety is resistant to every race of *P. manshurica.*

Frogeye Leaf Spot

Frogeye leaf spot is a common problem in the southern and central United States and can occur in some areas of the upper Midwest. It has been reported as far north as southern Wisconsin. The disease may cause severe defoliation during warm, humid weather. Frogeye leaf spot can be distinguished from other soybean foliar diseases by the reddish-brown or purple ring surrounding the round leaf spots.

Symptoms

Symptoms of frogeye leaf spot are most visible and typically seen on leaves, but can also occur on stems, pods, and seeds. Lesions on leaves begin as small, dark, water-soaked spots. They develop into brown spots surrounded by a darker reddish-brown or purple ring. The centres of the lesions turn light brown or light gray as they age. The centre of spots may turn white with black specks visible (fungal fruiting structures) or the centres may fall away leaving a 'shot hole' appearance. The lesions may eventually merge, covering large areas of the leaves and resulting in defoliation.

Conditions and Timing that Favour Disease

Frogeye leaf spot can occur at any time during the growing season, but seems to typically occur after flowering. Young leaves on the tops of plants tend to be most susceptible. Infection and disease development is favoured by warm, humid weather.

Causal Pathogen

Frogeye leaf spot is caused by the fungus *Cercospora sojina*. More than five races are known in the U.S. The pathogen overwinters in soybean residue and seeds.

Disease Cycle

Cercospora sojina survives in infected seed and plant debris from an infected crop. Infected seed may germinate poorly, and plants that do emerge from infected seed are often stunted and may have lesions on the cotyledons. These lesions produce spores that can be inoculum for leaf infections.

The fungus can also produce spores on the residue of a previous soybean crop. Although most soybean is grown in rotation with corn (meaning there is little soybean residue in newly planted soybean fields), enough soybean residue can remain to supply spores to begin an epidemic. Wind readily transports the spores of *Cercospora sojina* (whether these have been produced on residue or new lesions) from one field to another.

Spore production and infection requires warm, humid weather. Leaves are most susceptible to infection when they are just emerging and become less susceptible as they mature. This range of susceptibility can lead to a layered occurrence of disease in the plant canopy, depending on how conducive conditions were as each leaf layer emerged.

Frogeye leaf spot is a polycyclic disease, meaning that the number of lesions on the plant will continue to increase as long as the weather is favourable for infection. The greater the number of lesions, the greater the reduction of green leaf area, and the greater the reduction in yield. If favourable conditions for infection persist until late in the season, the fungus will infect pods and seeds.

Disease Management

To manage frogeye leaf spot, use resistant soybean varieties and pathogen-free seed. Rotate soybeans with a non-bean crop. Bury infested residue where feasible and where disease is severe. Foliar and seed treatment fungicides may provide some control.

Powdery Mildew

Powdery mildew occurs sporadically on soybeans, typically late in the season during periods of cool temperatures. The disease rarely appears to rarely cause yield loss, but it can potentially cause defoliation and reduced yields in susceptible varieties. Powdery mildew is differentiated from other foliar diseases by the white, powdery coating on infected leaves that looks similar to white flour sprinkled unevenly on the leaf surfaces.

Symptoms

All aerial plant parts can be infected by powdery mildew, although symptoms are most easily seen on the uppers surfaces of leaves. Infected leaves have white to light grey, powdery patches. These patches may enlarge and cover the surfaces of many leaves throughout a plant, however, infected leaves tend to be most common on the lower and middle leaves. Powdery mildew symptoms may vary among cultivars. Leaves on susceptible varieties may turn yellow, then brown, and fall from the plant.

Conditions and Timing that Favour Disease

Plants are most susceptible during the mid to late reproductive stages. Cool weather late in the growing season is most favourable for disease development. Rainfall is not known to increase the disease.

Causal Pathogen

Powdery mildew is caused by the fungus *Microsphaera diffusa*. Other hosts of this fungus include common bean, pea, and cowpea.

Disease Cycle

Cool weather (66-74°F) is most favourable for mildew development, and disease incidence is greater in seasons with cooler than normal temperatures. Rainfall does not seem to affect the disease. Plants are susceptible at any growth stage, but symptoms are rarely seen in the field until the mid- to late reproductive stages.

Agronomic Impact

Research studies have estimated yield loss by comparing yield of plots treated or not treated with a fungicide or comparing yield of resistant and susceptible cultivars during powdery mildew epidemics. Measured yield losses of 0 to 10 bushels per acre were estimated in Iowa studies, and 0 to 5 bushels per acre in Wisconsin. Late-planted soybean are at higher risk of yield loss than early-planted soybeans.

Symptoms and Scouting

White, powdery patches of the fungus that develop on cotyledons, stems, pods, and upper surface of leaves is a diagnostic sign of powdery mildew. Small colonies form initially, which can enlarge and coalesce to cover the entire surface of infected plant parts when conditions are favourable.

Occasionally, infected leaves may have yellow patches or browning tissue between veins, but these symptoms may be masked when the powdery fungal growth is abundant. Yellow spots and veinal necrosis can be signs of a resistant reaction to infection.

Management

- Crop rotation is not effective because the pathogen is readily introduced into fields by long-range dissemination of wind-blown spores.
- Powdery mildew is frequently more severe in late-planted soybean fields.
- Large differences in disease severity can be observed among soybean varieties. However, it is difficult for companies to breed for resistance because powdery

mildew pressure is low or nonexistent in most years. Generally, most determinate soybean cultivars are highly resistant to powdery mildew, while many indeterminate cultivars are susceptible.

- Several fungicides are labelled for powdery mildew and can be effective, if necessary.

Septoria Brown Spot

Septoria brown spot (also called brown spot) is common leaf disease of soybean across the Midwestern U.S. It's incidence can be high but it rarely develops to cause significant yield loss. Yield losses of 5-8 per cent may occur under severe conditions when much defoliation occurs. Where soybean rust may occur, it can create diagnostic problems because these two diseases can cause similar small, dark spots on leaves.

Symptoms

The first symptoms usually appear on the lower leaves and then progresses to the mid-to-upper canopy throughout the summer. Initial symptoms are small dark brown spots (<1/8" in size). It can develop on the first true leaves early in the season. The brown spots often enlarge and grow together into irregular brown areas, which often are associated with yellow patches concentrated more on one side of the leaf than another. The brown areas can contain tiny raised specks called pycnidia (visible with a hand lens) where spores are produced. Infected leaves may fall off prematurely.

Conditions and Timing that Favour Disease

Like most foliar diseases, Septoria brown spot is most common when conditions and leaves are wet and warm, ideally for extended periods of time. Because the pathogen survives and sporuates on soybean residue, minimum tillage and continuous soybeans may enhance this disease.

Causal Pathogen

Septoria glycines is a fungus that survives on crop residue and may be seed transmitted.

Disease Cycle

Septoria glycines overwinters on infected plant debris and occasionally on seed. The pathogen spreads from the soil to lower soybean leaves by splashing rain. Epidemics can occur in seasons with frequent rainfall. The spread of the fungus stops during hot, dry weather.

Because the brown spot pathogen infects aging leaves, soybeans weakened by other diseases or agronomic practices become more susceptible to this disease. It has been observed that relatively high levels of brown spot occur in fields with severe soybean cyst nematode damage, Fusarium root rot, and other conditions. If you find abundant brown spot, check whether another primary cause is present, such as nematodes.

Agronomic Impact

Brown spot normally does not affect plant growth, and soybeans can outgrow the disease in most years. The main effect of brown spot infection is premature defoliation of lower leaves. It is rarely reported to affect yield, but some yield loss may occur during very wet growing seasons.

Symptoms and Scouting

Symptoms of brown spot are many small, irregular, dark brown spots on both the upper and lower leaf surfaces. Adjacent spots (lesions) frequently merge to form irregularly shaped blotches and browning of the leaf edges or along the leaf vein. Infected leaves turn brown and yellow and may drop prematurely.

Brown spot can be mistaken for bacterial blight. Both diseases often occur in the same fields and even the same plant, and symptoms can be diffilcult to separate. Brown spot infection begins on older leaves, or leaves on the lower part of the plant, while bacterial blight occurs on upper new leaves. A characteristic yellow halo forms around each lesion caused by bacterial blight, especially in the early stages, whereas leaves infected by brown spot develop a more generalized leaf yellowing.

Disease Management

Septoria brown spot typically does not require management because it rarely causes significant losses. Soybean varieties are not available with resistance to this disease, but varieties can vary in their susceptibility. Rotation with non-legume crops and tillage may be beneficial, and foliar fungicides can provide some control under those rare conditions when an application may be warranted.

Soybean Mosaic Virus

Soybean mosaic virus (SMV) occurs widely, but has been rarely detected in several surveys in the Midwestern U.S. recently. SMV can cause yield loss, affect seed quality, and reduce seed germination and nodulation. Yield reductions are generally low and infections late in the season cause little damage.

Symptoms

Symptoms of plants infected with soybean mosaic virus can range from no apparent symptoms to severely mottled and deformed leaves. Mottling appears as light and dark green patches on individual leaves. Symptoms are most obvious on young, rapidly growing leaves. Infected leaf blades can become puckered along the veins and curled downward. Soybean mosaic virus can cause plant stunting, reduced seed size, and reduced pod number per plant. The disease is one of several factors associated with discolouration of seeds, causing a dark discolouration at the hilum. Symptoms of SMV may not apparent when temperatures are above 90ºF. Symptoms are often confused with growth regulator herbicide damage where the leaves will be elongated and which usually occurs in a pattern such as along a field edge. SMV can interact with bean pod mottle virus (BPMV) to create severe symptoms in plants infected with both viruses.

Conditions and Timing that Favour Disease

Plants can be infected with SMV at any time during the growing season. Plants infected when young tend to show more symptoms than plants infected when older. Higher activity or populations of aphids favour virus transmission.

Causal Pathogen

The causal agent of SMV is a virus. It has a wide host range including pea and snap bean. SMV is transmitted by aphids, sap, and by infected seed. Seed transmission rates appear to typically be below 5 per cent, but can be higher or lower depending on the cultivar.

Disease Cycle

SMV is sap and graft-transmissible. At least 32 aphid species, belonging to 15 different genera, transmit the SMV in a nonpersistent manner. Virus isolates may show some vector specificity. Infected plants resulting from transmission through seed play an important role in SMV epidemiology. Such plants are primary inoculum sources for SMV. In most cultivars, seed transmission is less than 5 per cent, but no transmission occurs in some cultivars while others can have levels as high as 75 per cent.

Disease Management

Use pathogen free seed. Planting early in the season may be helpful. Some cultivars may have some level of resistance to SMV. The value of insecticides to reduce SMV via controlling aphids is uncertain.

Alfalfa Mosaic

Alfalfa mosaic virus

Alfalfa mosaic, caused by *Alfalfa mosaic virus* (AMV), is a viral disease that is becoming increasingly common in soybeans. Alternate hosts of AMV include alfalfa, other legumes and solanaceous crops. AMV is transmitted by aphids.

Symptoms

Leaves have mottled patterns of bright yellow and dark green tissues. Newly emerged leaves may be smaller than usual with bright yellow spots and brown discolouration. Plants may be stunted. Plants infected by AMV do not produce seed with mottled seedcoats, unlike some other soybean viruses.

Alfalfa Mosaic Foliar Symptoms

Disease Development

AMV is transmitted by more than 15 species of aphids, including the soybean aphid (*Aphis glycines*). Reports of alfalfa mosaic in soybeans have increased in recent years and are believed to be associated with outbreaks of soybean aphids. The disease may be more prevalent on edges of fields, especially in fields bordering alfalfa.

Management

Variety Selection

Resistance to AMV has been identified in soybeans, but is not yet commercially available. However, current soybean varieties differ in tolerance to AMV, based on degree of symptom expression.

Foliar Insecticides

These are not likely to be effective in reducing transmission of AMV by aphids.

Bean Pod Mottle

Bean pod mottle virus

Bean pod mottle is a viral disease of soybean, snap bean and other legumes caused by *Bean pod mottle virus* (BPMV). Like many plant viruses, BPMV is spread by an insect. In the North Central region, the most important insect vector is the bean leaf beetle, *Cerotoma trifurcata*, which feeds on infected plants, then transmits the virus particles to the next plant on which it feeds.

Symptoms

Foliar symptoms include yellow and green mottled areas. Young leaves show symptoms more severely than older leaves, sometimes with a raised, blistered or distorted appearance. Symptoms can be transient and most obvious during periods of rapid plant growth and cool temperatures, but they may disappear during hot weather and during the reproductive stages of the crop. Symptoms may resemble injury from herbicide drift and are similar to those caused by other viruses. This makes it difficult to diagnose bean pod mottle and most other viral diseases based on symptoms alone.

Laboratory tests can be done at diagnostic clinics to distinguish among suspected viruses. BPMV is associated with green stem syndrome, a delayed maturity of the stems and petioles, which can make harvesting more difficult. Infection also decreases pod formation, reduces seed size, weight and number and may cause seed mottling.

Disease Development

There are three potential sources of BPMV: overwintered bean leaf beetles, perennial host species (e.g., *Desmodium* species) and infected seed (usually less than 0.1%). Although the level of virus transmission by overwintered beetles is low, beetles acquire BPMV from infected perennial host species and soybean seedlings infected via seed transmission. The presence of bean leaf beetles is an indicator for increased risk of BPMV infection. The firstgeneration peak in beetle numbers occurs during late V or early R growth stages - around early July. The second-generation peak occurs during pod-fill stages (R3 through R6) in August.

Management

Variety Selection

Although tolerance to BPMV infection has been identified in soybeans, commercial varieties are not clearly characterized for this trait. Currently, varieties differ in tolerance to BPMV, although the differences are not clearly studied.

Insecticide Seed Treatments

Consider planting treated seed if overwintering survival of bean leaf beetles is predicted. Also consider insecticide seed treatments if bean pod mottle has been confirmed in fields in previous years and bean leaf beetles have been present.

Foliar Applied Insecticides

Foliar applied insecticides can manage bean leaf beetle populations and may reduce incidence of bean pod mottle.

Cercospora Leaf Blight and Purple Seed Stain

Cercospora kikuchii

Cercospora leaf blight has become more prevalent in Iowa. Yield losses due to this disease are common in the southern United States, but serious losses have not been reported despite widespread distribution of the disease in the North Central region. Diseased plants are usually widespread within a field.

Symptoms

Foliar symptoms usually are seen at the beginning of seed set and occur in the uppermost canopy on leaves exposed to the sun. Affected leaves are discoloured, with symptoms ranging from light purple, pinpoint spots to larger, irregularly shaped patches typically only on the upper leaf surface. As disease develops, affected leaves may become leathery and dark purple with bronze highlights. Symptoms may be confused with sunburn. Discolouration may extend to the upper stems, petioles and pods. Infection of petioles and severe symptoms may lead to defoliation of the uppermost leaves and give the appearance of a maturing crop. However, petioles of fallen leaves remain attached to the stem, and lower leaves of the plant remain green.

Symptoms of purple seed stain are distinct pink to dark purple discolourations of seed. Discoloured areas vary in size from small spots to the entire surface of the seed coat; however, infected seeds may not show symptoms.

Disease Development

The fungus survives winter in infested crop residue and infected seed. Most early season infections do not cause symptoms but contribute to infection of foliage and pods later in the season. Warm and wet weather is favourable for infection. Foliar symptoms are the result of an interaction between a toxin produced by the fungus and sunlight. Weather conditions during flowering and plant maturity will affect the incidence of purple seed stain. Despite being caused by the same organism, there is no consistent relationship between the occurrence of Cercospora leaf blight and purple seed stain.

Management

Variety Selection

There are commercially available varieties resistant to Cercospora leaf blight. However, there are no known sources of resistance for purple seed stain.

Fungicides

Foliar fungicides are registered for Cercospora leaf blight. Applications made during pod-filling stages can reduce the incidence of purple seed stain, but may not affect soybean yield.

Crop rotation and tillage: Rotation to non-host crops such as alfalfa, corn and small grains and tillage to bury infested crop residue will reduce pathogen levels. If considering tillage, use proven conservation practices to maintain soil quality.

Phyllosticta Leaf Spot

Phyllosticta sojicola

Phyllosticta leaf spot is an occasional, minor disease of soybeans. It rarely affects yield.

Symptoms and Signs

Plants are susceptible to infection at all stages. Lesions most often occur on leaves and are circular, oval and irregular or V-shaped. Lesions appear gray or tan and have a narrow, dark margin. In older lesions, numerous small, black specks may be visible. These are pycnidia, the fruiting structures of the fungus. Disease also may progress to the petioles, stems and pods.

Disease Development

The fungus likely survives in infested crop residue. Cool, moist conditions favour disease development.

Management

Management is usually not needed. Crop rotation and tillage will reduce survival of *Phyllosticta sojicola*.

15

Soybean Viruses

General Information

A number of viruses affect soybean production in the southeast on an annual basis. Although yield loss from viruses is generally relatively low, individual fields may suffer significant losses in any given year. Viruses are infectious submicroscopic particles made up of DNA or RNA enclosed by a protein coat. Soybean mosaic virus (SMV) and bean pod mottle virus (BPMV) are the most common viruses infecting soybean in North Carolina. Soybean viruses are generally transmitted by insect vectors such as aphids or beetles, although Tobacco ringspot virus is also transmitted by the dagger nematode. Symptoms of the two most common viruses, SMV and BPMV, may overlap and soybean plants may be infected with both viruses. Tests are available to accurately identify each virus, but are used only rarely because taking corrective action is rarely possible.

Soybean Mosaic Virus – SMV

Soybean mosaic virus is the most common virus encountered in North Carolina. It may be seedborne or transmitted by aphids. SMV causes raised areas or puckuring on the leaf surface, stunting of the plant, and mottling of the seed. Seed mottling, however, may be caused by other factors. The severity of symptoms is related to the virus strain, soybean variety, and how early the plant is infected. Yield loss to SMV is generally related to time of infection. Virus transmission through seed may be as high as 30 per cent. When infected seed is planted aphids may spread the disease from infected plants to the remainder of the soybean crop. Wild hosts of SMV are relatively rare. Many soybean varieties are resistant to this virus including most varieties developed in North Carolina or Virginia, but strains of SMV that attack resistant varieties are fairly common. Symptom expression is also influenced by temperature. High temperatures limit symptom expression, whereas cool temperatures enhance development of leaf symptoms. Frequently, the crop may appear healthy until several days of cool weather in late summer or early fall, when the entire crop appears to be affected.

SMV Transmission

Infected seed is the most important way that soybean mosaic virus is introduced into a soybean field. Seed transmission depends on variety, ranging from 5-75 per cent. In most modern soybean varieties, rates of seed transmission are 0 per cent-5 per cent.

Once the virus is in the field, aphids can spread it from plant to plant as they feed. Over 30 species of aphids transmit SMV worldwide. The soybean aphid, (Aphis glycines) is one of the aphids vectors of SMV.

Synergistic Effect of Multiple Viruses Infections

Mixed infections of two or more viruses in a single plant result in more severe symptoms than single infections. High yield losses can occur with combined infection that would not occur with infection by a single virus.

Multiple virus infection also increases the level of seed transmission of SMV, depending how early in the season the plant is infected.

With the recent increase in incidence of bean pod mottle virus (BPMV) in the region, the potential for synergism between SMV and BPMV has increased.

Symptoms of SMV on Soybean

SMV-host interactions result in four distinct reactions, which include resistant, susceptible, late susceptible and necrotic. A host plant is considered fully susceptible to a virus ıf the virus can successfully complete replication, cell-to-cell movement and long distance movement. Similarly a host plant is resistant if the host can block one of these three processes. Disease symptoms can be seen in different parts of the plants including, roots, stems, petioles, leaflets, and seeds.

- **Susceptible (mosaic):** Generally, mosaic symptoms appear as yellowish vein-clearing along the small, branching veins of the first trifoliolate leaves 7 to 10 days after mechanical inoculation of unifoliolate leaves. These symptoms are transitory. Typical rugosity usually does not appear until the third trifoliolate leaf. More severe symptoms develop on subsequent leaves, which eventually show dark green enations along the main veins. Leaf margins frequently curve down at the side. The youngest and most rapidly growing leaves show the most severe symptoms. Plants infected early in the season in the field are severely stunted, with shortened petioles and internodes, and may mature later than non-infected plants.
- **Late Susceptible:** Late susceptible symptoms were first observed in the segregating populations of Columbia (R) × Lee 68 (S). Late susceptible plants express resistant reactions to virus for approximately 20 days after inoculation, but then susceptible symptoms appear as large mosaic islands on the first trifoliolate leaves. Apparently, the host delays viral replication or movement of virus due to partial dominance of the resistance gene and, therefore, this reaction can be considered a type of resistance.
- **Necrosis**: The necrotic reaction is a hypersensitive reaction of plants to pathogens, including viruses. The necrotic reaction, which can be classified into two subgroups, is often observed on soybean cultivars that have resistance genes:

1. **Local necrosis**: The hypersensitive reaction of the plant is limited to initially infected cells on the inoculated leaves. The formation of such localized necrotic spots, caused by host cell death in the vicinity of pathogen-infected cells, suggests that virus proliferation is restricted to the initial infected cell. Therefore, it is considered a resistant reaction
2. Stem tip (systemic) necrosis: In this case the hypersensitive reaction is not restricted to the initial infection site and can be systemic. The symptoms associated with stem tip necrosis include a brown discolouration of leaf veins, yellowing of the leaves, confined systemic necrotic lesions on leaves, stunting of the plants, browning of petioles, stem or stem-tips, bud blight, and defoliation, usually leading to plant death. Soybean cultivars that show systemic necrotic symptoms usually have necrotic lesions and/or veinal necrosis on inoculated leaves

Management

The only practical means for management of this virus disease of soybean is the selection and use of resistant varieties. Control of the aphid vector has not proved practical or reliable as a means of virus management.

Bean Pod Mottle Virus – BPMV

Bean pod mottle virus though generally less common than SMV can severely lower soybean yield in infected fields. BPMV causes mottling of the leaves, leaf distortion, stunting of the plant, and mottled seed. Bean pod mottle virus has also been implicated in "green stem syndrome", and this can result in additional yield losses. Green stem syndrome is the condition where the stems of mature plants remain green and leathery making harvest difficult. The severity of symptoms is related to the virus strain, soybean variety, and how early the plant is infected. Yield loss to BPMV is generally related to time of infection; early infection can result in severe losses. Virus transmission through seed is very low, generally less than 0.01 per cent. Like SMV, high temperatures limit BPMV symptom expression, whereas cool temperatures enhance development of leaf symptoms. BPMV is transmitted by several species of leaf feeding beetles, including bean leaf beetle. Overwintering beetles probably acquire virus from wild legume weed species. No varieties with resistance are available, but varieties do vary with regard to tolerance. Mixed infections of BPMV and SMV can result in severe stunting or death of the plant.

Symptoms

A typical leaf symptom of BPMV is a yellow and green blotchy appearance called leaf mottle. Young leaves show symptoms more severely than older leaves, sometimes with a raised or blistered appearance and distortion of leaves in the upper canopy.

Symptoms are most obvious during periods of rapid growth and cool temperatures. Sometimes symptoms resemble injury from herbicide drift. Symptoms go into remission during hot weather and later during the reproductive stages.

The symptoms caused by BPMV are similar to those caused by other viruses — this makes it difficult to diagnose BPMV and most other viruses based on symptoms alone.

Serological tests can accurately detect and distinguish among suspected viruses. Most diagnostic clinics in the North Central region are able to perform these tests

Management

The only practical means for management of this virus disease of soybean is the selection and use of tolerant varieties. Control of the leaf beetle vector has not proved practical or reliable as a means of virus management. Control of leguminous weeds that may harbor the virus or the use of trap crops has been has been suggested for management of this disease, but the efficacy of these tactics has not been verified or tested.

Risk Assessment

To determine if a virus problems exists in your field, look for the following signs:

- Moderate to high feedling actitivity by bean leaf beetles
- Lower than expected yields
- Mottled seed
- Presence of leaf symptoms: mottled, crinkled leaf symptoms typical of virus infection.

Tobacco Ringspot Virus – TRSV

Tobacco ringspot virus (TRSV) is fairly common in North Carolina but yield losses in production fields are generally insignificant. Principal symptoms include stunting, leaf distortion, and characteristic browning and curling of the terminal branch. The most obvious symptoms are the proliferation of buds and flowers, and lack of pods or poorly formed pods. Stems remain green and petioles may remain attached with black lesions. The stems remain green because the plants are sterile as a result of pod abortion. Infected plants will stand out in a mature soybean field because of the green stems. If there are large numbers of these green plants harvest may be more difficult. The primary impact of this disease is that soybean grown for seed from fields with this virus cannot be shipped to certain countries. Although the virus may be seedborne, this is probably not an important means of transmission since most infected plants are sterile. The dagger nematode can transmit this virus, but the virus does not move from the roots to the shoots and leaves of the soybean plant. Spread is probably by thrips, though no efficient vector has been identified.

Symptoms

Plants infected while less than 5-week old are stunted. The most striking symptom is the curving of the terminal bud to form a crook. Later, other buds on the plant become brown, necrotic, and brittle. Adventitious leaf and floral buds may proliferate excessively. The pith of stems and branches may show a brown discolouration, first near the nodes and then throughout the stem. Leaflets are dwarfed and tend to cup or roll, and the blades become more or less rugose and bronzed.

Pods generally are underdeveloped or aborted. Those that set before infection often develop dark blotches. Such pods generally do not produce viable seeds and drop early. Maturity is delayed in infected plants; they remain green and often stunted until harvested or killed by frost.

Causal Organisms

Tobacco ringspot virus is the type member of the nepovirus group of plant viruses and is related to arabis mosaic virus, grapevine fanleaf virus, tomato black ring virus, and tomato ringspot virus. The genome of TRSV is bipartite and consists of two single-stranded positive sense polyadenylated RNA molecules. Several strains of TRSV naturally infect soybean. Indicator plants can differentiate these strains.

Disease Cycle

The virus causes systemic infection in susceptible cultivars, moving from infected leaves to the tips of stems and into roots. Movement from roots to leaves is uncommon. TRSV is easily sap-transmissible. Nymphs of *Thrips tabaci* transmit it to soybean at a low level of efficiency. The nymphs appear to retain the virus for at least 14 days after acquisition. The dagger nematode *Xiphinema americanum* also is a vector of TRSV, but its efficiency in transmitting the virus to soybean is low. Even when it does occur, nematode transmission of TRSV to roots of plants may be of no significance, because the infection generally remains confined to the roots.

Seed transmission is the most important mode of long-range dissemination and carry-over from season to season. Systemically infected plants often produce infected seeds, which give rise to diseased seedlings. The extent of seed transmission depends on the time infection takes place; plants infected before bloom produce few or no seeds.

Management

Some varieties may have resistance to certain strains of the virus. Disease is generally more severe near pastures or at the edges of fields. Location of seed production fields away from pastures or borders that may harbor weeds that are infected with TRSV is the most practical strategy for minimizing disease.

Cowpea Chlorotic Mottle Virus– CCMV

The cowpea chlorotic mottle virus (CCMV) is occasionally found in North and South Carolina as well as Georgia. Symptoms are a distinct mosaic and stunting. Yield losses from this virus are probably not important since it generally appears on only scattered plants in a field. Bean leaf beetle and the spotted cucumber beetle are vectors for this virus. The virus probably survives in various weed species.

Hosts

Natural hosts include *Canavalia ensiformis*, groundnuts (*Arachis hypogaea*), *Phaseolus lunatus*, *P. vulgaris*, *Psophocarpus tetragonolobus*, soyabeans (*Glycine max*), tomatoes (*Lycopersicon esculentum*), *Vigna mungo*, probably aubergines (*Solanum melongena*), cowpeas cv. Blackeye (*Vigna unguiculata*), *Vicia faba* and *Vigna subterranea*. The virus also occurs in various weeds (Fabaceae), including *Stylosanthes* and *Tephrosia* spp. Many more hosts can be artificially inoculated.

Geographical Distribution

- **EPPO region**: Egypt, Israel.
- **Asia**: India (Karnataka, Maharashtra and probably elsewhere), Indonesia, Israel, Malaysia, Thailand, Yemen.
- **Africa**: Côte d'Ivoire, Egypt, Ghana, Kenya, Malawi, Mozambique, Nigeria, Sudan, Tanzania, Togo, Uganda, Zambia.
- **South America**: Brazil.
- **Oceania**: Fiji, Papua New Guinea, Solomon Islands.
- **EU**: Absent.

Biology

Unlike carlaviruses in general, CPMMV is transmitted in a non-persistent manner. The ability to transmit CPMMV is usually retained for a maximum of 20-60 min. Non-vector transmission is by mechanical inoculation. Seed transmission has been demonstrated in a number of hosts in different countries, but there are also negative reports. In practice it appears to be the main source of virus inoculum on the relatively short-lived hosts of this virus in tropical countries, though weeds may also act as reservoirs.

Symptoms

Symptoms vary on different hosts and in different seasons. On *Vigna unguiculata*, CPMMV causes diffuse chlorotic blotches on the primary leaves, systemic mottling and leaf distortion. On groundnuts, it causes necrotic lesions, chlorotic rings or line patterns followed by systemic leaf chlorosis, rolling and veinal necrosis. On soyabeans and on *Phaseolus* it causes vein mosaic and general leaf chlorosis, followed by apical necrosis, distortion and stunting. However, the first report of CPMMV in Tanzania was of mild symptoms on *Vigna mungo* and symptomless infection of *Phaseolus vulgaris*. On tomatoes, CPMMV causes mottling and inconspicuous banding of minor veins.

Morphology

CPMMV consists of usually straight filaments 650 nm long and 13 nm wide. In leaf cells of the host, filamentous particles aggregate to form sheets, bundles or brush-like inclusions.

Detection and Inspection Methods

Preparations of CPMMV are strongly immunogenic. The virus is detectable by ELISA and ISEM, but not by standard gel diffusion tests. Indicator plants include *Arachis hypogaea*, *Cajanus cajan*, *Canavalia ensiformis*, *Glycine max*, *Vigna unguiculata*, *Nicotiana clevelandii* (systemic mottle); *Beta vulgaris*, *Chenopodium murale*, *C. quinoa* (chlorotic local lesions).

Management

Some soybean varieties are resistant to this virus and should be used if the virus affects a significant portion of plants in a field.

16

Diseases of Stem

Anthracnose

Anthracnose is a stem disease that occurs during wet, warm, and humid conditions, although symptoms are often not seen until plants reach maturity. The disease typically has minimal effects on yield, but it can reduce yields, stands, and seed quality. Although the symptoms of anthracnose can be mistaken for pod and stem blight, the symptoms are different and both diseases may be present on the same plants late in the season.

Symptoms

The most common symptoms are seen late in the season as the plants approach maturity. Irregular brown spots develop in a random pattern on stems and pods. The infected areas are covered with tiny black spines (setae) that can be seen with a 10X hand lens. Brown cankers can appear on petioles and cause defoliation. Infection of pods results in few or small seeds per pod. Infected leaves may develop brown veins and curl up. In older plants, the stems, pods, and leaves may be infected without showing symptoms until the weather is warm and moist or plants reach maturity. Infected seeds may have no symptoms or may develop brown or gray areas with black specks. Seeds infected by anthracnose may not germinate. Infected seedlings develop dark, sunken cankers on the cotyledons, epicotyl, and radicle that cause damping-off.

Conditions and Timing that Favour Disease

Warm and moist conditions favour infection and disease development. Plants can be infected at any time during the season, but symptoms often don't appear until plants reach maturity in the upper Midwestern U.S.

Causal Pathogen

The primary pathogen that causes anthracnose in the Midwest is the fungus *Colletotrichum truncatum*, but other fungi may also be associated with anthracnose.

This pathogen overwinter in infected crop residue and infected seeds, and may be seedborne. It is a different pathogen than the one that causes anthracnose of corn, however, it has a wide host range that includes alfalfa, ragweed, and velvetleaf.

Disease Management

Rotate with a non-legume (non-host) crop. Use pathogen-free seed. Treatment of infected seeds with a fungicide may be beneficial. Fungicidal sprays may be helpful after flowering begins. Soybean varieties differ in their resistance to anthracnose.

Brown Stem Rot (BSR)

Brown stem rot (BSR) is widespread across the northern tier of the U.S, soybean producing states. The BSR pathogen infects the inner stem, and symptoms may or may not be visible without splitting stems of infected plants. BSR can cause significant yield reductions, and plants without visible symptoms on leaves may also suffer yield losses from 5-15 per cent BSR can cause premature senescence of infected plants. BSR can be confused with sudden death syndrome (SDS) based on the similar leaf symptoms for both diseases.

Symptoms

Symptoms of BSR usually don't appear until mid-August or later. BSR causes browning of the pith in the centre of the stem, especially near the lower nodes. The pith is typically brown in stems that are split, whereas the pith is white in healthy stems. Depending on summer environment, soybean cultivar, and type of the pathogen, leaves may also develop brown and yellow discolouration between the veins. The leaf symptoms can be confused with SDS symptoms, but these two diseases can be differentiated by the pith colour in the lower stem.

Conditions and Timing that Favour Disease

The BSR fungus infects through the roots and stem early in the growing season, but symptoms typically do not appear until August. BSR symptoms are favoured by cool, wet weather during pod-fill followed by hot, dry weather in mid-late August. Soybean cyst nematode may enhance BSR.

Causal Pathogen

Phialophora gregata, also named Cadophora gregata is a soilborne fungus. This pathogen overwinters in soybean stem residue and soil. Two different types of this pathogen (A and B) cause different symptoms. Type A typically causes pith browning and leaf symptoms, but type B usually causes only pith browning. Type B is common across the northern states in the Midwestern U.S.

Disease Management

The two most important tactics for management of BSR are the use of resistant soybean varieties and rotation to non-host crops such as corn. Because SCN may interact with BSR, resistance to SCN may also help to reduce BSR.

Green Stem Syndrome

Green stem syndrome refers to plants that maintain green stems and sometimes leaves well past the time when they are normally brown and mature. The plant stems remain moist while the pods and seeds have ripened. Green stem does not have a clear effect on yield, but the green stems make harvesting more difficult. The cause is unknown, and the incidence of green stem varies from location to location in a given year and can differ among soybean cultivars planted in one location.

Symptoms

Stems of plants remain green after the pods and seeds have ripened and are brown and ready for harvest. Occasionally the stems and leaves remain green after the pods have matured, which is well past the time when the whole plant is normally brown and dry.

Conditions and Timing that Favour Disease

Symptoms are typically first seen as the crop is maturing.

Causal Pathogen

The cause of green stem syndrome is unknown. This syndrome has been attributed to many different causes. These include plant viruses, low soil moisture, potassium deficiency, soybean population density, genetic mutations in soybean plants, and insect damage. Plant viruses, especially bean pod mottle virus (BPMV), were thought to be associated with green stem, but recent research has shown no cause and effect relationship between BPMV infection and green stem. Specific viruses are often not detected in plants with green stem, and plants with specific viruses often don't have green stem.

Disease Management

Plant soybean cultivars with relatively low susceptibility to green stem. The incidence and severity of green stem has been reported to vary among cultivars. Specific and proven management strategies are not known due to the uncertain cause of green stem syndrome.

Pod and Stem Blight

- **Pathogen:** Fungi. *Diaporthe phaseolorum* var. *sojae* and *Phomopsis longicola*
- **Symptoms:** No definite leaf or stem lesions are produced under field conditions. Fungal spore-bearing structures (pycnidia) appear as black specks in linear rows on dead stems and poorly-developed pods. Pod blight phase results in poor quality seeds and seed decay. Seedling blight may occur from seed infections.
- **Conditions:** Warm wet weather at R7 to R8 stages favours seed infection and decay.
- **Inoculum Survival:** Seed, infected crop residue.
- **Inoculum Dispersal:** Airborne spores.

Under some conditions this disease can cause yield loss and a significant reduction in seed quality. Pod and stem blight may be more common when harvesting is delayed during wet weather. Symptoms of pod and stem blight can be confused with anthracnose, and both diseases can occur together on plants late in the season.

Symptoms

Plants are usually infected by pod and stem blight early in the growing season. The pathogen may be present in green tissue without causing symptoms. The pathogen can infect all aerial parts of plant, but does not cause distinct lesions. Signs of infection appear on fallen petioles in mid-season and on pods and stems of plants nearing maturity. A key sign of infection is many small, black, raised dots (pycnidia) arranged in rows on infected stems, pods, and fallen petioles late in the season. In wet seasons, pycnidia may cover the entire plant at maturity. Upper portions of infected plants may turn yellow and die. Infected seed are cracked, shriveled, dull, and may have a gray mold on them. Seed infected by pod and stem blight may decompose after harvest and have low viability. Seedlings grown from infected seeds may often blighted.

Conditions and Timing that Favour Disease

Infection can occur throughout the season, although symptoms are not seen until later in the season. Wet, warm conditions and continuous planting of soybeans favours pod and stem blight. Insect damage or other injury to pods and seeds favours pod and seed infection.

Causal Pathogen

Pod and stem blight is caused by the fungus *Diaporthe phaseolorum* var. *sojae*. The seed decay is caused primarily by the related fungus *Phomopsis longicola* or other species. These fungi overwinter in soybean tissue residue and in infected seeds. Host range includes green bean, pepper, and tomato.

Disease Management

Rotate soybean with non-hosts such as wheat or corn. Use high quality, pathogen-free seed. Some soybean varieties may differ in resistance. Foliar or seed treatment fungicides may be of value under conditions that favour this disease. Harvest seed quickly after it matures.

Sclerotinia Stem Rot (White Mold)

White mold (also named Sclerotinia stem rot) is a common and destructive disease that tends to be sporadic across the northern U.S and Canada. Although it can be a serious problem in many areas, certain areas are more prone to this disease than others. For example, in the central Midwest white mold is especially common in SE Minnesota, NE Iowa, and NW Illinois. White mold is favoured by prolonged wet and cool weather when the plants are flowering in July. This disease is difficult to manage and resistant varieties are a partial solution to this perennial problem.

Symptoms

Lesions usually develop first at stem nodes during or after flowering. The lesions expand and the tops of the plants become grayish-green and then wilt and die. Infected stems often become soft and watery, and become covered with white moldy growth in moist conditions. Dry, dead stems can develop a bleached, white appearance. Hard, black sclerotia that look similar to rodent droppings develop on or inside infected stems and pods. Scattered dead plants can often be seen standing upright in affected fields, or plants can be killed in patches.

Conditions and Timing that Favour Disease

The occurrence of white mold varies widely from year to year and from location to location depending in a large part on weather conditions. Wet and cool weather during flowering is required for this disease to develop, and plants are usually killed after closure of the plant canopy. Other factors that may favour development of white mold include high plant populations, high fertility, narrow rows, protected fields and parts of fields where plants dry slowly, lack of air circulation under soybean canopy, and possibly early planting. Tillage has not been shown to be consistently associated with this disease.

Causal Pathogen

White mold is caused by the fungus *Sclerotinia sclerotiorum*. This fungus survives from year-to-year in soil or stems in the form of hard black masses of mycelium (sclerotia). The sclerotia germinate near the soil surface to form small tan-to-gray mushroom-shaped structures called apothecia, which produce ascospores that spread via air currents to infect dead soybean flowers. The infection then spreads into the stems. Seed lots can be contaminated with sclerotia, and seeds can be infected with the pathogen. The host range of this pathogen includes many broadleaf crops and other plants, but not corn or small grains.

Disease Management

Selection of soybean varieties with some level of resistance to white mold can be helpful in managing this disease. Low plant populations or wide rows may help to reduce white mold severity, but these tactics do not always make a difference. Where irrigation is used, reduce irrigation frequency during flowering . Seed should be free of *Sclerotinia* contamination and infection. Long-term rotation with corn or small grains may reduce white mold. Foliar fungicides may be helpful, but have generally performed inconsistently and may not be economically beneficial for managing this disease.

Stem Canker

Stem canker is a fairly common disease in many areas where soybeans are grown, but may not be recognized as much as it occurs. Stem canker can kill whole plants or parts of plants. It can be confused with Phytophtora rot. Two different kinds of stem canker are known, northern and southern, which seem to be geographically limited to some degree but their ranges may overlap. Soybean cultivars can have resistance to stem canker. This disease often appears to kill or damage scattered plants, but in some cases large areas can be killed and yield losses can be significant.

Symptoms

Early symptoms are reddish-brown lesions that appear at the base of branches or leaf petioles. These small lesions can develop into elongated, sunken, dark brown cankers that spread up and down the stem. Tiny black dots called perithecia (spore producing fungal structures) may appear on the stem singly or in clustered groups on plants killed by stem canker. Plant parts above the lesions may die. Reddish-brown discolouration may also occur inside the stem, and pods can abort. Leaves may develop necrosis and chlorosis between the veins and may remain attached after death. Lesions often develop at and remain darker at nodes, but may extend to the soil line and create a situation easily confused with Phytophthora rot.

Conditions and Timing that Favour Disease

Prolonged wet weather, especially early in the season favours stem canker. Symptoms of often seen from mid-July to harvest, especially in susceptible varieties. Reduced tillage may also favour this disease.

Causal Pathogen

Northern stem canker is caused by the fungus *Diaporthe phaseolorum* var. *caulivora*. Southern stem canker is caused by the related fungus *Diaporthe phaseolorum* var. *merdionalis*. These pathogens overwinter in infested soybean residue, and may be spread with infected seed.

Disease Management

Stem canker can be reduced by planting resistant varieties with resistance to this disease. Delayed planting and foliar fungicides may be beneficial. Tillage may reduce disease problems in fields where this disease has been a problem. Crop rotation with non-host crops such as wheat and corn may help to reduce stem canker.

17

Diseases of Root

There are several common root rot diseases that attack soybeans, causing varying degrees of damage from year to year. Each has characteristic symptoms that should make it possible to identify the trouble readily. All of the symptoms cause affected plants to wilt and turn brown, and usually to die prematurely. All are caused by common soilborne fungi.

Charcoal Rot

Charcoal rot is a soilborne root and stem disease of soybean that develops in the mid to late summer when plants are under stress, especially heat and drought stress. Infected plants may die prematurely and are often wilted and stunted. Significant yield losses can occur. The disease is common in the southern states and occurs in the Midwest in seasons with hot, dry conditions Charcoal rot was first confirmed in Minnesota in 1999 and North Dakota in 2002, and may be an expanding soybean disease in the northern Midwest. Many crops are affected by charcoal rot, including corn and sunflower.

Symptoms

Symptoms of charcoal rot generally occur during or after flowering, however, seedlings may also be affected. Brown lesions may form on the hypocotyl of emerging seedlings. After mid-season, leaflets on infected plants may be small and ultimately wilt and turn brown. The taproot and lower stem may become streaked with light gray. Small black specks may form beneath the epidermis and inside the lower stem and taproot to give them a charcoal-sprinkled appearance. Reddish-brown discoloration can also develop in the pith and vascular tissues of the root and stem.

Conditions and Timing that Favour Disease

Plants can be infected at any time during the growing season. Much infection may occur early in the season, but symptoms typically do not develop until after flowering when plants become stressed. Hot, dry weather favours disease development. Disease is most severe where plants have been growing under conditions of stress or injury.

Causal Pathogen

Charcoal rot is caused by the soilborne fungus *Macrophomina phaseolina*. This pathogen has a wide host range that includes corn, sunflower, and some weeds. The fungus overwinters in residue of host tissues and can survive for at least two years in dry soil. The pathogen can be spread by contaminated seed and soil.

Disease Management

Manage fields to reduce or avoid drought stress. Reduced tillage may reduce charcoal rot, perhaps due to cooler soils and less moisture stress. Rotation with crops that have relatively low susceptibility to charcoal rot, such as cereal grains, may be beneficial. Reduced seeding rates may also reduce drought stress and charcoal rot. Soybean cultivars may exhibit different levels of susceptibility, but none are fully resistant to this disease.

Fusarium Root Rot

Fusarium root rot is an important disease that occurs in many soybean production areas in the U.S. However, this disease may be difficult to diagnose because the causal agent(s) may either act as primary pathogens or they may colonize root systems along with other soilborne fungi. *Fusarium* species are often isolated from soybean roots that are also infected by other pathogens (e.g. *Pythium*, *Phytophthora*, and *Rhizoctonia*). *Fusarium* species are common and can survive for long periods in soil.

Symptoms

The lower taproot and lateral roots of infected soybean plants may appear brown to black in color and show cortical decay or vascular discoloration. Lateral roots may also die and decompose, and secondary roots may develop above them on the upper taproot. If root rot becomes severe, infected soybeans may develop foliar symptoms including stunting, marginal or whole leaf chlorosis (yellowing), wilting, and defoliation.

Conditions and Timing that Favour Disease

Cool temperatures and wet soils, particularly early in the growing season, often favour infection by *Fusarium* species. However, later in the growing season, as soil moisture becomes more limiting, soybeans may become stressed and may also be prone to infection by *Fusarium*. Factors such as the soybean cyst nematode, soil compaction, crop rotation history, soil pH, and soil type may be important for the development of *Fusarium* root rot. Flooding has been shown to reduce plant stand and increase levels of root rot.

Causal Pathogen

A number of *Fusarium* species have been found associated with root rot of soybean. The species most frequently associated with root rot on soybean are *F. solani* and *F. oxysporum*. Other *Fusarium* species include *F. acuminatum*, *F. chlamydosporum*, *F. compactum*, *F. culmorum*, *F. equiseti*, *F. graminearum*, *F.*

merismoides, *F. proliferatum*, *F. pseudograminearum*, *F. semitecum*, *F. subglutinans*, and *F. verticilliodes*. *Fusarium* species are widespread soilborne organisms capable of surviving for long periods of time as chlamydospores and as mycelium in plant residues and in soil.

Disease Management

Planting in well-drained soils and minimizing soil compaction may help to make conditions less favourable for infection by *Fusarium* species. Minimizing stress and injury to plants caused by soybean cyst nematode, herbicides, iron deficiency, and other plant pathogens may also help to reduce Fusarium root rot. Fungicidal seed treatments are often recommended when planting into fields with a history of fungal root rot problems and may aid in controlling Fusarium root rot.

Phytophthora Rot

- **Pathogen:** Fungus. *Phytophthora sojae*
- **Symptoms:** Seed rot and pre-emergence damping-off. Root and stem rot of older seedlings. In more mature plants chlorosis and wilting of leaves, with a dark brown discoloration on lower stem progressing upward from the soil line. Root rot of older plants may also occur. Affected plants are clustered in field.
- **Conditions:** Heavy soils and soil saturation for more than 24 hours promote disease. Disease is more severe with reduced-till. Highest risk with no-till.
- **Inoculum Survival:** Soil, infected crop residue.
- **Inoculum Dispersal:** Soilborne spores.

Symptoms

Phytophthora root and stem rot, caused by the soilborne fungus *Phytophthora sojae* (synonyms *P. megasperma* f. sp. *glycinea* and *P.m.* var. *sojae*) may attack plants at any stage of growth. The disease, which is favoured by cool and rainy weather, may kill the seedlings before emergence; or they may shrivel and die after emergence, leaving gaps in the rows. Older plants may develop dull dark brown lesions extending upward on the stem from the soil line, occasionally to the tenth node. The taproot becomes dark brown, and the entire root system may be rotted. Infected plants usually turn yellow, wilt, and die. The withered leaves commonly remain attached to dead plants for a week or more. *Phytophthora* is found most often in heavy clay soils that are poorly drained and compacted, especially in low areas where surface water has been standing for several days. This disease is also favoured by reduced tillage and early planting. Plants are often killed in sections of the rows. Plant losses and yield reductions may approach 100 per cent in very susceptible soybean cultivars. The severity of loss depends on cultivar susceptibility, rainfall, drainage, soil type, and tillage.

Disease Cycle

The *Phytophthora* fungus overseasons primarily as dormant, thick-walled oospores in crop debris or soil. Large numbers of oospores are formed in infected roots and stems of susceptible and tolerant soybean cultivars. Oospores are thought to germinate in the spring in wet soils, forming sporangia which contain numerous motile zoospores. Optimal temperature for oospore germination is 75° F (24° C). Zoospores are released into soil water where they swim about and are attracted to soybean roots by normal plant exudates. Optimum temperature for zoospore production is 68° F (20° C) with a minimum of 41° F (5° C). Zoospores adhere to roots, form a cyst, and germinate. Under less ideal conditions, oospores and sporangia in the soil may germinate and infect roots directly (optimum 77° F or 25° C) without forming zoospores.

Leaf infection may result when soil particles containing the *Phytophthora* fungus are deposited on the leaves during wind or rainstorms. If the weather remains cloudy and damp, severe leaf infection occurs and the fungus grows internally toward the petiole and then the stem.

The severity of Phytophthora rot of soybeans may increase if there are high populations of other root-rotting fungi in the soil (e.g. *Pythium* or *Fusarium* spp. and *Rhizoctonia solani*), because damaged roots are more susceptible to infection. Infection of soybean roots by the nematodes also increases the severity of Phytophthora root rot.

There are many races of *Phytophthora sojae*, which greatly complicates the development of resistant cultivars by conventional breeding methods. The races can be distinguished on eight soybean differential cultivars. Resistant cultivars are resistant to only certain races. However, this resistance is high and is effective from planting to plant maturity. Tolerant cultivars are susceptible in the seedling stage but are not susceptible to any race past this growth stage. The level of tolerance may vary from high to low.

Control

1. Grow well adapted, high yielding, resistant or highly tolerant cultivars.
2. Plant in warm soil (65° F [18° C] or more) that is well drained and fertile. Avoid growing susceptible cultivars in low lying areas in poorly drained soil or where Phytophthora rot has appeared in the past. Also avoid deep planting and an excessive seed rate.
3. Where feasible, use tillage or tiling to improve drainage and soil water absorption. Reduced tillage, especially no tillage, often has higher disease levels. Fields with heavy residues tend to warm more slowly in the spring and may have higher soil moisture levels, conditions which favour disease development.
4. Apply a seed and/or soil fungicide to fields with known history of disease. For details, see "Condensed Plant Disease Management Guide for Field Crops" chapter in the *Illinois Pest Control Handbook.* These treatments will control only the seedling blight phase.

PYTHIUM ROOT ROT, DAMPING-OFF, SEED DECAY

Symptoms

Pythium rot is caused by at least five species of the cosmopolitan soilborne fungus *Pythium*. Species of *Pythium* generally cause seedling diseases that may induce seed decay and damping-off (seedlings fail to emerge or they emerge then wilt and collapse), especially in wet seasons with high levels of rainfall before and after planting. Pythium rot is most severe in poorly drained soils. Infected plants have dark areas extending up the stem several inches from the soil line. The diseased areas usually become translucent, soft, and watery. These areas tear away when the plants are pulled from the soil.

If dry weather sets in, the plants appear dry and shredded. Usually, the roots are badly decayed. Infected plants normally occur singly or in small groups scattered throughout a field. *Pythium* usually causes little reduction in yields. Infection by *Pythium* species is often followed by infection by other root- and crown-rotting microorganisms which can mask typical symptoms.

Disease Cycle

Pythium fungi are common inhabitants of the soil that colonize crop residues and attack a wide range of crop plants. The fungi survive in soil and plant residue as dormant, thick-walled oospores and as mycelium in crop residues. When the soil is cool (50 to 59° F, 10 to 15° C) and wet, the oospores commonly germinate and produce a sporangium in which zoospores are formed. After escaping from the sporangium, the zoospores swim about in the soil water and are attracted to seeds or to the roots of seedlings where they encyst and later form a germ tube that penetrates and causes infection. At higher temperatures (77 to 97° F, 25 to 36° C), the oospores may germinate directly and form one or more germ tubes that penetrate the seed coat or the root and stem tissues directly. Seedlings up to 10 days old are more susceptible to damping-off than older plants.

Disease Management

1. Plant high-quality, crack-free seed capable of at least 85 per cent germination in a warm or standard test and 70 per cent in a cold test.
2. Plant in warm soil (above 65° F, 18° C) that is well drained and fertile and well prepared. Where feasible, turn under weeds or cover crops several weeks before planting.
3. Apply a seed or soil fungicide. For details, see the "Condensed Plant Disease Management Guide for Field Crops", chapter in the current Illinois Pest Control Manual. Fungicide seed protectants will often increase emergence, especially when conditions do not favour seedling growth and development. However, seed or soil fungicides will not improve emergence of damaged or low-quality seed.
4. Do not plant carryover seed or seed that has a high percentage of cracked seed coats.
5. Avoid excessive irrigation for the first 10 to 15 days after planting.

Rhizoctonia Root and Stem Rot

Rhizoctonia root and stem rot is a common soybean disease that typically causes most damage to seedlings, but can also damage older plants. It can kill and stunt plants to result in significant yield losses, or the lesions can be superficial and have minimal effects on plant health. *Rhizoctonia* is a fungal pathogen that infects many different plants in the northern U.S., but only some types of this pathogen infect soybean.

Symptoms

Rusty-brown, dry sunken lesions on stems and roots near the soil line are a characteristic symptom of *Rhizoctonia* infection. Lateral roots may be decayed. Seedlings or older plants may develop these infections and become stunted, yellow, and may wilt. The infections can be superficial and cause no clear damage to plants, or they can girdle the stem and kill or stunt plants.

Conditions and Timing that Favour Disease

Rhizoctonia root and stem rot occurs primarily in early to mid summer. Infected plants typically appear in patches in a row or field. Several different conditions can favour this disease including, high soil moisture, warm soil temperatures, soil types with high amounts of organic matter, and delayed emergence. Plant stress from herbicide or hail injury or the soybean cyst nematode (SCN) also may favour this disease.

Causal Pathogen

Rhizoctonia solani (a soilborne fungus). This fungus has a wide host range that may include soybean, corn, alfalfa, and other crops; but only some types of this pathogen infect soybean. The most common strains of this pathogen (anastamosis groups also referred to as 'AG') that infect soybean are AG-2-2 and AG-4. Different AG groups can have different optimal conditions for growth and infection.

Disease Management

Encourage seedling health with good agronomic practices and the use of high quality seed. Avoid or reduce plant stress, for example from herbicide injury and SCN infection. Crop rotation and tillage may be of value where disease has been severe. Some seed treatment fungicides may reduce *Rhizoctonia* infection for a few weeks after planting. Soybean cultivars may have different levels of tolerance, but none are fully resistant to this disease.

Soybean Cyst Nematode (SCM)

Soybean cyst nematode (SCN) is one of the most significant pathogens of soybean in most places where soybean is grown. It is widespread in Minnesota and has continued to spread into new areas and counties. Yield loss from SCN can exceed 30 per cent. Soybean cyst nematodes are microscopic roundworms that infect the roots of soybean and other plants. Above-ground symptoms are not always visible, even with yield loss of 15-30 per cent. Thus, SCN can be present in a field for years before it is identified. When symptoms are present, they are non-specific and similar to symptoms from other pathogens or abiotic stresses. Infection by SCN can also potentially increase other soil-borne soybean diseases such as brown stem rot, sudden death syndrome, and Fusarium root rot.

Symptoms

Juvenile (microscopic) nematodes enter the plant roots and start to feed. As they continue to feed on the roots, they swell as they mature. SCN is best diagnosed by gently digging roots from the soil and looking for females and cysts that are visible to the unaided eye or with a hand lens. Tiny white to yellow lemon-shaped females may be seen on roots starting the end of June and then throughout the rest of the season. The bodies of the females are white and fairly easy to see in the early and middle of summer, but turn brown late in the season and become more difficult to see.

Infected plants may become discolored (chlorotic), stunted, or necrotic due to feeding by the female nematodes. These symptoms tend to be more extreme in fields with high levels of SCN and when plants are stressed due to low fertility or drought. Highly infested areas in fields may be oval to somewhat elliptical in outline, with the most severe damage in the centre with less damage toward the margin.

Conditions and Timing that Favour Disease

Moisture and fertility stress can enhance the disease. High soil pH can favour SCN. Planting continuous susceptible soybeans favours SCN

Causal Pathogen

SCN is caused by the nematode *Heterodera glycines*. Cysts on roots can contain hundreds of eggs that are eventually released into the soil and can remain viable for years until a suitable host plant is found. Host range includes soybean and numerous legume and weed species. Many types of SCN (HG types, previously called races) occur that are pathogenic to different sources of resistance to SCN. Nematodes can be spread by anything that moves soil, such as water, wind, and machinery.

Disease Management

Soil samples should be taken and sent to a diagnostic laboratory to determine if SCN is present and what the population is in the soil. Soybeans should be rotated with non-host crops. Resistant soybean varieties should be planted, and different resistant varieties should be rotated. If available, cultivars with different sources of SCN resistances should be included in the rotation. Weeds, moisture, and fertility should be managed to reduce plant stress.

Sudden Death Syndrome

Sudden death syndrome (SDS) is an important disease of soybeans throughout much of the U.S. SDS has been spreading north and west into states including Minnesota, Nebraska, and Wisconsin. SDS also appears also to be spreading across soybean production areas of Minnesota. Severe SDS can result in yield losses greater than 50 per cent. SDS is primarily a root disease but typically also affects leaves and causes defoliation. SDS often occurs in fields infested with the soybean cyst nematode (SCN).

Symptoms

The first symptoms are typically on leaves in late July or early August in the Midwestern U.S. Leaf symptoms often begin as scattered yellow, diffuses pots between veins. The spots typically expand between veins to become brown lesions surrounded by chlorotic areas, and the leaves may be cupped or curled. Leaves detach from the petioles as the disease progresses. Brown to grey discolored areas develop in the vascular tissue of the lower stem, and can typically be seen by removing the epidermis of the stem of fresh plants. The pith remains white, which is a diagnostic feature that distinguishes SDS from brown stem rot (BSR). SDS also cause root rot, and roots may have surface blue fungal growth in moist conditions.

Conditions and Timing that Favour Disease

Infection of roots may occur early in the season, but symptoms of SDS usually don't develop until late July or in August. Infection and disease development are favoured by early planting; cool and wet soil; SCN infection, and susceptible varieties.

Causal Pathogen

Fusarium virgulifome (previously named *Fusaium solani* f.sp. glycines). This is a soilborne fungus that appears to primarily infect soybean, although snap and lima bean may be infected. This pathogen overwinters in soil and may survive for long periods of time in soil.

Disease Management

The key in most areas is planting soybean varieties with the highest level of SDS resistance. Varieties should also be resistant to SCN, and crops should be rotated to manage SCN populations. Other tactics include reducing excessive soil moisture with drainage, minimizing compaction, and staggering planting dates.

18

Bud Blight of Soybean

Bud blight of soybean is an important viral disease occurring in severe form during the rabi season and causing economic loss to the growers. The results of experiments on survey, purification, identification by electron microscopy, ELISA and PCR; transmission studies by mechanical, seed and insects; physical properties, host range; development of serodiagnostic techniques, DAS-ELISA and immunodiffusion test, management of the disease are presented hereunder.

The disease incidence was very high in *rabi/summer* where the highest incidence was recorded at Ugarkurd village with 22.5 per cent and a lowest incidence of 10.0 per cent was recorded at Nayanagar village. At Main Agricultural Research Station, Dharwad the disease incidence was 7.5 per cent. In Bagalkot district, the minimum disease incidence was recorded at Kumbarhalla village with 1.5 per cent and maximum incidence of 5.2 per cent at Nagaral village. In Belgaum district, the lowest incidence of 1.0 per cent was noticed at Ankalgi village, whereas highest incidence of 3.8 per cent was recorded at Anigol village. In Bidar district, the disease ranged between 0.8 to 6.8 per cent. The lowest incidence of 0.80 per cent was recorded at Udbal village whereas, highest incidence of 6.8 per cent was recorded at Janti village. In Dharwad district, the disease ranged between 1.0 to 2.5 per cent. The disease incidence was minimum with 1.0 per cent at Hangarki village, whereas maximum incidence of 2.5 per cent at Aminbhavi village.

The disease incidence ranged between 2.5 to 4.5 in Haveri district, where the highest disease incidence was recorded at Basrikatti village with 4.5 per cent and the lowest incidence of 2.5 per cent at Kunduru village. The highest incidence was recorded at Ugarkurd with 35.0 per cent and a lowest incidence of 12.5 per cent at Nayanagar village of Belgaum district. At Main Agricultural Research Station, Dharwad the disease incidence was 9.5 per cent.

Symptomatology

Seedlings of soybean (MACS-124) and cowpea (C 152) were raised under glasshouse conditions in insect proof nets. Soybean and cowpea seedlings were mechanically inoculated with the virus causing bud blight of soybean collected from the field. The infected cowpea seedlings developed necrotic ring spots within 5-6 days. Where as on soybean mild necrotic rings developed on leaves. After 25 days soybean showed typical curving of the buds (hook like). Virus from both soybean and cowpea were back inoculated to soybean seedlings in glasshouse which showed characteristic bud blight symptoms as that of in field conditions.

Virus Purification

Virus was partially purified as described in material and methods. The virus was maintained under insect proof glasshouse condition on cowpea (C 152) and the cowpea leaves showing chlorotic rings were used for the purification of virus.

Identification of the Virus

Electron Microscopy

The presence of virus particles in the purified preparation was confirmed by electron microscopy. The electron micrograph showed typical virus particle of isometric shape resembling Tobacco streak virus.

Direct Antigen Coating - Enzyme Linked Immuno Sorbent Assay

The virus causing soybean bud blight reacted positively with antiserum raised against *Tobacco streak virus* (TSV) but not with *Groundnut bud necrosis virus* (GBNV) antiserum. Positive reaction was observed in both positive controls i.e., TSV infected sunflower with TSV antiserum and GBNV infected groundnut with GBNV antiserum. Both negative controls i.e., buffer and healthy samples exhibited negative reactions. The results revealed that soybean bud blight was caused by *Tobacco streak virus*.

Polymerase Chain Reaction i.e., RT-PCR

Total RNA was isolated from infected and healthy soybean samples along with TSV (from sunflower) and GBNV (from groundnut) which were maintained on cowpea (C 152) and also a healthy cowpea sample. C-DNA was synthesized using reverse transcriptase enzyme. From these samples, coat protein was isolated using specific forward and reverse primers of TSV and GBNV separately. The amplicon of TSV-CP gene was confirmed by electrophoresis on 1.0 per cent agarose gel and ~ 400 bp band was found in infected soybean and cowpea infected with TSV confirming the presence of CP gene of TSV, where as no band was observed in cowpea infected with GBNV, healthy soybean and healthy cowpea, where as ~ 800 bp band was found in cowpea infected with GBNV but not in infected soybean, cowpea infected with TSV (sunflower) and healthy cowpea when the primer of GBNV was used.

Cloning

The coat protein (CP) gene was amplified by PCR in order to generate large quantity of DNA. The electrophoresed product of TSV-CP ~ 400 bp band was eluted and used for ligation in PTZ57R/T a cloning vector having 2.88 kb size with T over hang. Transformation of *E. coli* strain DH5a with ligation mixture resulted in several colonies carrying the recombinant DNA on an artibiotic (AMP 100) containing medium which included recombinant as well as self ligated vectors. White colonies obtained on the X-gal and IPTG were used for screening the recombinant clones. The recombinant colonies were selected based on blue-white colony assay. White colonies were produced due to the insertion of TSV-CP gene in multiple cloning sites, which resulted in disruption of *Lac Z* expression.

In the absence of insert, the Lac Z gene is switched on by adding the inducer isopropyl β-D-thiogalactopyranoside (IPTG). Its presence causes the enzyme β-galactosidase to be produced. The functional enzyme is able to hydrolyse a colourless substance 5-bromo 4-chloro 3-indolyl β-galactopyranoside (X-gal) to a blue insoluble material. Thus, bacteria carrying recombinant plasmids are unable to synthesize functional b-galactosidase enzyme producing white coloured colonies. Hence, bacterial colonies carrying the recombinant DNA molecules are colourless and can be easily identified from the non-recombinant blue colonies.

The transformed clones consisting of coat protein (transformed) gene were grown separately on Luria broth and they were further analyzed and confirmed by colony PCR with a produced of ~ 400 bp as resolved and analyzed on gel-electrophorosis. Further confirmation was also done by restriction analysis using Xba1 and Bam H1 restriction enzymes, which released a fragment of ~ 400 bp TSV-CP gene.

Sequencing

The clones consisting of the coat protein gene of causal virus were sequenced using M13 universal forward and reverse primers. The results revealed that the cloned DNA fragment of 398 bp long was obtained. The results of the BLAST revealed the query matching with reported TSV coat protein gene sequences from different geographical locations. The highest homology of 99.7 per cent was found with CP gene sequence of DWD-8, GWD-2, Latur, Beed, Solapur, Raichur and Coimbatore followed by 99.4 per cent with DWD-2, DWD-2-3, DWD-14 and Gulbarga.

The amino acids composition of coat protein gene of TSV UASD showed lowest per cent of Histidine and Tyrosine (0.76%) and highest amount of Alanine (13.74%). The sense strand molecular weight of DNA was 122.68 kD and of antisense was 123.3 kD. The molecular weight of DNA duplex was 254.97 kD. The sense strand molecular weight of RNA was 127.78 kD and of antisense strand was 128.3 kD. The molecular weight of RNA duplex was 256.09 kD.

The frequencies of nucleotide observed was Adanine 97 (24.2%), Guanine 97 (24.4%) Cytosine 114 (28.6%) and Thiamine 90 (22.6%). The results of electron microscopy, ELISA, RT-PCR and gene sequencing revealed that *Tobacco streak virus* might be the causal agent of soybean bud blight disease. Hence it can be designated as TSV-Sb a strain of Tobacco streak virus.

Management of Bud Blight Disease of Soybean

To know the efficacy of different insecticides along with border crop (sorghum), to manage soybean bud blight disease through vector control, experiments were conducted at Agharkar Research Institute (ARI), Pune and Main Agricultural Research

Station (MARS), Dharwad. At 40 days after sowing (DAS), lowest disease incidence of 2.0 per cent and thrips population of 2.42 per leaf was recorded in treatment comprising border cropping with sorghum + spray with imidacloprid (T_6), which was significantly superior over control, which registered 11.17 per cent disease incidence and 10.85 thrips per leaf.

However, this treatment was on par with the treatment involving border cropping + spray with interprid (T_9), which recorded the disease incidence of 2.33 and a thrips population of 2.88 per leaf and also with the treatment comprising imidacloprid spray (T_1), which recorded a PDI of 2.83 and 2.99 thrips per leaf and the treatment with interprid spray (T_4) with PDI of 3.17 and a thrips population of 3.82 per leaf. Raising of border crop (T_5) and spraying with either acetamprid or thiomethoxam alone failed to abate the thrips population and the disease incidence, however these are statistically superior over control treatment. The observations made at 60 DAS revealed that the trend of superiority/similarity of treatments was continued, but with an increase in both PDI and thrips population. At 60 DAS, the PDI ranged from 6.17 (T_6) to 24.83 (T_{10}) and the thrips population from 5.59 (T_6) to 19.69 (T_{10}).

The border cropping treatment (T5) resulted in least per cent decrease in PDI over control of 31.94 and the treatments receiving spray of insecticides either by imidacloprid or interprid in combination with border cropping registered higher per cent decreased disease over control ranging from 77.31 (T_6) to 73.92 (T_9) than insecticides or border cropping alone. Lowest disease incidence of 1.83 per cent and a thrips population of 1.67 per leaf were recorded in treatment comprising of border cropping + spray with imidacloprid (T_6) at 40 DAS, which was significantly superior over control, which recorded PDI of 11.20 and 12.18 thrips per leaf. However, this treatment was on par with the treatment comprising of border cropping + interprid which recorded PDI of 2.0 and a thrips population of 2.07 per leaf (T_9) and also with the treatment (T_1) receiving imidacloprid spray alone which recorded PDI of 2.17 and a thrips population of 2.43 per leaf, which was also on par with treatment (T_4) with PDI of 2.83 and a thrips population of 3.73 per leaf. All the treatments except control were significantly superior over border crop alone (T_5) which recorded the PDI of 8.17 and a thrips population of 9.67 per leaf. However it was statistically superior over control treatment (T_{10}).

The trend of superiority/similarity of treatments was continued as the observations made at 60 DAS, but with an increase in both PDI and thrips population. The PDI ranged between 5.67 (T_6) to 25.83 (T_{10}) and the thrips population between 4.22 (T_6) to 18.30 (T10) per leaf. The treatments receiving spray of insecticides either by imidacloprid or interprid in combination with border cropping recorded higher per cent decrease in PDI over control ranging from 79.73 (T_6) to 77.78 (T_9) than insecticides or border cropping alone. The treatment with border cropping alone (T_5) resulted in least per cent decrease in PDI over control of 31.53 per cent.

Note: T_1 - Imidacloprid spray, T_2 - Acetamprid spray, T_3 - Thiamethoxam spray, T_4 - Interprid spray, T_5 - Border crop with sorghum alone, T_6 - Border crop with sorghum + T_1, T_7 - Border crop with sorghum + T_2, T_8 Border crop with sorghum + T_3, T_9 Border crop with sorghum + T_4, T_{10} Control.

At 40 DAS, the lowest disease incidence of 2.72 per cent and a thrips population of 3.39 per leaf were recorded in treatment comprising of border cropping + imidacloprid spray (T_6), which was significantly superior over control, which recorded 12.33 per cent disease incidence and 13.10 thrips per leaf. However, this treatment was on par with the treatment involving border cropping + interprid spray (T_9) which recorded a PDI of 2.83 and 3.37 thrips per leaf and followed by the treatment comprising of imidacloprid spray with 3.17 PDI and 4.34 thrips per leaf, which was also on par with treatment (T_4) registered PDI of 3.67 and 4.68 of thrips per leaf.

The observations made at 60 DAS revealed that the trend of superiority/similarity of treatments was continued, but with an increase in both PDI and thrips population. At 60 DAS, the PDI ranged from 4.78 (T6) to 26.28 (T10) and the thrips population was 5.11 (T_6) to 18.44 (T_{10}). The border cropping alone treatment (T_5) resulted in least per cent decrease in PDI over control of 30.50 per cent and the treatments receiving spray of insecticides either by imidacloprid or interprid in combination with border cropping registered higher per cent decrease in PDI over control ranging from 80.58 (T_6) to 78.42 (T_9) per cent than insecticides or border cropping alone.

Attempts were made to develop management strategies by using different insecticides alone and in combination with sorghum border cropping. These insecticides in combination with sorghum were evaluated for their efficacy in keeping disease incidence low by controlling thrips which are responsible for the spread of the disease. During *Kharif*, border crop with sorghum in combination with Imidacloprid spray was best which not only kept the vector population low but reduced the per cent mean disease incidence (4.08%) accounting 77.31 per cent decrease in disease over control. Border crop with sorghum in combination with Interprid spray was the next best treatment which reduced mean per cent disease incidence (4.69%) accounting to 73.92 per cent decrease in disease incidence over control with reduced thrips population.

During *rabi*/summer, lowest per cent mean disease incidence (3.75%) was observed in the treatment composed of sorghum border cropping with Imidacloprid accounting to 79.73 per cent decrease in disease incidence over control. Next best treatment was sorghum border crop with Intreprid spray which recorded the per cent mean disease incidence of 4.11 per cent accounting to 77.78 per cent decrease in disease incidence over control.

The next best treatment was sorghum with Interprid spray which recorded 4.17 per cent mean disease incidence with 78.42 per cent disease inhibition over control by reducing the thrips population.

Similarly, the spread of sunflower necrosis disease could be minimized by spraying Imidacloprid (0.025%). Use of border crop's like sorghum reduced the incidence of disease from 18 to 7 per cent. Similarly spray of imidacloprid @ 0.05 per cent at 30 DAS reduced the incidence of disease from 27 to 5 per cent. Seed treatment with imidacloprid (5g/kg) + spray (@ 0.25ml/L) at 30, 45 and 60 days after sowing and sorghum as a border crop, by way of reducing the vector movement kept the sunflower necrosis disease incidence at low.

As there were many controversial reports regarding the etiology of soybean bud blight disease in India as *Tobacco ring spot virus*, *Peanut bud necrosis virus* and *Tobacco streak virus*. To resolve the above problem, studies were undertaken to identify the actual cause of the disease under study by applying serodiagnostic and molecular technique like RT-PCR and gene sequencing. From the study it was evident that the disease under study was caused by Tobacco streak virus in Karnataka which was designated as TSV-Sb. It can be managed by border cropping (sorghum) + imidacloprid (@ 0.25 ml/lit) spray. Further the varieties like NRCS 7, MAUS 71 shown resistant reaction can further be tested in hot spots with heavy disease load and can be included in integrated disease management schedule, if found promising.

19

Insects and Pests of Soybean

This chapter describes insects and pests that affect only soybeans. The insects and pests listed below affect soybeans as well as other crops.

JAPANESE BEETLE (*Popillia japonica*) - Soybeans, Forages

Description

Japanese beetle grubs can be distinguished from other grubs by the wide, shallow V-shaped raster pattern. The grubs are also much smaller in size than European chafer and June beetle grubs. The adult beetles are approximately 13 mm (½ in.) in length and can be easily identified by their bright, metallic-green head and coppery wings tinged with green edges. They have 12 white tufts of hair along the boundary of their wings.

Life Cycle

Japanese beetles have only one generation a year. They over-winter as third instar larvae below the frost line. Once the soil has warmed up above 15°C, the larvae migrate to the surface and feed on plant roots until mid- to late June, after which time they pupate to become adults. Adults emerge in early July and live for approximately 40 days. Once mated, females lay their eggs in the soil, which hatch in a few weeks. Larvae begin feeding on roots, molting through three instars before preparing for over-wintering by migrating below the frost line by early October.

Damage

Both the larval and adult stages can feed on field crops. This pest is most commonly found in the Niagara/Hamilton region, though it is known to be present across Ontario. Soybean and hay fields in particular tend to experience some root-feeding damage from the larvae. Adults will also feed on soybeans, dry edible beans, fruit crops and ornamental plants, causing leaves to appear skeletonized.

Scouting Technique for Larvae (Grubs)

Scout for grubs on the sandier knolls of the field and in the areas where past injury was evident. Using a shovel, dig up approximately 1 square foot of soil (30 cm^2), about 7-10 cm (3-4 in.) deep, in at least five areas of the field.

Scouting Technique for Adults in Soybeans

Scout 20 plants in at least five areas and compare the damage found to Fig. 19.1, Defoliation Chart for Soybean Leaf-Feeding Insects.

Action Threshold for Larvae (Grubs)

No thresholds are available for Japanese beetle grubs, though two or more larvae indicate that control may be necessary.

Management Strategies for All Crops:

- Use insecticide seed treatments in fields with a history of damage by the larvae.
- Avoid planting early in cool, wet springs. Plant in ideal soil and weather conditions to help promote rapid germination and seedling growth.
- No rescue treatments are available for grubs. Tillage can help kill some of the larvae and expose them to their predators such as birds, skunks and raccoons.
- For further recommendations on adults.

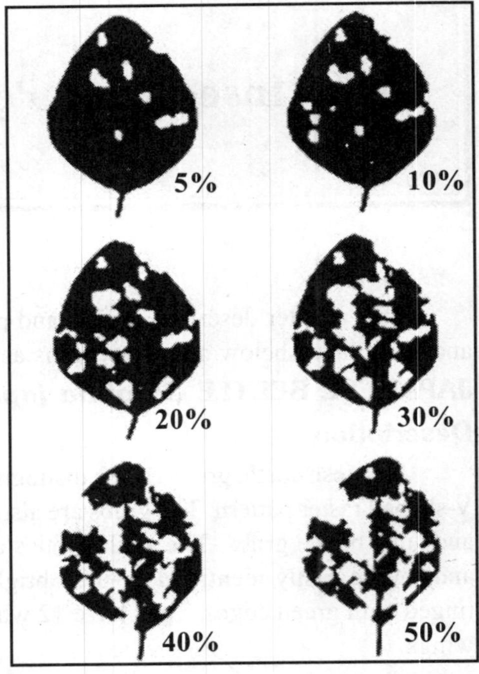

Fig. 19.1: **Defoliation Chart for Soybean Leaf-Feeding Insects**

5% defoliation - 6 or 7 spots; 10% defoliation - approximately 12 spots and outer edge of leaf defoliated; 20% defoliation - larger spots of defoliation; 30% defoliation - much larger areas of defoliation; 40% defoliation and 50% defoliation - very little of leaf remains intact.

JUNE BEETLE (*Phyllophaga* spp.) - Soybeans, Forages

Description

June beetle larvae can be distinguished from other white grubs by their oval-shaped raster pattern, where two rows of rasters run parallel to each other. The adult is slightly larger, roughly 20 mm (3/4 in.), than European chafer and is reddish-brown to black in colour. The June beetle is also known as the true white grub or June bug.

Life History

June beetles have a 3-year life cycle. Adults emerge from the soil mid-May to mid-June and lay eggs. Adults tend to congregate at dusk in large masses on trees and shrubs to mate. Eggs are laid in moist soil and hatch within a few weeks. First instar larvae begin feeding on plant roots and molt into the second instar before migrating deep into the soil to over-winter. Once the soil warms up the following spring (Year Two), the second instars begin feeding and will remain as larvae throughout the year, molting once into the third instar. The second year of their life cycle is therefore the most destructive. Larvae again prepare to over-winter by migrating deeper in the soil once temperatures drop, until the following spring. In Year Three, the third instar larvae feed on roots for a short time before pupating and becoming adults. These adults will remain dormant in the soil for the rest of the season and only emerge the following spring.

Damage

Damage depends on which year of the life cycle the majority of the larvae are in. The second year of the life cycle is the most damaging, because there is a full growing season of the larval stage. Soybeans and forages tend to experience the most injury from this insect, especially when the crop is still young. Adults can feed on tree species and ornamental plants such as roses but do not feed on field crops.

Scouting Techniques

Scout for grubs on the sandier knolls of the field and in the areas where injury was evident in previous years. Using a shovel, dig up approximately 1 square foot of soil, (30 cm^2) about 7-10 cm (3-4 in.) deep, in at least five areas of the field. Sift through the soil by hand, breaking up any clumps and count how many grubs are in each sample.

Action Threshold

No thresholds are available for June beetle grubs, though two or more larvae indicate the need for control.

Management Strategies for All Crops

- Use insecticide seed treatments in fields with a history of damage, particularly if grubs appear to be mainly in the second year of their life cycle when the majority of the feeding will take place.
- Avoid planting early in cool, wet springs.
- Plant in ideal soil and weather conditions to help promote rapid germination and seedling growth.
- No rescue treatments are available. Tillage can help kill some of the larvae and expose them to their predators such as birds, skunks and racoons.

Management Strategies for Forages

- Avoid planting forages in infested fields, particularly if grubs appear to be mainly in the second year of their life cycle, when the majority of the feeding will take place.
- Plant fields with a history of crop loss due to grubs to another field crop that has an insecticide seed treatment available for grub control. Re-assess the grub population following this control tactic to determine if forages can be planted in that field again.

- A well-managed pasture with a good mix of legume and grass species may help reduce stand loss, as grubs tend to feed more on the grass species. Over-seeding or reseeding may be required for a few years to compensate for what the grubs have taken out.

SEEDCORN MAGGOT (*Delia platura*) - Corn, Dry Edible Beans, Soybeans

Description

The seedcorn maggot is a small, yellowish-white, headless, legless larva. The body tapers to the front with two small mouth hooks protracting. The maggots burrow into germinating seeds and the below-ground parts of emerging seedlings, producing weak seedlings. The adults resemble a small housefly that is slender, light grey and approximately 5 mm (1/5 in.) in length.

Life History

The seedcorn maggot over-winters in the pupal stage. Adults emerge in early spring. Once mated, female adults (flies) search for an egg-laying site from April until the middle of June. The females are attracted to moist soils that give off an odour of decaying organic matter, such as crop residues, areas where manure has been applied or freshly tilled soil. Weeds are also attractive to females. The adults lay their eggs in the soil. The larvae then develop in the soil and organic residue, feeding on germinating seeds.

Damage

Seedcorn maggot is usually a problem during cool, wet springs when germination is delayed. The maggots feed on the swollen, ungerminated seed. They can be found in the cotyledon, embryo and hypocotyl. They can also mine the stem of the young seedling. Slow emergence and/or reduced stand establishment can occur. Damaged seedlings that germinate often die or lag behind.

Scouting Technique

Unlike wireworm, seedcorn maggot damage is usually found over a generalized, large portion of the field. Nothing can be done to rescue a damaged field except replanting if necessary. High-risk factors include freshly tilled soil with heavy crop residue, recently applied manure, recently tilled green manure, deep planting and early planting followed by cool, wet spring conditions. Look for signs of poor stand emergence and feeding damage at the base of the newly emerging plants.

Action Threshold

No threshold is available at this time.

Management Strategies

- Consider insecticide seed treatments or in-furrow, soil-applied insecticides in early-planted fields where large amounts of manure or residue have been recently incorporated.
- Use good-quality seed that will emerge quickly.

- Plant in good soil conditions when cool wet weather is not in the forecast to ensure rapid seedling emergence.
- There are no rescue treatments available. Use an insecticide seed treatment or in-furrow insecticide in fields requiring replanting.

SLUGS (*Deroceras reticulatum*) - Corn, Soybeans, Newly Seeded Forages, Canola

Description

Juvenile and adult slugs are soft-bodied, legless, greyish or mottled in appearance and have a slimy or gelatinous covering that protects them from drying out. They are essentially snails without a shell. The head has two pairs of tentacles. Slugs usually range from 1-3 cm (1/3 in.) in length but can reach up to 10 cm (4 in.).

Life History

There is one generation per year but two populations, one maturing as adults in spring and one maturing as adults in fall. Therefore, damage can occur both in the spring and the fall on young developing plants. Both eggs and adults over-winter. Juvenile slugs hatch from eggs in the spring and the fall and are the most damaging stage of the pest. Slugs are most active during cool and wet periods in spring and fall and prefer environments with high humidity and relatively cool temperatures. Debris, such as crop litter or manure, provides them with shelter from the sun.

Damage

Slugs feed above or below ground, depending on the moisture level. They can feed on germinating seeds and seedlings, with no real preference for a plant part.

Slugs feed on lower parts of larger plants, partly or completely eating through leaves, resulting in ragged holes that cause a skeletonized appearance on leaves.

Feeding can resemble hail damage, and severe defoliation can result. If slug populations are high, they may feed on germinating seeds, hollowing them out before they can emerge. Higher-risk fields include no-till corn, soybeans and canola, especially fields with considerable crop residue, wheat fields underseeded with red clover, newly seeded alfalfa and fields following forages, especially grasses. Knowing the slug population of each field in the fall will indicate how significant the problem will be the next spring. It is the same population that over-winters and feeds in the spring.

Scouting Technique

Scout for slugs at night or in the early morning hours, when they are active (nocturnal). Look for gaps in the stand, stripping of leaf tissue and/or small holes chewed in the leaves. Check under debris and clumps of soil. A certain sign of slugs is a slimy, silver-coloured trail on the plants or soil. To determine population levels, take small pieces of plywood, approximately 0.6-0.9 m (2-3 ft) long, or roofing shingles and position them on the soil surface in fields that have been harvested. Use 10-15 boards randomly scattered across the field to provide a good indication of population levels. These boards will act as shelters for the slugs. Visit the boards every 5 days for approximately 1 month, counting the number of slugs present under the boards. Morning is the best time to look, since slugs will still be in their shelters.

Action Threshold

No action thresholds are available. If slugs are commonly found under monitored boards as described above, the field should be considered at high risk for slug injury in the spring. Scout these fields again in the spring to confirm risk. Young seedlings and germinating seeds are most impacted.

Management Strategies

- Planting into conditions that help the crop grow quickly can avoid heavy slug damage.
- Tillage can be used against slugs since the elimination of the crop cover exposes the slugs to dehydration and predation by birds and mammals. Zone tillage or row sweepers can help speed up the drying of the row area, thus deterring slug feeding. Moving trash away from seedlings may help reduce damage.
- There are presently no economically feasible chemical methods available for slug control in field crops. Slug baits are available for field crops but are very expensive and are only recommended for use in small problem areas of the field. Apply baits shortly after May 24 to achieve the highest potential for success.
- Experiments with 28 per cent nitrogen/water mixtures or foliar potash applications have proven to be inconsistent and are not encouraged.

TARNISHED PLANT BUG (*Lygus lineolaris*)

Description

Tarnished plant bug (TPB) adults are approximately 5 mm (1/5 in.) in length, mottled, yellowish-to-reddish-brown in colour and have a small triangle shape on their back. The nymph stage does not resemble the adults but can be misidentified as aphids, though they lack the cornicles ("tailpipes") that aphids possess. Nymphs are yellowish-green, wingless and lack the distinctive triangle-shape on their back. Older nymphs develop four small black dots on the thorax and one on the abdomen.

Life History

TPB have several host crops but tend to move into canola and dry edible beans when alfalfa is being cut. They over-winter as adults in the leaf litter and plant debris within fields, woodlots, fencerows and ditch banks. Once temperatures warm up, adults migrate to other host crops to feed and lay eggs. Several generations occur within the summer. It is usually the later generations that enter the edible bean crop once other host crops are no longer suitable for feeding. TPB tend to be more of a prevalent in hot, dry years.

Damage

The adults and later stages of nymphs are the more damaging stages. TPB have piercing-sucking mouthparts that they use to pierce into the plant tissue and inject saliva that breaks down some of the plant tissue. Feeding on flowers can cause flower abortion. Feeding during pod stages results in scarring, malformation and dimpling or pitting of the pods. Sap may ooze from the feeding sites on the pods, which increases the risk of pod disease development. TPB can also drill directly into the seed, causing pick, reducing seed quality. In sunflowers, TPB injury causes kernel brown spot.

Scouting Technique

Monitor fields weekly during the early-pod and seed-filling stages. Monitor intensely after neighbouring alfalfa fields have been cut. Take 20 sweeps in a 180° arc in 5 areas of the field to determine the average number of adults and nymphs per sweep. TPB prefer pigweed in flower, which can be monitored to help indicate when TPB are present in and around the field. Border rows are apt to have higher populations, so ensure that sweeping takes place.

Action Threshold for Dry Edible Beans

A treatment may be required when an average of one to two tarnished plant bugs per sweep is found during the pod stages.

Action Threshold for Canola

No thresholds have been validated for Ontario, though other jurisdictions recommend spraying canola when two tarnished plant bugs per sweep can be found after petal fall, but prior to pod maturity.

Action Threshold for Sunflowers

One tarnished plant bug adult or nymph per nine heads prior to or at bloom warrant control in fields for confectionary production.

Management Strategies

- Several parasitic wasps help control TPB. Use a foliar insecticide only when threshold has been reached, because insecticides are extremely detrimental to these parasitoids.
- Spray in the very late evening or early morning when bees are less likely to be foraging in the crop.
- Contact local beekeepers at least 24 hours in advance so that they can move their hives prior to spraying.
- Control weeds, particularly pigweed, which can attract TPB to the field.

SOYBEAN APHID (*Aphis glycines*)

Description

The soybean aphid is a small (pinhead-size), pale yellow aphid with black cornicles ("tailpipes") and a pale yellow tail. Adults may be winged or wingless. Nymphs are smaller than the adults and are wingless. Eggs on buckthorn are small, football-shaped and yellow when first laid but turn a dark brown similar to the colour of the buckthorn branch. Eggs are usually laid along the seams of the buckthorn bud.

Life History

The soybean aphid, a pest originally from Asia, was first discovered in North America in 2000 and in Ontario in 2001. This insect has two hosts that it requires to complete its life cycle. The soybean aphid survives as eggs on the twigs of buckthorn species. In the spring, nymphs hatch from these eggs, and the aphids undergo two generations as wingless females on the buckthorn. The third generation develops into winged adults that migrate to soybean plants. The aphids then continue to produce wingless generations until the soybean plants become crowded with aphids and the plants experience a reduction in quality. Once crowded, winged forms are produced to disperse to less-crowded soybean plants. There can be as many as 18 generations of aphids per year on soybeans. Like most aphids, the soybean aphids are all female, born pregnant and give birth to live nymphs. Males are only born in the fall so that the females and males can mate to produce the egg on buckthorn.

Damage

Aphids have piercing-sucking mouthparts that suck juices and nutrients from the plant. Lower populations of aphids can live and feed on soybeans without causing yield loss. Once populations reach threshold levels, especially in dry years when the plants are stressed, aphids can cause the plants to abort flowers, become stunted, reducing pod and seed production and quality. Yield loss by soybean aphid is greatest when soybeans are in the early R stages (R1-R2), when flowers can abort and impact pod establishment. Peak infestations during the pod fill stage (R3) and beyond can result in smaller seed size and a reduction in seed quality. Aphids also excrete a sticky substance called honeydew, which can act as a substrate for grey sooty mould development. This insect may also be a vector of soybean mosaic virus.

Scouting Technique

Early-season aphid infestations tend to concentrate on the newly emerging leaves and upper trifoliates of the plant. Later in the season, once into the reproductive stages of soybeans, the aphids tend to migrate down to the middle or lower canopy, possibly due to heat and predator abundance experienced at the top of the canopy. Because of this movement within the canopy through the season, taking full plant counts is still the best method to estimate the number of aphids per plant and relate that to the threshold.

Scout each field every 7-10 days from early June until early September or until the crop is well into the R6 stage of soybeans. Scout fields more frequently (every 3-4 days) as aphid populations approach the threshold. Look at 20-30 random plants across the field. Avoid field edges. Estimate the number of aphids per plant in that field. A minimum of two field visits is required to confirm that aphid populations are increasing.

Action Threshold

The threshold for soybean aphids is 250 aphids per plant and actively increasing on 80 per cent of the plants from the R1 up to and including the R5 stage of soybeans. This threshold gives an approximate 7-10-day lead time before the aphids would reach the economic injury level, where cost of control is equal to yield loss. When soybean aphid populations are not actively increasing above 250 aphids per plant, natural enemies are keeping up with the aphid population. More aphids per plant are needed once soybeans are in the R6 stage. Beyond the R6 stage, economic return from any insecticide application is not likely. Soybean aphid colonies typically start on the underside of the leaves. Once populations begin to increase on the plants, aphids can then be found on the stems and pods of the plant. This is usually a good indication that aphids have reached threshold.

Management Strategy

- There are several natural enemies, including the lady beetles (ladybugs), minute pirate bug, syrphid fly larvae and parasitic wasps that are helpful in controlling this pest. A pathogen can also infect the aphids but requires warm, moist conditions to become established.
- When soybean aphid populations are not actively increasing above 250 aphids per plant, natural enemies are keeping up with the aphid population. Do not use an insecticide in this case, as it will kill the natural enemies and enable the aphid population to increase above threshold levels.
- Before applying an insecticide to control aphids, scout for spider mites to ensure that populations are not present. If they are, select the appropriate insecticide that will kill the mites and the aphids, so that the mite population is also controlled and will not flare up shortly after application.

TWO-SPOTTED SPIDER MITE (*Tetranychus uricae*)

Description

The adult mite is barely visible to the naked eye, roughly 0.5-1.0 mm (1/25 in.) in length, rounded, eight-legged and yellowish-brown with two dark spots on the sides of the abdomen. The larvae look like the nymphs and adults but have six legs instead of eight. Nymphs look similar to the adults, with eight legs. Over-wintering females are orange/red.

Life History

Spider mites generally over-winter as adult females in sheltered areas, such as plant debris and field margins. Harvested wheat fields underseeded to red clover are another important over-wintering site. Red clover provides food for mites until freeze-up, allowing the mites to survive in the field. In late-April, as the weather turns warm, mites become active in search of food and egg-laying sites. Spider mites disperse by crawling, so infestations tend to spread slowly from field edges. Non-mated female mites will mass at the top of the plants and spin webs that serve as a "balloon," allowing strong winds to pick them up and carry them off to another site. Spider mite females can reproduce without mating. A single unmated female can be the start of a new colony. Under hot, dry, windy conditions, infestations can spread very quickly. There can be up to seven generations per year, with generation development overlapping. Frequent rain and cool weather reduce mite populations in soybeans.

Damage

Mites feed on individual plant cell contents on the underside of leaves through stylet-like mouthparts. Each feeding site causes a stipple. Severe stippling causes yellowing, curling and bronzing of the leaves. Eventually, the leaf will dry up and fall off. Upon close examination, fine webbing on lower surfaces of the foliage can be seen. Damage is more severe in hot, dry weather and usually occurs in mid-July (after winter wheat harvest). Spider mites usually start at the edges of the field, but windy days can carry them in from other sites, with pockets starting up deeper into the field.

From the road, these pockets may have been confused for drought stress. High-risk factors include neighbouring winter wheat stubble fields, hay fields and ditch banks and fencerows that harbour over-wintering mites. No-till fields of soybeans following winter wheat underseeded to red clover are also at risk.

Scouting Technique

Scout fields weekly, starting the first week of July. Infestations tend to occur shortly after wheat harvest and when municipalities mow road sides. Infestations usually move in from the edge of fields as hot spots. Look for tiny white stipples on the upper surface of leaves in the mid-canopy. Pull these leaves from the plant and shake them onto a white piece of paper to see the actual mites moving around. You will need a 10X hand lens to actually see the mites.

Action Threshold

Four or more mites per leaflet or one severely damaged leaf per plant prior to pod fill indicates that control is necessary.

Management Strategies

- If mite numbers exceed the action threshold, an insecticide may be necessary.
- Use border sprays to keep early infestations under control. This will help prevent the spread of mites to other parts of the field and may reduce the need for further treatment.
- If rain is in the forecast, delay spraying. Prolonged wetness will usually reduce the number of mites to insignificant levels.
- Use of drought-tolerant varieties will minimize the effect of spider mites. Natural enemies help keep mites at low levels when conditions are unfavourable for the mites. Natural enemies of mites include ladybird beetles, thrips and predaceous mites. Cool temperatures and high humidity can promote the development of a pathogen that can provide natural control.

Defoliating Insects

Soybeans are able to compensate for large amounts of foliage loss due to insect feeding, and often little effect on yield is observed. Soybean plants not only continue to put out new leaves at the top to compensate for the feeding but leaves positioned below the feeding injury sites actually grow larger, increasing their surface area, since they are getting more sunlight through the canopy. However, the most critical stage for soybeans is bloom (R1) to pod-fill (R4), when seed development is highly dependent on photosynthesis. Should large amounts of defoliation occur throughout the plant during these stages, yield can be affected, particularly in dry years.

To estimate damage thresholds for leaf-feeding insects on soybeans, determine the percentage of defoliation occurring in each soybean field. In 10 areas of the field, pick trifoliate leaves from five plants in the middle of the canopy. Discard the least and most damaged leaflets from each trifoliate collected.

Defoliation is often overestimated. Most of the defoliating insects feed on the tops of the plants and field edges first so that upon first inspection of the field, it appears that there is a lot of defoliation. Make sure to inspect trifoliates from the middle of the canopy to get a good assessment of defoliation.

BEAN LEAF BEETLE (*Certoma trifurcata*) - dry Edible beans, soybeans

Description

The bean leaf beetle (BLB) adult is around 5 mm (1/5 in.) in length, with or without four black spots (parallelogram shaped) found on the wing covers. Adult beetles can vary in colour but are most often yellow-green, tan or red.

A small, black triangle is visible at the base of the wing covers (the prothorax - behind the head). The margins of the wing covers have a black border.

The bean leaf beetle is often confused with the spotted cucumber beetle or lady beetles. A small black triangle is visible at the base of the wing covers (behind the head) of the bean leaf beetle.

Life History

There are two generations of BLB per year, not including the over-wintering population that enters the soybean crop from their over-wintering sites in early spring. The BLB overwinters in the adult stage in woodlots, leaf litter and soil debris. In late-April, the over-wintering adults become active and begin feeding on nearby alfalfa fields until the first cutting of alfalfa or soybeans emerge. Mated females then lay lemon-shaped, orange-coloured eggs in small clusters in the soil at the base of the soybean plants. Egg-laying occurs until mid-June. There is then a distinct period between the end of June to mid-July when there is little to no adult activity in the field, since most of the population is now in the egg and larval phase. Newly hatched larvae feed on roots and other underground plant parts for about 30 days before pupating. The first generation adults begin to emerge from the soil in mid-July and feed on the soybean foliage and pods. This generation lives for approximately one month, laying eggs that will become the second generation adults. A second generation of adults emerges mid- to late August and feeds on the pods until the plants senesce. The adults then migrate to alfalfa fields if available or move to their over-wintering sites.

Table 19.1: Standard Damage Thresholds for Soybean Insect Defoliation

Soybean Development	% Defoliation
Pre-bloom (i.e., vegetative stages)	30%
Bloom (R1) to pod-fill (R4)	15%
Pod-fill to maturity (R5-R6)(unless pod feeding observed)	25%

Damage to Soybeans

Defoliation injury by bean leaf beetle adults is generally not serious in Ontario. The exception is damage caused by over-wintering adults to young soybean plants (V1-V2). Adult feeding appears as small round holes between the major leaflet veins. Cotyledons and seedling plants can be clipped off by heavier populations. Late-season pod feeding is another concern. BLB feed on the surface of the pod, leaving only a thin film of tissue to protect the seeds within the pod. These pod lesions increase the pod's susceptibility to secondary pod diseases such as alternaria. Pods may also be clipped off the plant, but this is not the primary cause of yield loss. The most important concern is that BLB is a vector of bean pod mottle virus. The virus causes the plant and seed to become wrinkled and mottled, reducing the quality of the seed.

Damage to Dry Edible Beans

BLB prefer soybeans, though they can cause injury in dry edible beans, particularily in dry years when populations are high. BLB rarely enter the edible bean crop until mid-season. Defoliation typically does not reach threshold in Ontario. Adult feeding appears as small round holes between the major leaflet veins. Cotyledons and seedling plants can be clipped off by heavier populations. Late-season pod feeding is the main concern in dry edible beans. BLB feed on the surface of the pod, leaving only a thin film of tissue to protect the seeds within the pod. These pod lesions increase the susceptibility to secondary pod diseases such as alternaria. Pods may also be clipped off the plant. However, this is not the primary cause of yield loss.

Scouting Techniques

Soybean Seedling Stage

Select at least five sampling sites from across the entire field at random. At each sampling site, slowly walk down 4.5-6 m (15-20 ft) of row and carefully count all beetles. Do not disturb the plants, but check closely enough that you can see the underside of the leaves. Calculate the average number of beetles per metre (foot) of row.

Beyond Soybean Seedling Stage

In 10 areas of the field, pick trifoliate leaves that are fully expanded from the centre of the plant canopy from five plants. Discard the least and most damaged leaflets from each trifoliate collected. Determine the per cent defoliation that has occurred, using.

Soybean R5-R6 Stage

Thresholds have not yet been validated for Ontario. Thresholds are based on the per cent of pods with feeding damage. Assess pods on 20 plants in five areas of the field. Avoid the field edge. Determine the number of pods with feeding injury or clipping and make note of the presence of adults.

Prior to the Dry Edible Bean Pod-Fill Stages

Determine the level of defoliation taking place. In 10 areas of the field, pick trifoliate leaves that are fully expanded from five plants in the middle of the plant canopy. Discard the least- and most-damaged leaflets from each trifoliate collected. Determine the per cent defoliation that has occurred, using.

Dry Edible Bean Pod-Fill Stages

Thresholds are based on the per cent of pods with feeding damage. Assess pods on 20 plants in five areas of the field. Avoid the field edge. Determine the number of pods with feeding injury or clipping and make note of the presence of adults.

Damage Thresholds

Soybean Seedling Stage (VC-V2)

Thresholds for bean leaf beetle are 16 adult beetles per foot of row in early seedling stages. If plants are being clipped off, take action.

Soybean R5-R6 Stage of IP, Food Grade and Seed Fields

If 10 per cent of the pods on the plants have feeding injury and the beetles are still active in the field, a spray is warranted. However, remember to consider days-to-harvest intervals. Japanese beetles can also defoliate soybeans. For other foliar feeding insects in soybeans, including redheaded flea beetle, corn rootworm adults, grasshoppers, thistle caterpillars and others, follow the same scouting techniques.

Action Thresholds for Dry Edible Beans

Substantial yield loss does not take place until up to 35 per cent defoliation occurs before bloom and 15 per cent after bloom. Thresholds during pod fill have not been validated in Ontario yet. However, with higher value and stringent quality standards in dry edible beans, if 5 per cent-8 per cent of the pods inspected have feeding scars, control may be necessary. Ensure that adults are still presently active in the field before a spray is applied.

Management Strategies for Soybeans

Plant fields with a history of early-season bean leaf beetle activity and fields planted earliest in the area with insecticide-treated seed. Before applying a foliar insecticide, determine the level of soybean aphid and or spider mite pressure in the field. Certain insecticides can have more impact on the natural enemies than on intended pests and can cause aphid or spider mite populations to flare up.

Management Strategies for Dry Edible Beans

Treat the seeds planted in fields with a history of early-season bean leaf beetle activity or fields planted earliest in the area with insecticide seed treatments. Use foliar insecticides when defoliation thresholds have been reached.

POD-PIERCING INSECTS

Green Stink Bug (*Nezara viridula*), Brown Stink Bug (*Euschistus servus*)

Description

There are two types of stink bugs that can injure beans: Southern green stink bugs and brown stink bugs. The Southern green stink bug adults are large (about 1.8 cm (3/4 in.) long), light-green, shield-shaped bugs with fully developed wings. Brown stink bugs are smaller than the green stink bug, approximately 1 cm (1/3 in.) in length, and are a mottled brown-grey in colour. Adult stink bugs are shaped like a shield. The nymphs (juveniles) can look very different from their adult stage, having very short, stubby wing pads, and are often a different colour than the adults. In particular, green stink bug nymphs have a flashy display of black, green, orange and yellow. Eggs are laid in tight clusters, are yellowish white and barrel-shaped.

Life History

Southern green stink bugs do not over-winter in Ontario but are blown up from the southern U.S. by mid-summer. Brown stink bugs can over-winter in Ontario and may be present in other crops in early summer. Stink bugs are first found in soybean fields during August and early September.

The brown stink bug adult should not be confused with the spined soldier bug, which is a beneficial and feeds on caterpillars and other insect pests. To tell these two apart, look at their feeding beak or needle-like mouthpart. The beak of the brown stink bug is slender to pierce through delicate plant tissue. The beak of the spined soldier bug is thicker so it can harpoon into its insect prey. The soldier bug adult also has more pointed ("spined") shoulders than the brown stink bug, though this may be hard to notice unless you have them side by side to compare.

Damage

Both adults and nymphs have piercing and sucking mouthparts for removing plant fluids. Stink bugs feed directly on pods and seeds. However, their injury is difficult to assess because their mouthparts leave no obvious feeding scars on the outside of the pod. Instead, they inject digestive enzymes into seeds, causing the seed to dimple or shrivel. The feeding wound provides an avenue for diseases to gain entry into the pod. Seed quality is reduced. Indirect effects can include delayed maturity (green bean syndrome) of injured plants, though stink bugs are not the only cause for green bean syndrome.

Scouting Technique

Use the drop-cloth technique in row plantings, and the sweep-net technique for narrow row and drilled beans.

The drop-cloth method involves using a 90 cm (36 in.) long piece of white cloth positioned on the ground between two rows of soybeans. Vigorously shake the plants over the cloth in each of the two rows. Count the number of adults and nymphs and divide the number by 6 to obtain the average number of stink bugs in a 30-cm (1-ft.) row. Repeat this in at least four more areas of the field. Be careful not to disturb the plants prior to shaking them on the cloth.

Using a 38-cm (15-in.) diameter sweep net, take 20 sweep samples (in a 180°-arc sweep) in five areas of the field. Determine the average number of adults and nymphs per sweep by dividing the total count by 100.

Action Threshold

Control may be warranted in IP food grade and seed soybeans if an average of one stink bug per 30 cm (1 ft) of row or 0.2 bugs per sweep is found during the late R5-R6 stages.

Management Strategies

- Apply foliar insecticide if thresholds are reached.
- Be aware of the preharvest intervals for products.
- Some natural enemies parasitize or feed on stink bug eggs.

20

Nematode Management in Soybean

Nematodes that Attack Soybean

Soybean (*Glycine max*) has been grown relatively little in Florida in recent years, but the rise in value may cause some growers to consider growing the crop again. Part of that consideration should include knowledge of the severe nematode problems of soybean in Florida. Growers should be aware that nematodes are a major pest problem in soybean production, and in addition, seriously increase nematode risks to other crops that may follow soybean.

Nematodes attacking soybean include all the root-knot (*Meloidogyne* spp.) nematode species that occur in Florida. In addition, reniform (*Rotylenchulus reniformis*), lesion (*Pratylenchus* spp.) and sting (Belonolaimus longicaudatus) nematode populations are increased by soybean production. Each of these nematodes can be limiting factors in the production of soybean as well as other crops in Florida. Soybean cyst nematode (*Heterodera glycines*), important in previous years, only affects soybean among Florida agronomic crops. It has not been detected in Florida for many years since the decline in soybean production and the shift of much of the previous soybean acreage to cotton, a non-host of soybean cyst nematode.

Diagnosis

The presence or potential for nematode problems in soybean could be suggested by one or more of the following:

1. Cropping history of the field, e.g. two or more years of cotton production or other nematode-susceptible crops;
2. Above-ground symptoms including off-colour and/or stunted plants in spots or large areas of a field;
3. Below-ground symptoms such as small knots on roots or stunted and swollen root tips.

Above-ground Symptoms

Above-ground symptoms of nematodes attacking soybean resemble those caused by many other kinds of root injury, such as disease or general nutrient deficiency. Irregular, oval shaped areas in the field may contain plants that are stunted and yellowed. Plants with nematode-damaged root systems wilt more easily under moderately dry conditions and recover more slowly than healthy plants when water becomes available. Severity of damage is unevenly distributed in the field. Near the end of the season, leaves of nematode-affected soybean plants may prematurely yellow and drop before those of healthy plants. Frequently, lines of these damaged plants may stretch along rows following the direction of usual soil cultivation.

Root Symptoms

All nematodes affecting soybean reduce feeder roots and cause root stunting. To clearly see root symptoms, roots should be carefully dug with a shovel for close examination. Below-ground symptoms differ, depending on the nematodes causing them, and are not always distinct enough to use as a sole basis for diagnosis.

Root-knot nematode infections cause the roots of soybean to swell into galls. These may not be obvious until the latter half of the soybean season. Root galling caused by nematodes on soybean may resemble Rhizobium nodules, and these can be confused when diagnosing a root-knot nematode problem. Rhizobium nodules on soybean roots grow on one side of the root, can be easily removed from the root and are a pink colour inside. Root-knot nematode galls, on the other hand, grow around the small roots, are firmly attached, and are not pink on the inside.

Roots infected with soybean cyst nematode (SCN) usually have reduced Rhizobium nodulation and are short, sparse, and dark in colour. Small period-sized dot-like cysts on the roots can be seen with very careful examination. These are the developing females of soybean cyst nematode and can range in colour from white to creamy yellow to dark brown.

Other nematodes may cause soybean roots to be stunted or pruned, and the roots are usually darker in colour than healthy roots. Sting nematodes stop root growth, giving the appearance that roots have been cut off. Reniform nematodes are the most difficult to diagnose in the field and produce overall stunted root systems with few feeder roots. Extensive root decay caused by common fungi or bacteria often follows nematode injury, especially by lesion nematodes. A laboratory analysis is usually necessary to confirm cyst, reniform, lesion, and sting nematodes on soybean.

Nematode Assays

Soybean is such an excellent host for many important plant-parasitic nematodes that a field planted to this crop should be sampled before any cash crop is planted at the same site. Samples should not be taken when the soil is dusty dry or soggy wet. Two sampling strategies may be employed. A general survey should be performed immediately after soybean has been harvested. A soil core to 10 inches deep should be taken for every one acre in a 10-acre block containing a uniform soil type and cropping history. In a more definitive strategy where a nematode problem is suspected, several soil cores from within and immediately around a poor growth site should be taken while soybean is still growing. Include portions of damaged roots with the soil sample.

Prior to taking samples, contact your County Extension agent for information concerning available sampling tools, shipment bags and proper procedures for submitting samples. The cores should be thoroughly mixed and a 1-pint sample extracted and placed in a sealed plastic bag and kept cool (not frozen) before immediate shipment to an advisory laboratory.

Field Mapping

With the advent of GPS systems, some growers are now routinely collecting soil samples from their fields with sampling area sizes of 1-5 acres. These are then placed on maps and variable rate nematicide applications are made only where the nematicide is needed to improve yield. On one north Florida farm, intensive sampling and variable rate nematicide application have saved the grower up to 60 per cent of nematicide costs by only targeting nematode problems areas in his fields.

Root-knot nematodes can be monitored by observing root galling on susceptible crops. Carefully lift plants at regular intervals throughout a field and note on a field map the extent of galling at each site. This provides far more detailed information about the distribution of problems than can be obtained from lab analysis of one or two composite soil samples. Crop species and varieties on which galls are found can also give valuable clues to which root-knot nematode species are present in each location.

Management

Nematode management for soybean and following crops depends upon identifying and monitoring nematode populations to choose tactics for each field. Careful choice and integration of crop rotation, other cultural practices, resistant varieties, and nematicides are required. The kinds of nematodes present and their distribution in fields must be known to:

- identify fields that cannot be planted profitably, or where a different crop has better profit potential;
- plan optimum crop rotations to minimize losses for following crops and reduce populations;
- select appropriate resistant varieties; and
- recognize fields where nematicide use might pay for soybeans or other crops.

Crop Rotation

Soybean generally is not a suitable rotational option for the nematode management in other crops. Soybean should not be planted either before or after cotton as both are hosts to important nematode pests including southern root-knot, reniform, and sting nematodes. The susceptibility of soybean to nematodes is so great that, even if planted as a forage, growing soybeans for more than one consecutive season could cause damaging levels of nematodes for subsequent crops. Unless sting nematodes are in a field, a crop of soybean should be followed by a summer planting of a grass crop such as field corn, sorghum, or bahiagrass, etc. These crops are the most likely to reduce populations of root-knot and reniform nematodes. Rotation is a good tool to help keep relatively low populations from becoming too high, or for gradually reducing high populations over several years. It should not be expected to abruptly reduce a nematode population, since:

- some of a nematode population will survive the winter without a host
- most crop plants can support at least a little nematode reproduction
- most planted fields have weeds that support nematode reproduction

Soybean is the only common agronomic crop that supports soybean cyst nematode (SCN). However, some leguminous weeds, some varieties of field peas (southern peas), and most edible beans apparently can support SCN reproduction, so avoid them in a rotation intended to reduce SCN and do not follow soybeans with these crops. An additional problem is that some of the eggs within a cyst of SCN may remain dormant for many years. There may well be enough (perhaps 5%-10% of the initial number) to initiate a new population 2 or 3 years after the cyst is produced, and a very few may well survive as long as 5 years. Therefore, rotation cannot be expected to reduce a high population of SCN rapidly, nor to eliminate a population.

Reniform nematode populations are likely to increase where cotton and soybean are grown frequently, and also will build up on many vegetables. Rotations to reduce reniform nematodes should include corn, sorghum, other grasses, and/or peanut. Unfortunately, rotations are of little value for reducing lesion or sting nematode numbers, because they live well on so many different plants, including most grasses, soybean, most vegetables, and cotton. Lesion nematodes reproduce well on peanut and tobacco in Florida; sting does not.

Soybean is often planted behind a winter small-grain crop such as rye, wheat, or oats. A winter grain crop can help prevent erosion and weed growth, and provides income from the field twice per year rather than once. However, root-knot nematodes can infect new roots of many small grains planted while the soil is warm enough (above 65°F) to allow nematode infection of the grain crop before soil temperatures drop in winter. Rye, triticale, most wheat varieties, and barley can support root-knot nematodes; many varieties of oats support less or no reproduction. Reproduction in these grains may not actually increase root-knot nematode numbers, but may interfere with their normal overwinter decline. If planting is delayed until soil temperatures are lower, root-knot nematodes should not be able to reproduce in small grains.

Use of crop rotation systems that include bahiagrass has been increasing, and this perennial grass is a non-host for nematodes affecting soybean. However, weeds must be managed in the bahiagrass or nematode populations will be maintained in such a system resulting in damage to the following soybean crop. A two-year bahiagrass rotation is sufficient to manage plant-parasitic nematodes in a future soybean crop providing weeds are controlled early and regularly in the first year bahiagrass and this is continued throughout the life of the rotation.

Resistant Varieties

Considerable effort has been expended over the years to develop soybean varieties with resistance to soybean cyst and root-knot nematodes. There are soybean varieties with resistance to one or more of the three common species of root-knot nematodes and some populations of soybean cyst nematode (SCN). Some varieties resistant to SCN also are resistant to the reniform nematode. However, no variety is "nematode proof", and mixed populations of more than one nematode make choosing resistant varieties more difficult. In root-knot nematode resistant soybean varieties, the resistance is considered “quantitative” and is governed by a large unknown number of genes. Resistant varieties, therefore, may allow root-knot nematodes to survive and reproduce but at a lower level than susceptible varieties. This does not cause the resistance in a particular cultivar to fail but a considerable soil population of root-knot nematodes will remain following cultivation of a resistant soybean. Alternatively, soybean cyst resistance in soybean is considered “qualitative”. Here resistance is conferred by a few dominant soybean genes. Compared to root-knot nematode, essentially no soybean cyst nematodes develop within a resistant cultivar. If soybean cyst-resistant cultivars are monocultured for a few years, resistance-breaking cyst nematodes will cause failure of that particular line of resistance.

Soybean varieties or lines are no longer tested in Florida for nematode resistance traits. However, when buying seed, consult with seed dealers and soybean seed companies to determine variety resistance to the three root-knot nematodes (Javanese, peanut and southern) commonly found in Florida soybean fields.

Nematicides

There is little or no justification for using nematicides on soybeans produced for forage. For the grain market, growers should carefully consider costs and commodity price expectations before choosing nematicides for nematode management in soybean.

Temik 15G is available for use on soybean, but using this nematicide is subject to several use restrictions in general and more specifically in Florida. Before applying the product, read the label carefully, and in addition, request information from the Florida.

21

Relationship between *Meloidogyne incognita* and *Rotylenchulus reniformis* as Influenced by Soybean Genotype

Root-knot (*Meloidogyne incognita* (Kofoid & White) Chitwood) and reniform *(Rotylenchulus reniformis* Linford & Oliviera) nematodes are pathogenic to soybean (Gly*cine max* (L.) Merr.). These species share the same geographic and host ranges in Louisiana, where nematode damage has reduced soybean yield 4 per cent to 8 per cent annually during 1988-1993.

The replacement series approach, originally proposed by plant ecologists for use in competition studies, has been used successfully in several subdisciplines of plant pathology. This approach recently has been adapted for use in competition studies involving phytoparasitic nematodes. Replacement series experiments are designed to quantitatively assess the relative impact of inter- and intra-specific competition between two species at a single community density.

Target species are introduced alone or together in various ratios. At the end of the experiment, relative nematode yields (number of each species in mixed culture divided by number in nonmixed culture) are calculated for each species. Inhibition or stimulation of a species can be visualized by plotring the relative nematode yields against the input proportion of that species. If inter- and intra-specific competition are equal, final nematode population sizes for each species should be directly proportional to the percentage of that species initially introduced.

In replacement series experiments, showed increased *M. incognita* reproduction in the presence of *R. reniformis*. This was evidenced by relative yields for *M. incognita* populations in soil that were significantly higher than predicted at all ratios at which this species occurred together with *R. reniformis*. Relative nematode yields for *R. reniformis* populations in soil did not differ from predicted yields, which indicated no effect of *M. incognita* on reproduction by *R. reniformis*. These experiments, however, were limited to the soybean cultivar Davis, which is susceptible to

M. incognita. The objective of this research was to determine if the relationship between *M. incognita* and R. *reniformis* documented on a susceptible soybean cultivar was similar to that found on a soybean cultivar resistant to *M. incognita.*

Materials and Methods

General procedures: Two experiments were conducted in a greenhouse where temperatures ranged from 22 to 35° C. Supplemental incandescent and fluorescent lighting (ca. 260 μE . s^{-1} . m^{-2}) provided a minimum of 14 hours of continuous light daily. These studies utilized 15-cm-diam. clay pots that contained approximately 1.6 kg of a soil mixture composed of three parts fumigated (67% methyl bromide, 33% chloropicrin) Convent silt loam soil (Aeric Fluvaquent, coarse-silty, mixed, nonacid, thermic) and two parts autoclaved sand.

Two experiments were conducted in microplots. Each microplot consisted of a 30-cm-diam, clay pot that contained approximately 15 kg of fumigated (32.7% sodium methyldithiocarbamate, 67.3% inert ingredients; 18.8 ml fumigant in 882 ml water per pot) Mhoon silt loam soil (Typic Fluvaquent, fine-silty, mixed, nonacid, themaic). Microplots were set into the ground to the depth of the pot rim and spaced 1 m apart.

The entire microplot area was sheltered by a polyethylene-covered quonset hut frame, open at both ends, and covered with black shade cloth. Plants in microplots received 516 pE. s -1- m -2 of light (approximately 30% of full sunlight). Supplemental lighting was not used in the microplot area.

Seeds of Davis (susceptible to both nematode species) or Buckshot 66 (resistant to *M. incognita,* susceptible to *R. reniformis)* soybean were treated with a commercial preparation of *Bradyrhizobium japonicum* (Kirchher) Jordan (Nitragin; Nitragin, Milwaukee, WI) and sown in flats. Seedlings of uniform size were selected when plants were at growth stage V1, and a single seedling was transplanted to the centre of each test pot for greenhouse tests or to a 10-cm-square multi-pot for microplot tests. Plants were fertilized with 120 ml of a 23-19-17 N-P-K fertilizer solution (RapidGro; Chevron, San Ramon, CA) 3 days after transplanting. Plants received approximately 26 ppm N, 20 ppm P, and 33 ppm K.

Populations of *M. incognita* race 2 and R. *reniformis* were derived from single egg masses and maintained on tomato *(Lycopersicon esculentum* L. 'Rutgers') in a greenhouse. Inoculum consisted of vermiform nematodes obtained from soil by wet-sieving and centrifugal-flotation. Soil in each pot was infested with the required number of each species by pipetting nematodes suspended in tap water into two depressions made in the soil. Tap water was pipetted into depressions in control pots. Each depression was 1 cm in diam., 4 cm deep, and 5 cm from the base of the stem on opposite sides of the plant. After infestation, the depressions were filled with additional fumigated soil.

In greenhouse tests, pots remained undisturbed until harvest. In microplot tests, the plant and soil from the multi-pot were transferred 10 days after infestation into a depression of comparable size made in the microplot soil. Pots then remained undisturbed until harvest.

At the end of each experiment, five soil cores (2.5-cm-diam.) from the soil surface to the bottom of the pot were collected from each pot, mixed thoroughly, and subsampled (150 g). Nematodes were extracted with wet-sieving and centrifugal-flotation. Numbers of juveniles, males, vermiform females, and swollen females collected on a 38-pm-pore sieve were recorded for each species.

Plant stems were cut at the soil surface, and the root-soil mass was removed from each pot. Root systems were freed from soil by washing gently in tap water. Severity of galling caused by *M. incognita* was rated according to the following scale: 0 = no galls, 1 = galls < 3 mm in diam. with no reduction in the number of feeder roots, 2 = galls 3 to 10 mm in diam. with no reduction in the number of feeder roots, 3 = galls 11 to 20 mm in diam. with no or slight reduction in the number of feeder roots, 4 = galls > 20 mm in diam. with moderate reduction in the number of feeder roots, and 5 = galls > 20 mm in diam. with major reduction in the number of feeder roots. Incidence of galling caused by *M. incognita* was rated according to the following scale: 0 = no galls, 1 = galls confined to 25 per cent or less of the root system, 2 = galls appearing on 26 per cent to 50 per cent of the root system, 3 = galls appearing on 51 per cent to 75 per cent of the root system, and 4 = galls appearing on 76 per cent or more of the root system.

Nematodes were extracted from a subsample (2 g) removed at random from each root system. Root tissue was combined with 60 ml of 0.5 per cent NaOC1 and ground for 10 seconds at maximum speed in a blender fitted with a 500-ml stainless steel container. The slurry was poured onto nested 75- and 25-pm-pore sieves, and vermiform and swollen individuals of each nematode species were counted.

Eggs collected on the 25-pm-pore sieve could not be identified to species, so egg counts were not included in population totals. *Replacement series experiments:* The relationship between *M. incognita* and *R. reniformis* was examined on Davis and Buckshot 66 soybean.

Experiments on each cultivar were conducted twice, i.e., once in the greenhouse and once in microplots. Numerous test-by-treatment interactions were detected in the initial analyses, so each test was analyzed independently. All four tests were established in randomized complete block designs with five (microplot) or 10 (greenhouse) replications. *Meloidogyne incognita* and R. *reniformis* were introduced alone or in combination at an initial community density of 1,000 individuals/pot when plants reached growth stages V2 to V3. Soil was infested with nematodes at one of the following *M. incognita:tL reniformis* ratios: 0:0, 100: 0, 75:25, 50:50, 25:75, or 0:100. Experiments were terminated 91 to 93 days after nematodes were introduced, when soybeans were at growth stages R4 or R5 in greenhouse tests, or R6 in microplot tests. At harvest, plants were divided into root and shoot portions by cutting the stem at the soil line.

Soybean roots and shoots were dried at 70° C for 4 days, and weighed after galling assessment and collection of tissue samples for nematode extraction. Soil samples were processed and nematodes were counted. Relative nematode yields were based on the total number of nematodes of each species extracted from soil and roots, expressed per gram of dry root tissue. For these experiments, relative nematode yield was calculated by dividing the number of nematodes of a species extracted from mixed culture by the number of nematodes of the same species recovered from unmixed culture.

Data presentation and analyses: To examine the relationship between *M. incognita* and *R. reniformis,* differences between the predicted relative nematode yield lines (representing equal interspecific and intraspecific competition) as defined by the replacement series, and the relative nematode yield lines plotted using calculated relative nematode yield values, were determined by lack-of-fit regression with the "Fit Model" module of SAS JMP version 3.0. Paired t-tests using the "Fit Y by X" module of SAS JMP version 3.0 were used to determine at which ratio(s) the predicted and calculated relative nematode yield values differed.

Plant weights were subjected to analysis of variance, Fisher's protected LSD, and orthogonal polynomial contrasts with the "Fit Model" mad "Fit Y by X" modules of SAS JMP version 3.0. Galling indices for plants inoculated with *M. incognita* were examined by orthogonal polynomial contrasts with the "Fit Model" module of SAS JMP version 3.0.

Results

Meloidogyne incognita and *R. reniformis,* separately or concomitantly, did not impact shoot or root weight of Davis or Buckshot 66 soybean in greenhouse tests. In microplot tests, 'Davis' shoot weights were lowest on plants inoculated with high levels (100:0, 75:25) of *M. incognita.*

Shoot weights increased in a linear fashion (t = 4.35, P> |t| = 0.0008) as the proportion of *M. incognita* in the inoculum decreased. Plants inoculated with mixtures of *M. incognita* and *R. reniformis* had heavier roots than the uninoculated control in microplot tests. A quadratic relationship (t = -3.06, P> |t| = 0.0090) was detected among all inoculated treatments, with heavier root systems on plants infected by mixtures of nematodes. Where *M. incognitawas* included in the inoculum, root weight increased in a linear manner (t = -2.47, P> |t| = 0.0357) as the level of *M. incognita* decreased. In the microplot test, 'Buckshot 66' plants inoculated with low levels (25:75, 0:100) of *M. incognita* had heavier shoots than plants inoculated with moderate to high levels of *M. incognita,* though weights in both groups did not differ from uninoculated controls. Root dry weights were not influenced by the nematodes at any ratio on 'Buckshot 66' in the microplot test. Orthogonal polynomial contrasts did not reveal any trends in shoot or root weight related to nematode infestation on 'Buckshot 66'. Incidence and severity of galling were generally greater on 'Davis' than on 'Buckshot 66' in both greenhouse and microplot tests. Galling was so severe on 'Davis' that feeder roots were almost completely absent in the microplot test. On 'Davis', orthogonal polynomial contrasts revealed a cubic relationship between the proportion of *M. incognita* in the inoculum and gall incidence (t = -2.33, P > |t| = 0.0378) and severity (t = -2.85, P> |t| = 0.0146) in the microplot test. For both indices, minimum values were associated with the 50:50 ratio. In the greenhouse test, gall incidence decreased linearly in proportion to lower levels of *M. incognita* in the inoculum (t = 3.03, P > |t| = 0.0053). No relationship between nematode ratio and severity of galling was detected on 'Davis' in the greenhouse. On 'Buckshot 66', no relationships between nematode ratio and either incidence or severity of galling were detected in greenhouse or microplot tests.

On 'Davis', relative *M. incognita* yields in the greenhouse test were significantly higher than predicted (F = 4.26, P = 0.0099), notably at the 50:50 ratio. Relative nematode yields *of R. reniformis* were not influenced by infection of the same host by *M. incognita* (F = 0.60, P = 0.6171). In the microplot test, both *M. incognita* and *R. reniformis* relative nematode yields were lower than predicted (for *M. incognita, F* = 3.28, P = 0.0422; for R. *reniformis, F*= 12.80, P ~< 0.0001) (Fig. 3B). Significant reductions in relative nematode yields occurred at the 50:50 ratio for *M. incognita* and at the 75:25 and 25:75 ratios for R. *reniformis*. On 'Buckshot 66', no significant differences were detected between calculated and predicted relative nematode yields for either species in greenhouse or microplot tests.

Discussion

The genotype of the soybean host influenced the relationship between *M. incognita* and *R. reniformis*. In the greenhouse test, the susceptibility of 'Davis' to *M. incognita* increased when *R. reniformis* infected the same host, as evidenced by higher relative nematode yields of *M. incognita.* In the microplot test, enhanced *M. incognita* reproduction probably began early in the season, resulting in severe galling, destruction of feeder roots, and dramatic population declines for both species, reflected in the relative nematode yields observed 91 to 93 days after infestation.

The reduction in shoot weight seen in the microplot test also may be attributable to the significant damage caused by the large *M. incognita* population. The microplot infestation method may have concentrated high numbers of nematodes in a small area, thereby increasing the potential of individual nematodes to locate and infect roots at the beginning of the experiment. In addition, the microplot environment was less subject to temperature and moisture fluctuations, which can impact nematode population development, than was the greenhouse environment. A combination of these factors may have contributed to the apparent increase in susceptibility to *M. incognita* on 'Davis' in the microplot test. In spite of these factors, enhanced susceptibility to *M. incognita* was not observed on 'Buckshot 66', which remained resistant to this species even when colonized by *R. reniformis*. Host resistance, therefore, is a key factor in determining the nature of the relationship between *M. incognita* and *R. reniformis*.

The relationship between *M. incognita* and *R. reniformis* was defined based on vermiform and swollen individuals because these life stages could be readily classified as one species or the other. Eggs, however, were not identifiable to species; therefore, egg counts were not included in population totals. Preliminary hatch, morphology, and differential staining studies were conducted in an attempt to identify eggs to species, but we were not able to identify a reliable method by which the entire egg cohort could be classified. In our experience, rootassociated populations of *M. incognita* are generally larger than root-associated populations of *R. reniformis*. This inequality would be exaggerated on a cultivar susceptible to *M. incognita,* when *R. reniformis* and *M. incognita* occur in the same community. The ability of one nematode population to influence the reproduction of a second nematode population is a key factor affecting interspecific competition. The results of the current study support those of researchers, who first reported that infection of Davis soybean by *R. reniformis* consistently increased *M. incog'nita* reproduction. The stimulatory effect of *R. reniformis* on *M. incognita* is not an isolated example of enhanced reproduction by nematodes in coexistence. Increased reproduction of *Belonolaimus longicaudatus* in the presence of *Hoplolaimus galeatus* on cotton, *Hoplolaimus columbus* in the presence of *M. incognita* or *Scutellonema brachyurum* on cotton, *Criconemella xenoplax* in the presence of *Meloidogyne hapla* on grape, *Pratylenchus brachyurus* in the presence of *M. incognita* on tobacco cv. NC 2512, and *Paratrichodorus minor* in the presence of *P. brachyurus* on soybean have been documented. Mutual stimulation of *P. minor* and *Pratylenchus zeae* on corn *and H. columbus* and *S. brachyurum* on cotton also have been reported. Further studies are required to elucidate the mechanism behind the stimulatory effect of *R. reniformis* on *M. incognita* on 'Davis' soybean in this system.

It is widely believed that *Rotylenchulus* is replacing *Meloidogyne* throughout the soybean production region in the southern United States. Our current findings that show an increase in the *M. incognita* population in the presence of *R. reniformis* on susceptible 'Davis' seem to contradict this.

However, an explanation may be found in examining results from the resistant cultivar Buckshot 66, which did not support enhanced reproduction by *M. incognita* even when coinfected by R. *reniformis.* Soybean culfivars resistant to *Meloidogyne* spp. are employed commonly in nematode management programmes. Because R. *reniformis* has a longer infective period and a shorter life cycle than *M. incognita,* it has greater potential to reach a damaging population level on cultivars resistant to *M. incognita.* In addition, commercial soybean cultivars resistant to *R. reniformis* are lacking. Consequently, planting *M. incognita*-resistant soybean likely favours *R. reniformis* over time.

The influence of the host is evident in other nematode-host-nematode systems as well. Inoculation with *M. incognita* inhibited subsequent penetration of tomato roots by *P. brachyurus* but stimulated penetration of cotton roots by the latter species. Researchers documented inhibitory, neutral, and stimulatory associations among *M. incognita, P. brachyurus,* and *M. hapla* on tobacco, which differed in both nature and magnitude depending on the host cultivar. The associations were species-specific, as *M. incognita* did not have the same impact on *P. brachyurns* as did another root-knot nematode species, *M. hapla.* In split-root experiments, researcher reported that inoculation of root-knot nematode-resistant tobacco with *Meloidogyne arenaria* or *M. hapla* masked the resistance of that cultivar to *M. incognita* race 1 when this species was subsequently introduced. Researcher found that infection by *Ditylenchus dipsaci* reduced the resistance of the alfalfa culfivar Vernal 298 to *M. hapla.* The galling of soybean induced by a combination of *M. incognita* and *M. javanica* was significantly greater than when either species was tested independently.

Relationships defined on one host may be quite different on other cultivars or host species. However, host suitability is not the only factor capable of influencing the ecological association among nematode species. Edaphic factors such as soil texture, soil moisture, and temperature, nematode population densities, timing and method of nematode inoculation, pesticide application, and the influence of other biological entities within the system may alter nematode relationships. To fully document the interrelationships between two nematode species, the species should be evaluated under a range of biotic and abiotic conditions.

22

Manure Management

Overview

The numbers of livestock are increasing for many livestock operators, while the number of cropland acres are remaining constant. This trend has resulted in many producers considering manure applications for soybeans. Research studies in Minnesota have evaluated pre-plant manure applications for soybeans. The overall effects of manure for soybeans have been positive, but there are situations that have the potential for negative effects, if not properly managed.

Field Selection

Soybean fields should not be selected for manure applications until after all the non-leguminous crops have been considered. Soybeans do not require applied nitrogen (N), and their phosphorus (P) demand is less than that of corn and small grains. If soybean fields are being chosen for manure applications, the greatest agronomic return will be on those fields that test low for plant nutrients, or that could benefit from the addition of organic materials, or both.

Observation and research have also indicated that preplant manure applications can magnify or promote most current pest problems in a field. While this primarily applies to the soybean disease of white mold, preplant manure can increase most organisms. The manure creates an environment that promotes disease growth (i.e. lush vegetative growth). Manure's nutrients and weed seed population can also stimulate and expand a weed problem in certain fields. Manure should not be applied to fields with known white mold histories or other pest problems.

Application Method

For air and surface water quality reasons all manure should be injected or otherwise incorporated into the soil. Agronomically, there is also good justification for not broadcasting the manure and leaving it on the soil surface. Soybean seed germination and early seedling growth are very sensitive to ammonia and salts which are contained in animal manure.

Corn or small-grain crops are not so easily affected. Therefore, it is important that the germinating seed or young seedling does not come in direct contact with zones of concentrated manure, or injury can result. To avoid this injury risk, either inject the manure beneath the seeding zone, or thoroughly incorporate the manure into the entire topsoil zone — each of these methods minimize "hot" areas created by the manure. Tillage for seedbed preparation will usually alleviate these concerns. The application method has a direct influence on the amount of Nitrogen (N) that will be available to the soybean. Table 22.1 lists the N availability amounts for the year of application, and predicted availability the following year. Regardless of the method of application one is using, it is of utmost importance that the manure be uniformly applied to the field.

Rate Selection

The rate of manure to be applied should be calculated so that the amount of available N supplied by the manure does not exceed the amount of nitrogen (N) that is removed by the soybean crop. Applying manure at greater rates will result in creating an environmental liability from excess N. Also, excessive manure rates can also enhance any of the potential agronomic concerns created by manure applications such as excessive lodging, diseases such as white mold, seedling injury, and others. Three things to consider when determining rates of manure application are:

1. the amount of nutrients in the manure
2. the availability of N in the manure which is based on your method of application
3. the nutrient needs of the soybeans

The following equation provides this calculation:

Rate (1000 gal/A) = {Nutrient Need (lb/A) × [(Manure content, lb/1000 gal)/ Availability, %]}

Or

Rate (tons/A) = {Nutrient Need (lb/A) × [(Manure content, lb/ton)/ Availability, %]}

Supplemental Fertilizer

There is no need for commercial fertilizer when manure is applied for soybeans. Most often, phosphorus (P) is the primary nutrient recommended for soybeans, and with even the lowest rates of manure applied to the soil, the P needs are met. All other nutrients are applied at rates that exceed nutrient recommendations. Table 22.1 lists some of the micronutrient quantities excreted per animal, per year. Most animal manure will supply a complete set of nutrients.

A concern is often raised that if manure (or commercial N fertilizer) is applied to soybeans, the nodules will become inhibited and not function for the remainder of the growing season; thus, prompting the notion that midto late-season N applications need to be made. Although manure N will greatly decrease the activity of soybean's nodules, once soil N levels become low the nodule activity will increase to meet the demand of the soybean.

Table 22.1: Manure Nitrogen Availability and Loss as Affected by Method of Application and Animal Species

Species	Broadcast Incorporation *1			Injection	
	None	<4d	<12 hr	Sweep	Knife
% Total N					
Dairy					
Avail. Yr 1	20	40	55	55	50
Avail. Yr 2	40	40	35	40	40
Lost (*2)	40	20	10	5	10
Swine					
Avail. Yr 1	35	55	75	80	70
Avail. Yr 2	15	15	15	15	15
Lost	50	30	10	5	15
Beef					
Avail. Yr 1	25	45	60	60	50
Avail. Yr 2	35	35	35	35	40
Lost	40	20	5	5	10
Poultry					
Avail. Yr 1	45	55	70	NA	NA
Avail. Yr 2	25	25	25	NA	NA
Lost	30	20	5	NA	NA

*1 These categories refer to the length of time between manure application and incorporation.

*2 Lost refers to estimated volatilization and denitrification processes.

Manure applications for soybean fields can be made with minimal risk if proper precautions are taken. Selecting fields that will benefit from manure's nutrients and that have few pest problems will be advantageous. Manure should be applied at agronomically-based rates that account for method of application, and the nutrient needs of the soybean crop. Avoid seeding soybeans into an area that contains a relatively high concentration of manure. No supplemental fertilizer will be required.

23

Weed Management

Overview

Weeds growing with soybeans compete with the crop for light, moisture, and nutrients. Uncontrolled, weeds reduce soybean yields and interfere with harvest. A 1992 report of the Weed Science Society of America estimated that weeds cause more than a $52 million loss in Minnesota soybean production each year.

An effective weed management programme requires understanding potential weed problems, and planning, to control weeds in a timely manner. Soybeans are very competitive with weeds once the soybeans develop a canopy, but early emerging weeds, if left uncontrolled, can cause significant yield loss. Early season weed control (generally before weeds reach 4 inches in height) is the key to providing soybeans with a competitive advantage by minimizing the impact of weeds. The most effective control programmes include a variety of control practices in an integrated weed management system.

Common Weed Problems

Annuals

Summer annual grass and broadleaf weeds such as foxtails, woolly cupgrass, tall waterhemp, common ragweed, and common cocklebur can be problems in soybeans. These weeds germinate in the spring and summer and produce seed before they die in the fall. A well-timed cultivation or herbicide treatment can greatly reduce annual weed populations. Annual weeds have a fairly predictable pattern of emergence, but their germination depends on soil moisture and temperature.

Winter Annuals and Biennials

Winter annual weeds such as mustards and horseweed (marestail), and annual/ biennial weeds such as biennial wormwood, are a problem in no-till soybeans. These weeds germinate in the fall and become a noticeable problem by early to mid-summer of the next growing season. They can be controlled with tillage or burndown herbicide treatments before soybean planting.

Perennials

Perennial weeds that regrow each year from an established rhizome or root system are very competitive and difficult to control. Perennial broadleaf weeds such as Canada thistle, common milkweed, and hemp dogbane are difficult to manage in soybeans. Spot spraying, weed wipers, or herbicide resistant crops tolerant to nonselective herbicides such as Roundup, will help manage these perennial broadleaf weeds. Crop rotation, or treatment in the fall, best manages these weeds after soybean removal.

Weed Identification

Proper weed identification is the foundation of a successful weed management programme. Being able to identify weeds at the seedling stage of development is a critical component of profitable soybean production because. in weed control, timing is everything.

Integrated Weed Management

Effective weed control usually results from a combination of cultural, mechanical, and chemical practices. The ideal combination for each field will depend on a number of considerations including

1. The kinds of weeds present,
2. The level of weed infestation,
3. The soil type,
4. The cropping system,
5. The availability of time and labour to complete the control tactic in a timely manner.

Weed-Soybean Competition

Weeds are vigorous competitors with soybeans. Weeds usually germinate and emerge with the soybeans; therefore, soybeans do not get ahead of the weeds Soybeans are relatively short and consequently susceptible to shading from taller weeds. Weeds can also compete with soybeans for nutrients and water. Since soybeans are especially sensitive to moisture deficiencies in early- to mid-summer, nearly-complete weed control must be accomplished within four to five weeks after soybean emergence in order to avoid yield losses due to early emerging weeds. Planting narrow rows, and following production practices that encourage vigorous soybean growth, will increase the crop's competitive advantage over the weeds. The idea is to "shade out" late emerging weeds. In a wider row spacing, a producer should strive to have the soybeans lapped in the row middles as soon as possible. Generally, weeds that emerge four to five weeks after the soybean planting date will not be competitive with the soybean crop.

Crop Rotation Practices

Crop rotation can be an important component of a weed management programme. For example, most annual broadleaf weeds can be more easily and economically managed in corn than in soybeans. The opposite is true for most annual grass weeds. Crop rotation can encourage (over time) the use of different types of herbicides, with different sites of action. This helps to prevent the development of herbicide resistant or tolerant weeds.

Tillage Practices

Several tillage practices aid weed management in soybeans. Seedbed preparation immediately prior to planting will kill weeds that have germinated. In the absence of seedbed tillage, a burndown herbicide treatment is often required. Killing the weeds that germinate prior to, or at the time of soybean planting, regardless of the tillage system employed, is important because these will be the most competitive weeds.

For pre-emergence herbicides to be effective, they must be moved into the soil by rainfall before the weed seeds germinate. If rainfall has not been sufficient for herbicide activation, the weed seedlings should be controlled with a rotary hoe, or harrow, as soon as they emerge. Cultivation of weed escapes is also an effective and economical weed control tool. Cultivation should be done when weeds are small (1 inch) and the cultivation should be shallow (1 to 2 inches) to avoid soybean root damage.

Herbicides

Herbicides are used on almost all soybean acreage because they are an efficient weed management tool. However, far too many growers equate weed management solely with herbicides. University of Minnesota research trials indicate weed management is most consistently successful and economical when a diversity of weed management tools are used in an integrated approach. For example, one cultivation following your planned herbicide programme, or a sequential pre-plant incorporated/ postemergence herbicide programme, is more consistently successful than a one pass post-emergence weed control programme. Also, a more diversified weed management approach will prevent unwanted weed species shifts.

Selecting Herbicides

Selection of an appropriate herbicide or combination of herbicides should be based on consideration of the following factors:

- Label approved for use
- Ground and surface water pollution concerns
- Use of the crop
- Crop and variety tolerance
- Potential for soil residues that may affect following crops
- Kinds of weeds
- Soil texture
- Soil pH

- Soil organic matter
- Potential for drift problems
- Tillage practices
- Herbicide performance
- Herbicide cost
- Availability of a fully-adapted herbicideresistant crop

Timing

Proper application of chemicals is essential for obtaining satisfactory results. Carefully follow the suggested rates on the labels for specific soil and weed situations. Apply herbicides at the weed and crop stages specified. Delayed applications usually result in poorer weed control, and may injure the crop.

Weather

Weather conditions will also affect herbicide performance. Temperature and moisture affect the weed control and crop injury potential of a herbicide. Temperatures below 50° F and above 90° F often limit the soybean's ability to degrade the herbicide, and application may result in crop injury. Dry soil conditions or cold temperatures (below 50° F) may limit the weed's ability to take up enough herbicide to provide adequate weed control. Heavy rainfall may move a herbicide downward in the soil, resulting in poor weed control or crop injury. When applying herbicides, observe label precautions regarding weather conditions, as well as crop and weed size.

Early Pre-plant Treatment

Emerged weeds must be controlled at planting for soybeans to be successful. Certain herbicides can be applied before soybeans are planted in the spring to control emerged weeds, and/or for residual control of late-emerging weeds. Many residual herbicides applied early need to be applied before weeds germinate. They usually require precipitation or incorporation for herbicide activation. If weeds have already emerged at treatment time in no-till planted soybeans, addition of a burndown herbicide with foliar activity is often required. Early pre-plant herbicides need enough residual activity to control weeds before and after planting, or else they require follow up treatments of post-emergence herbicides, or cultivation.

Pre-plant Incorporated Herbicides

Certain residual herbicides can (or must) be applied and incorporated into the soil before planting to control susceptible weeds. These pre-plant herbicides need to be incorporated thoroughly to the proper soil depth, as directed on the label. Incorporation is more uniform with dry, mellow soil than with damp or cloddy soil. Pre-plant-incorporated herbicides are less dependent on rainfall for their effectiveness because they have been mechanically placed in the weed emergence zone. Avoid furrowing too deep at planting time, and thereby moving too much treated soil out of the planted row, or weed escapes will occur in the row.

Pre-emergence Herbicides

Some residual herbicides can be applied to the soil surface after the crop is planted, but before soybean and weed emergence. Rainfall or irrigation of about 0.5-0.75 inch of water is required after application to move the herbicide into the soil where it can be absorbed by the germinating weeds. Too little or too much rainfall after herbicide application can cause poor weed control. In Minnesota, the south central and southeastern sections of the state have the greatest probability of timely rainfalls that will successfully activate pre-emergence herbicides. In southwestern, west central, and northwestern Minnesota, the probability of such a timely rainfall is lower, and pre-plant- incorporated herbicides tend to be the more effective soil-applied herbicide option. Also, if there is insufficient rain, a rotary hoe can be used to control small weeds and help incorporate the herbicide.

Pre-emergence herbicides can also be applied in a band over the row at planting time. Band applications are generally 12 to 14 inches wide. With a planned cultivation after crop emergence to control weeds between the rows, banding provides an opportunity to reduce herbicide inputs without sacrificing yields.

Post-emergence Herbicides

Post-emergence herbicides control weeds after the crop and weeds have emerged from the soil. Some post-emergence herbicides have soil residual activity (e.g. Pursuit) and some do not (e.g. Roundup Ultra). Application rate, weed and crop size, environmental conditions, and adjuvants (effectiveness enhancements) greatly influence post-emergence herbicide performance. Post-emergence herbicides are most effective when applied to small weeds that are actively growing. Application to larger weeds or plants growing under environmental stress may result in poor weed control and increased crop injury.

In Minnesota, it takes approximately four weeks for an annual weed such as giant foxtail to reach four inches in height. In five weeks, giant foxtail can be five to six inches tall, and in six weeks the foxtail may be eight inches tall. For many herbicides the ideal foxtail height for postemergence application is three to four inches. Therefore, the window of opportunity for effective post-emergence control is approximately one week. Many post-emergence herbicides require adjuvants to improve plant uptake. Without the necessary adjuvants poor weed control may result. However, using the wrong type of adjuvant, under the wrong environmental conditions, can also increase herbicide crop injury potential. Use adjuvants according to herbicide label recommendations.

Herbicide Mode of Action

Herbicide mode of action is the process by which herbicides kill weeds. Different herbicides can affect different plant processes, resulting in the death of the weed (and not the soybeans). Herbicide mode of action is also a convenient way to categorize the numerous herbicides in the marketplace. Herbicides can be classified into families based on their chemical similarity. In some cases, herbicides from different families target the same biochemical process (site of action) within the plant and result in the same herbicide crop injury response in the plant. Herbicide mode of action explains how a herbicide kills a plant, and herbicide site of action tells you what plant process is affected.

Learning herbicide mode of action processes will help you understand the events that relate to herbicide effectiveness. For example, the ways temperature can influence the effectiveness and crop injury potential of a particular herbicide.

Understanding herbicide mode of action will improve:

1. Crop injury diagnostic skills.
2. Herbicide selection and application skills.
3. Herbicide resistance management strategies.

Herbicide Resistant Weeds

Weed species, and different biotypes within species, vary in susceptibility to herbicides. A population that is initially susceptible to a herbicide, but contains a small percentage of resistant biotypes, may develop into a resistant population. Selection for resistance is most likely with the repeated use of a highly effective herbicide programme. It is important to use different weed management tactics (e.g. herbicides, cultivation, rotary hoeing), crop rotation, and employing herbicides that affect different sites of action in the target weeds.

Herbicide Resistant Soybeans

Herbicide resistant soybeans allow the use of herbicides that would otherwise seriously injure or kill the soybeans. Herbicide resistant soybeans that have been developed include STS soybeans (for use with Reliance STS) and Roundup Ready soybeans (for use with Roundup Ultra). In the near future, Liberty Link soybeans should be available (for use with Liberty). Reliance STS is a broadleaf herbicide, and Roundup Ultra and Liberty are broad-spectrum herbicides that have grass and broadleaf weed activity. STS soybeans were developed by conventional breeding techniques. Roundup Ready and Liberty Link soybeans were developed through genetic engineering. As with any weed management practice, use of a herbicide resistant crop, and the corresponding herbicide, should be part of an integrated weed management programme.

Weed Management Checklist

- In the fall, identify weeds and map their locations before harvest.
- During the season, start scouting 10 days after planting.
- Shorten the scouting interval if growing conditions are favourable for weeds—weeds can grow too large for optimum control in less than a week.
- To favour soybeans in competition with weeds, grow a vigorous crop that closes the canopy quickly.
- Rotate crops to prevent increases in weed problems.
- Rotate transgenic and non-transgenic crops.
- Herbicide rate, timing, and method of application depend on weed species present, their size, and the growing conditions.

24

Herbicide Resistant Weeds

Introduction

Resistance of weeds to herbicides is not a unique phenomenon. In fact, resistance to pesticides is a world wide problem that is not confined to any single pest category. The first report of insects resistant to insecticides was in 1908, of plant pathogens resistant to fungicides in 1940, and of weeds resistant to herbicides (triazines) in 1968. By 1991, 120 weed biotypes that were resistant to triazine herbicides and 15 other herbicide families were documented throughout the world. Results of a 1992 North Central Weed Science Society survey of the north central United States and Canada reflect a world wide trend of increasing appearance of herbicide resistance. Twelve states or provinces reported biotypes of 19 weed species resistant to triazine herbicides. Five states or provinces reported biotypes of three weed species resistant to lipid biosynthesis inhibitors, 10 states or provinces reported biotypes of four weed species resistant to amino acid biosynthesis inhibitors, four states or provinces reported biotypes of two weed species resistant to dinitroaniline herbicides, and Manitoba reported resistance of a wild mustard biotype to growth regulator herbicides. Indeed, pests have proven to be ecologically and biochemically adaptable to agrichemicals.

Why Worry About Herbicide Resistance?

In corn, soybean, and small grains there are many herbicide options. Why then should a crop producer be concerned whether a weed biotype is resistant to a particular herbicide? There are several reasons. Many herbicide options could quickly be lost for several crops if a weed biotype is resistant to more than one herbicide (i.e. cross resistance). Obviously, a loss of herbicide options could have important economic and environmental consequences to agriculture. Also, in an era of high re-registration costs for older herbicides and high development costs for new herbicides, the possibility for replacement of the herbicides lost due to resistance diminishes. Finally, in most cases, it will not be easy nor inexpensive to assess resistant weed biotypes. Due to cross resistance, many resistance problems may have to be solved by trial and error, which could be quite expensive to the crop producer.

The herbicide resistance issue does have solutions and perhaps the best place to start is to consider herbicides as a resource that needs to be preserved. Strategies for resistance prevention follow from there.

Definitions

Site of action refers to the biochemical site within the plant with which the herbicide directly interacts. Some herbicide site of action interactions are well understood, others are unknown. Many of the well-known sites of action are enzymes or proteins essential to plant growth and development. Also, some herbicides are believed to act at multiple sites.

Metabolism refers to the biochemical processes within the plant that generally modify herbicides to less toxic compounds. Differential rates of metabolism between crops and weeds is a primary method of crop selectivity to herbicides. One metabolic process may affect several different families of herbicides.

Herbicide families are a convenient way of organizing herbicides that share a common chemical structure and have similar herbicidal activity. Two or more herbicide families may affect the same site of action and therefore express similar herbicidal activity and injury symptoms.

A biotype is a group of plants within a species that has biological traits that are not common to the population as a whole. For example, the Pursuit resistant corn hybrid Pioneer 3377 IR is a biotype of Pioneer 3377 and atrazine-resistant common lambsquarters is a biotype of common lambsquarters. Therefore, in most instances, specific biotypes are not easily recognizable by casual observation.

Selection intensity in regard to herbicide resistance is the degree to which weed control measures (e.g. herbicides) in a cropping system give a competitive advantage to a weed or crop biotype resistant to a particular herbicide.

Herbicide susceptibility means a particular weed or crop biotype is killed by the recommended use rate of the herbicide.

Herbicide resistance refers to the inherited ability of a weed or crop biotype to survive a herbicide application to which the original population was susceptible. Currently, the three known resistance mechanisms that plants employ are: an alteration of the herbicide site of action, metabolism of the herbicide, and removal of the herbicide from the target site (sequestration).

Herbicide cross resistance refers to a weed or crop biotype that has evolved a mechanism or mechanisms of resistance to one herbicide that also allows it to be resistant to other herbicides. Cross resistance can occur with herbicides within the same or in different herbicide families and with the same or different sites of action. For example, after the extensive use of herbicide A in a field, selection of a weed biotype resistant to herbicide A is found to also be resistant to herbicide B although herbicide B was never used in that field.

Herbicide multiple resistance refers to a weed or crop biotype that has evolved mechanisms of resistance to more than one herbicide and the resistance was brought about by separate selection processes. For example, after a weed or crop biotype developed resistance to herbicide A, then herbicide B was used and resistance evolved to herbicide B. The plant is now resistant to herbicides A and B through two separate selection processes.

How Does Selection of Resistant Weed Biotypes Occur?

Selection for change in weed populations begins when a small number of plants (a biotype) within a weed species have a genetic makeup that enables them to survive a particular herbicide application. Where this difference in genetic makeup originated is not clear. However, herbicides are not known to directly cause the genetic change (i.e. mutation) that allows resistance. The resistant biotype, therefore, is present in low numbers in natural populations and when a herbicide is applied, most of the susceptible weeds die but the few resistant weeds survive, mature, and produce seed. If the same herbicide continues to be applied and the resistant weeds reproduce, the percentage of the weed population that is resistant will increase.

It is difficult to predict exactly which weed species will have biotypes resistant to a given herbicide. However, we have learned from previous pesticide resistance problems that the occurrence of herbicide resistant weeds is linked directly to the herbicide programme used, the weed species present, and the crop management practices employed.

Selection Intensity - The Key to Prevention

Selection intensity acts, in a sense, like a filter that can screen out susceptible weed biotypes while leaving resistant biotypes. Herbicides by definition are effective weed killers; therefore, they have the potential to exert heavy selection intensity on weeds. The more susceptible a weed species is to a given herbicide (i.e. the greater the weed control) the greater the selection intensity. As a result, the rate of selection for resistance can be quite rapid if the same herbicide or herbicides with the same site of action are repeatedly used in a particular field.

With such highly effective herbicides, one would think that the increase in the number of herbicide resistant biotypes would be readily observable. This is not the case. Resistant biotypes generally are only detectable when they make up about 30 per cent of the population. During the first several years of a weed control programme that relies on only one herbicide, the proportion of resistant biotypes is very low (less than 1% of the population). As long as the application of this herbicide continues and the resistant biotypes reproduce, the proportion of the population that is resistant will increase. It is very common to go from excellent control of a particular weed species to very poor control within one growing season. A gradual decline in performance is seldom seen. In field situations, resistance to sulfonylurea herbicides has been reported to occur after 3 to 5 years of repeated use. With triazine herbicides, resistance has generally appeared after seven or more years of repeated use. Therefore, depending upon the proportion of the population that was initially resistant to a herbicide, repeated use of a product for more than two years could develop a herbicide resistance problem.

Herbicide Factors that Increase Selection Intensity

The herbicide characteristics that affect herbicide resistance are as follows:

1. Herbicides that act on a single site of action.
2. Herbicides that are applied multiple times during the growing season.
3. Herbicides used for several consecutive growing seasons or repeated application of herbicides with the same site of action to the same or different crops.
4. Herbicides used without other weed control options (e.g. cultivation) and are considered "stand alone" weed control programmes.

Single Site of Action Herbicides

Several herbicide families interfere with only a single site of action. Herbicides that interfere with single sites of action are generally more likely to select for resistant weeds because a change in only one gene may be enough to affect a herbicide's binding potential to the site of action. Therefore, it is more probable that a resistant weed population will develop if a difference of only one gene is required.

Multiple Site of Action Herbicides

Based on the line of reasoning presented for single site of action herbicides, if a herbicide has multiple action sites it is less likely existing biotypes will have the genetic differences at all of the sites of action that will result in resistance. Therefore, it is less likely that weeds will evolve resistance to herbicides with multiple action sites.

Herbicide Cross Resistance and Site of Action

A change in a site of action that results in resistance to a particular herbicide may or may not result in resistance to other herbicides that are active at the same site of action. The reason for this is there can be many different binding sites at a particular site of action (e.g. an enzyme) and those binding sites can be very herbicide specific. Therefore, several different herbicides may bind to the same enzyme but at different sites on the enzyme. As a result, it is not possible to predict herbicide cross resistance; however, the greatest potential for herbicide cross resistance exists among herbicides of the same family and having the same site of action.

To illustrate cross resistance, both the imidazolinone (e.g. Pursuit and Scepter) and sulfonylurea (e.g. Classic) herbicide families are ALS enzyme inhibitor. However, imidazolinone resistant (IR) corn hybrids are resistant to imidazolinone herbicides and are cross resistant to the sulfonylurea herbicides. The imidazolinone tolerant (IT) corn hybrids are resistant to Pursuit and soil-applied Scepter but are not cross resistant to sulfonylurea herbicides.

Herbicide Resistance via Altered Metabolism

Regardless of whether a herbicide is active at single or multiple site(s) of action, it is often metabolized by crops or weeds before reaching the primary site(s) of action. Therefore, the rate at which a herbicide is metabolized plays a key role in determining crop injury and weed control. The genetic regulation of a metabolic process will influence the likelihood of developing herbicide resistance due to altered metabolism. For example, a change in only one gene has altered the rate of metabolism of atrazine in some biotypes of atrazine-resistant velvetleaf (*Abutilon theophrasti).* Most metabolic processes are thought to be controlled by multiple genes, thereby reducing the probability but not eliminating the possibility of weed biotypes that are resistant to herbicides due to enhanced metabolic capabilities or altered metabolic processes. Metabolic resistance could be especially challenging if it were to occur, because a metabolic process often affects several families of herbicides that do not share a common site of action. Regardless of the resistance mechanism, the key to prevention of herbicide resistance is to reduce the selection intensity.

Weed Characteristics that Favour Resistance

Weeds, by their nature, have a diverse genetic background that gives them the ability to adapt to many different environments. For example, the repeated mowing of a lawn selects for low growing plants that avoid or are not affected by repeated cutting. Therefore, it should not be surprising that weeds can adapt to certain herbicide programmes. Weeds with a diverse genetic background may have a resistant biotype that has a 1 in 1 million chance of occurring within a weed population. Although these odds sound remote, a 1 in 1 million chance of occurrence can translate into a high probability of selecting for a herbicide resistant weed biotype unless proper methods to reduce selection intensity are used.

As a herbicide resistant biotype becomes more predominant in the weed population, two factors increase in importance:

1. Weed reproductive capability.
2. Weed seed dispersal mechanisms.

The greater the reproductive success of the resistant biotype, the greater its potential to spread and become a dominant part of the population. Due to the extended viability of most weed seeds, once established, a herbicide resistant biotype will be difficult to eliminate from the population, even if extensive remedial weed control measures are used. Weeds such as kochia can tumble for miles spreading seed onto previously uninfested land. As a result of the diverse seed dispersal mechanisms of weeds, it is apparent that a farm manager must always use good herbicide resistance management strategies to prevent resistant biotypes from developing on the land and prohibit the establishment of resistant weed biotypes spreading from adjacent lands or from custom harvesting equipment and other machinery.

Diagnosing Herbicide Resistant Weeds

Before assuming that any weeds surviving a herbicide application are resistant, rule out other factors that might have affected herbicide performance. Several factors would be misapplication, unfavourable weather conditions, improper timing of herbicide application, and weed flushes after application of a non-residual herbicide. If resistance appears to be a likely possibility, check for the following:

1. Are other weeds listed on the product label controlled satisfactorily? Chances are only one weed species will show herbicide resistance in any given field situation. Therefore, if several normally susceptible weed species are present, reconsider factors other than herbicide resistance as the cause of the lack of weed control.

2. Did the same herbicide or herbicide with the same site of action fail in the same area of the field in the previous year?
3. Do field histories indicate extensive use of the same herbicide or herbicide site of action year after year?

If one or more of these three situations apply, it is possible that the weeds are resistant to the herbicide. If resistance is suspected, control the weeds with a labeled herbicide having another site of action or use appropriate nonchemical weed control methods to prevent the weeds from going to seed. Next, contact your local crop consultant or extension agent, state weed specialist, and the appropriate chemical company to develop a comprehensive weed control programme to manage the problem.

Herbicide Resistant Crops

Recent research efforts have been directed at breeding herbicide resistance into crops. For minor-use crops it may be more economical to breed herbicide resistance into a crop than to develop new selective herbicides for current crop varieties. For major-use crops such as corn, soybeans, and wheat, herbicide resistant crops may be useful where difficult to control weeds or environmental conditions dictate the use of specific herbicides to which the crop is normally susceptible.

The use of herbicide resistant crops could enhance the potential for selecting for herbicide resistant weeds unless careful management practices are followed. The key, once again, is selection intensity. Misuse of herbicide resistant crops could encourage the use of a single herbicide or herbicide family over several crop rotations, thereby enhancing the selection intensity for herbicide resistant weeds.

Herbicide resistant crop varieties or hybrids need to be carefully evaluated for other performance characteristics (e.g. yield) and these characteristics should be compared to all other suitable hybrids or varieties in the marketplace, whether they have herbicide resistance or not. This will ensure that crop producers are getting the best overall agronomic value for their money. It will also be very important that accurate records be kept of the exact planting location of the herbicide resistant crops to avoid herbicide misapplication.

Management Strategies for Avoiding and Managing Herbicide Resistant Weeds

The following list of strategies for avoiding and managing problems with herbicide resistant weed biotypes has developed. Keep in mind that reliance upon any one strategy is not likely to be effective. The crop producer must use the following strategies in carefully selected combinations if herbicide resistant weed problems are to be avoided or properly managed.

1. Use herbicides only when necessary. Where available, herbicide applications should be based on economic thresholds. Continued development of effective economic threshold models should be helpful.
2. Rotate herbicides (sites of action). Do not make more than two consecutive applications of herbicides with the same site of action to the same field unless

other effective control practices are also included in the management system. Two consecutive applications could be single annual applications for two years, or two split applications in one year.

3. Apply herbicides in tank-mixed, prepackaged, or sequential mixtures that include multiple sites of action. Both herbicides, however, must have substantial activity against potentially resistant weeds for this strategy to be effective. Remember that in the past, weeds that were selected for herbicide resistance often were not the primary target species. It may be expensive to apply herbicide combinations that duplicate a wide spectrum of weed control activity. Many of the more economical herbicide combinations may not be adequate.
4. Rotate crops, particularly those with different life cycles (e.g. winter annuals such as winter wheat, perennials such as alfalfa, summer annuals such as corn or soybeans). At the same time, remember not to use herbicides with the same site of action in these different crops against the same weed unless other effective control practices are also included in the management system.
5. Planting new herbicide resistant crop varieties should not result in more than two consecutive applications of herbicides with the same site of action against the same weed unless other effective control practices are also included in the management system.
6. Combine, where feasible, mechanical weed control practices such as rotary hoeing and cultivation with herbicide treatments.
7. Include, where soil erosion potential is minimal, primary tillage as a component of the weed management programme.
8. Scout fields regularly and identify weeds present. Respond quickly to changes in weed populations to restrict spread of weeds that may have been selected for resistance.
9. Clean tillage and harvest equipment before moving from fields infested with resistant weeds to those that are not.
10. Encourage railroads, public utilities, highway departments and similar organisations that use total vegetation control programmes should be encouraged to use vegetation management systems that do not lead to selection of herbicide resistant weeds. Resistant weeds from total vegetation control areas frequently spread to cropland. Chemical companies, state and federal agencies, and farm organisations can all help in this effort.

25

Insect Management

Overview

Insects and mites rarely threaten soybean production in Minnesota. This pleasant situation has resulted from the introduction of clean soybeans from Korea and China without importing insect pests. The pests highlighted in this chapter have adapted to soybeans from other native U.S. plants. Consequently, insect problems are infrequent and localized. For example, infestations over the last 10 years have included two-spotted spider mites in 1988, grasshoppers in 1989-90 and 1997-98, green cloverworms in 1991, thistle caterpillars in 1992, seedcorn maggots in 1993, and white grubs in 1998. Infrequent infestations pose three problems:

- Since few people are scouting for these insects, infestations may not be detected promptly
- Even if symptoms are noticed, growers and crop advisors may have difficulty diagnosing problem insects and mites.
- Sporadic problems mean most growers or crop advisors lack management expertise, especially for spotty problems that may occur only once every 10 to 20 years

Geographical variation is typical with migratory insect problems, such as green cloverworms and potato leafhoppers, which are more common in southern Minnesota. There can also be drought-related insect problems such as grasshoppers and two-spotted spider mites, which are more common in western Minnesota. No area is immune to insect outbreaks. As soybean acreage expands in northern Minnesota, more insect problems could emerge. This chapter reviews the insect pests that potentially affect soybean production in both northern and southern Minnesota.

Types of Insect Damage

Insects and mites attacking soybeans can be grouped by the type of damage they cause, and can be categorized as *stand-reducing, leaf-feeding,* and pod-feeding.

Stand-reducing insects attack germinating seeds or the roots or underground stems of young plants, and they can cut off the plants. Examples include seedcorn maggots, wireworms, white grubs, and cutworms. Three factors influence stand reduction and management decisions. First, because the seed rises out of the ground during emergence, its exposure to seed-feeding insects is greatly reduced. Second, because the growing point rapidly moves above ground, the risk of stand loss from cutworms is increased. Third, soybeans compensate quite well for stand loss; reductions in stand from 160K to 105 K may not cause detectable yield loss. While rescue treatments are not available for most stand-reducing insects, if promptly detected, cutworm infestations can be easily controlled with insecticides.

Stand Reducing Insects

Cutworms

There are a number of species of cutworms which are variable in colour. All have a hardened shield on top of the body behind the head. Cutworms are active just under the soil surface and will curl into a ball if disturbed (not to be confused with white grubs, or Japanese beetle grubs, which are C-shaped). Cutworms can attack seedling plants by girdling or cutting through young stems. Some cutworms, such as the dingy cutworm, also prefer to lay eggs in soybean fields, and can contribute to high populations in corn if it follows in the rotation.

Seedcorn Maggot

The larvae are typical maggots, less than ¼ inch long, legless and cylindrical, tapering to a point at the head, dirty-white to creamy-yellow in colour. Seedcorn maggots feed underground on cotyledons and can also burrow into seeds. Damage from this insect is accentuated when cool, wet weather delays sprouting and emergence. The adult flies, similar to house flies, are attracted to decaying organic matter.

White Grubs

White grubs are white to cream-coloured C-shaped grubs (¼ inch to 1¼ inches long) that feed on the fibrous roots of soybeans. The predominant grubs in Minnesota have a long life cycle of generally 3 years. They attack soybeans following sod throughout the state. In western Minnesota one species may attack soybeans in sandy soil near cottonwoods, poplars, or willows. Their root pruning can lead to stunting and death of plants. No rescue treatments are available and soil insecticides are labeled for white grubs in soybeans. If a problem is anticipated, or if abundant grubs are detected at tillage, consider planting corn with a soil insecticide.

Wireworms

Wireworms are rarely a problem for soybeans, but they can attack germinating seeds and the soft, underground part of the stem. Damage has been reported when soybeans follow sod, such as pasture or Conservation Research Programme (CRP) land that was reclaimed for crop production. Low-lying areas of fields already in production can also experience problems, particularly if weather after planting is cool and wet enough to delay germination. Seed treatments are typically recommended in these higher-risk situations.

Table 25.1: Yield Loss (%) from Stand Reduction

Original	Stand Dead and Missing Plants (1000s/acre)												
(1000s/acre)	17.5	18	35	52	70	87	104.5	122	139	157	174	191.5	209
209	1	2	5	8	13	19	26	35	49	62	78	100	
191.5	2	3	6	11	17	24	32	47	62	77	100		
174	2	5	8	14	22	31	45	60	77	100			
157	3	7	11	19	28	43	59	76	100				
139	5	8	15	25	39	56	75	100					
122	6	11	20	35	53	73	100						
104.5	8	15	31	50	71	100							
87	9	25	45	68	100								
70	18	37	64	100									

Leaf-feeding insects remove or damage leaves, which may affect future growth, pod-set, or pod-fill. Examples of defoliating insects include grasshoppers, bean leaf beetles, and several caterpillars (green cloverworms, yellow woollybears, thistle caterpillars or webworms). Each defoliating insect produces a unique type of feeding damage. In contrast, the potato leafhopper uses its piercing/sucking mouthparts to damage leaf plumbing. Two-spotted spider mites suck out leaf cells.

Leaf feeding is initially obscure but may rapidly escalate. Defoliation always appears worse than the resulting yield loss, because soybean canopies have more leaf area than they need to produce a good bean crop.

Table 25.2: Yield Loss (%) from Soybean Defoliation

Growth	Stage % Defoliation									
	10	20	30	40	50	60	70	80	90	100
VE-V4	–	–	1	3	4	5	6	7	13	20
V5-12	–	1	2	4	5	6	7	9	15	22
R1-2	–	2	3	5	6	7	9	12	16	23
R2.5	1	2	3	5	7	9	11	15	20	28
R3	2	3	4	6	8	11	14	18	24	33
R3.5	3	4	5	7	10	13	18	24	31	45
R4	3	5	7	9	12	16	22	30	39	56
R4.5	4	6	9	11	15	20	27	37	49	65
R5-5.5	4	7	10	13	17	23	31	43	58	75
R6	1	6	9	11	14	18	23	31	41	53

Keep in mind that hail is a one-time event, whereas ongoing insect defoliation or mite injury at the same level causes more yield loss. Factors affecting good canopy formation, such as drought, disease, or stand loss will accentuate defoliation impacts on yield. Soybean susceptibility to defoliation also varies with growth stage. The greatest susceptibility occurs during pod-fill.

Table 25.3: Action Thresholds for Adult and Nymphal Grasshoppers

	Nymphs/yd²		Adults/yd²	
Rating	**Margin**	**Field**	**Margin**	**Field**
Light	25-35	15-25	10-20	3-7
Threat	50-75	30-45	21-40	8-14
Severe	100-150	60-90	41-80	15-28
Very severe	200+	120+	80+	29+

Warning

Do not overreact to insect defoliation. Carefully examine the extent of defoliation that has actually occurred. Make sure the insect infestation has not matured before committing to an expensive (and useless) insecticide application.

LEAF FEEDING INSECTS

Bean Leaf Beetle - see Pod Feeding Insects

Grasshoppers

Grasshopper populations develop during dry springs following long, warm autumns. Under moderate or high moisture, fungal diseases normally keep grasshopper populations in check. Grasshoppers tend to prefer to lay their eggs in untilled soil, such as roadsides and ditches. Damage, therefore, will likely first occur at the margin of fields. An exception is soybeans planted in last years soybean or alfalfa fields; certain grasshopper species will lay eggs in both cropping systems. Grasshopper nymphs look very much like adults, but lack fully developed wings. Grasshoppers feed on leaves and, as soybeans mature, on developing pods.

Scouting for grasshoppers should start early in the growing season (late April, early May), because early detection is often instrumental in control. Scouting should start at field edges, fence rows, dirt roads, and ditches. Consider field-edge applications unless grasshoppers occur throughout the field. Thresholds can be based on either grasshopper numbers or soybean defoliation. Thresholds based on grasshopper populations can be estimated by scouting the field and treatment decisions. Thresholds based on defoliation include treating when defoliation inside the field exceeds 30 per cent prebloom, or 20 per cent blooming-to-pod-fill. (Be aware that certain species of grasshoppers will lay eggs in soybeans and alfalfa.) This migratory moth is common throughout the soybean-growing areas of the eastern United States and the Great Plains, but seldom reaches pest status. The caterpillar is green with white and typically has two generations per year. Because it attacks early in the season, however, plants usually compensate for foliage loss before pods are set. Many entomologists consider the green clover worm a valuable food source for beneficial insects and diseases. This reservoir of beneficials often controls pests of more economic importance later in the season. Treat only if defoliation reaches 40 per cent in prebloom 20 per cent during bloom and pod-fill, and 35 per cent from pod-fill to harvest.

Japanese Beetle

The Japanese beetle has a wide variety of plant hosts and will attack soybeans both early and late in the growing season. A soybean-feeding variant does not occur in Minnesota at this time. Adult beetles feed on foliage, skeletonizing the leaves. They are long, have a hard shell, are metallic green, and have bronze-coloured wing covers. Small white squares (actually tufts of hair) are visible around the outside edge of the wing covers.

Potato Leafhopper

Potato leafhoppers are very small (~1/8 inches), wedge-shaped insects. They are bright green, quick moving, and have piercing/sucking mouthparts. When feeding, they inject a toxic saliva which causes localized stippling, yellowish to reddish-yellow discolouration of leaves (especially at the tips), leaf crinkling and cupping. This injury may appear similar to herbicide damage. Extensive feeding damage can result in plants that are stunted. The thick pubescence on soybean leaves tends to prevent this small insect from getting close enough to implant its mouthparts. However, young plants without heavy pubescence are vulnerable to leafhopper attack. Stressed plants are also more vulnerable to injury from potato leafhopper than are healthy plants. In addition, due to this insect's host preference, soybean fields adjacent to alfalfa fields should be considered at a greater risk from potato leafhopper infestation due to movement when alfalfa is cut. Scout for potato leafhopper by examining fields with two trifoliolates or less, and treat if populations exceed 1/plant at V2, or if seedling plants with dying leaves are present.

Saltmarsh and Woolybear Caterpillars

These hairy, robust caterpillars may be white or multicoloured, solid, or banded. They often feed in the upper canopy where they are noticeable, so populations are frequently overestimated. Smaller larvae tend to feed in the lower canopy or on the underside of leaves, so early infestations can go unnoticed. This insect is only an occasional problem in Minnesota, except for drought years.

Two-spotted Spider Mites

In most years, spider mite populations are kept in check by fungal diseases and predators. Both mortality factors require cooler temperatures and higher humidities. In very warm, dry years spider mite populations can rapidly increase and cause widespread damage through soybean fields. Early infestations will kill soybeans, while later infestations cause premature senescence and reductions in yields up to 40 per cent-50 per cent.

Soybeans planted next to alfalfa are at high risk during favourable mite conditions, and should be scouted first. Look for stippling and bronzing of soybean leaves. Fully grown adult mites will be barely visible to the naked eye on the underside of leaves, while younger stages will have to be observed with a hand lens. Treat only in outbreak conditions when mites are present throughout the field, and stippling is present on leaves.

Reinfestations may occur because some of the insecticides used may not be effective against eggs. The eggs will hatch in several days, and the infestation may begin again, so continued scouting is recommended. Border-treating fields may be effective if the problem is caught early enough. Be advised that if an outbreak has occurred, subsequent rain alone may not solve the problem of spider mite infestations, because the fungal diseases which attack them will be too late.

Thistle Caterpillars

The caterpillars of the painted lady butterfly rarely cause problems in soybeans unless an unusually large spring migration of the butterflies occurs from the U.S. desert Southwest or Mexico. The caterpillars are commonly found on thistles, but will also attack early vegetative soybeans. The larvae (up to 1.5 inches long) feed on the top leaves and web them together with silk. Their appearance is quite distinctive. The body is black with yellow spots and has numerous multi-pronged spines. Treatment is recommended if defoliation exceeds 50 per cent.

Webworms

These are green caterpillars with 3 dark spots arranged in a triangle on the side of each body segment. At least one hair originates from each spot. The larvae web leaves with silk, and skeletonize leaves by feeding. This insect is rarely a problem in Minnesota, and has never reached economic threshold levels here.

Pod-feeding insects attack developing pods, or even cut pods off the plant. Examples include grasshoppers and bean leaf beetles. Because the soybean's investment in yield is nearly completed, this type of attack is the most destructive. Pod-feeding is difficult to anticipate. Equivalent infestation levels may or may not produce economic loss. Assessment of seed damage or pod loss can indicate when to treat an infestation. However, this approach can only prevent further losses from that point on.

Pod Feeding Insects

Bean Leaf Beetle

These small (¼ inch) yellowish-buff to reddish beetles usually sport four distinct black spots on their back. A small proportion of the beetles lack spots, but all colour forms have a black triangle at the base of the wing covers. The bean leaf beetle attacks soybeans throughout the growing season. Overwintering adults colonize early-emerging soybean fields, but beetle feeding on cotyledons and unifoliolate leaves does not reach economic threshold. There is one generation in the north and two in the south of Minnesota per year. Larvae feed underground on soybean roots and nodules, but this feeding does not appear to affect yield. Emerging adults from the first generation feed on soybean leaves in July and should be treated if defoliation exceeds 35 per cent and beetles are still feeding. Adults from the second generation should be treated in late August if defoliation exceeds 25 per cent during pod-set and pod-fill. These adults also feed on pods, which affects seed development and allows disease entry. Consequently, these beetles should be treated if damaged pods exceed 10 per cent, or if adults exceed 0.5 per plant, during pod-fill. Heavy populations should be watched closely and treated aggressively if pod clipping is noted.

Insect Interactions of Soybeans with Other Crops

Cutworms

Dingy cutworm and black cutworm problems in corn are more severe following soybeans. Dingy cutworms prefer laying eggs in soybeans and alfalfa when adults are active in August and September. Consequently, crops following soybeans have a higher risk of attack from this cutworm. The black cutworm migrates north each spring. Arriving moths lay eggs in crop and weed residue, and soybean residue is a preferred egg-laying site. The timing and extent of tillage have important implications for risk of cutworm attack. Ridge-till and no-till corn after soybean often have the most severe infestations.

Stalk Borer and Giant Ragweed

Giant ragweed has emerged as a weed control problem in some soybean herbicide programmes. This weed is a preferred egg-laying site for stalk borers. Corn planted the next year may suffer severe infestations, particularly if the weed control programme in corn forces any stalk borers in giant ragweed into corn. While stalk borers are more commonly recognized as an insect problem in corn, they may also attack soybeans.

Crop Rotation and Corn Rootworms

Rotation to a non-corn crop, such as soybeans, is a highly-preferred and effective way to avoid corn rootworm problems. Recently, corn rootworms have demonstrated their capability to survive crop rotation. The northern corn rootworm retains its egg laying preference for corn, but a larger proportion of eggs overwinter two or more years. The western corn rootworm has shifted its egg laying to soybeans in the eastern portion of the corn belt. These problems could affect crop rotations throughout the corn belt.

Insects cause sporadic and localized outbreaks in Minnesota soybeans. Yield losses may occur through stand reductions, defoliation, and pod feeding. Because outbreaks are infrequent, growers and crop advisors may fail to recognize or diagnose an emerging outbreak. The critical times to scout soybeans for insect problems include the first two weeks of emergence for stand loss problems, late July and August for defoliation, and late August and September for pod feeding. Learn to recognize the insects and their injury symptoms.

26

Scouting

Overview

Scouting is an important component of making informed crop management decisions. Scouting is time-consuming and expensive, but failing to scout will cost the grower through yield loss, or unnecessary insecticide applications, neither of which is acceptable. By knowing the kind, number, and location of insect, weed, and disease damage within a field, the producer can make sound decisions about insect management and can often save several times the cost of scouting.

Scouting techniques are designed around the pest's life history and the crop's growing stages. They must provide an accurate representation of pest populations before damage is done to the crop. To properly scout for pests, the grower must know where they live, what they look like, and how to find and count them. Information on pest life cycles, and the timing and type of damage inflicted to the crop is essential.

Frequency of Samples

Scouting should be conducted throughout the growing season. The frequency of sampling depends on the nature of the pest threat. Scouting is ideally done weekly, but sample periods can be lengthened in cooler weather, or shortened in higher temperatures. This requires a significant amount of time, and this is another reason to develop simple and fast scouting methods.

Number and Location of Sample Sites

There should be a sufficient number of samples taken to accurately reflect the population of the pests within a field. Scouting location and pattern depends on the within-field distribution of the pest being monitored. Obviously, other factors such as field size, shape, and access will also influence how and from where samples are taken.

There are three general scouting patterns:

1. If the pest is evenly distributed throughout the entire field, a transect in a circular, "W", or adapted "Z" pattern should be used. These patterns have been designed to ensure that the entire pest population has an equal opportunity to be sampled.
2. Some pests are associated with particular field conditions, such as low/high, wet/dry, or low/high organic content. Sampling effort must, therefore, be concentrated in these areas.
3. Some pests generally concentrate on the edges of fields, but may get into the field as well. Scouting the margins of fields first will provide a good indication as to whether sampling within the field is required. Be aware that most of these species have different action thresholds within the field and at the edges.

Sampling Methods

There are a number of standard techniques to sample insects, weeds, and plant diseases. The most common method of scouting for pests is simply conducting visual inspections. This technique generally involves selecting a number of plants, leaves, stems, or roots and examining them for the presence of pests or damage. This may require the dissection of plant material or simply walking through the sample area. Visual inspections can be quantitative, or presence/absence, depending on the species being monitored. Generally, presence/ absence techniques are used where thresholds are very low, or numbers are very high, and actual counts would not be possible. In either case, careful examination of the plant material is necessary.

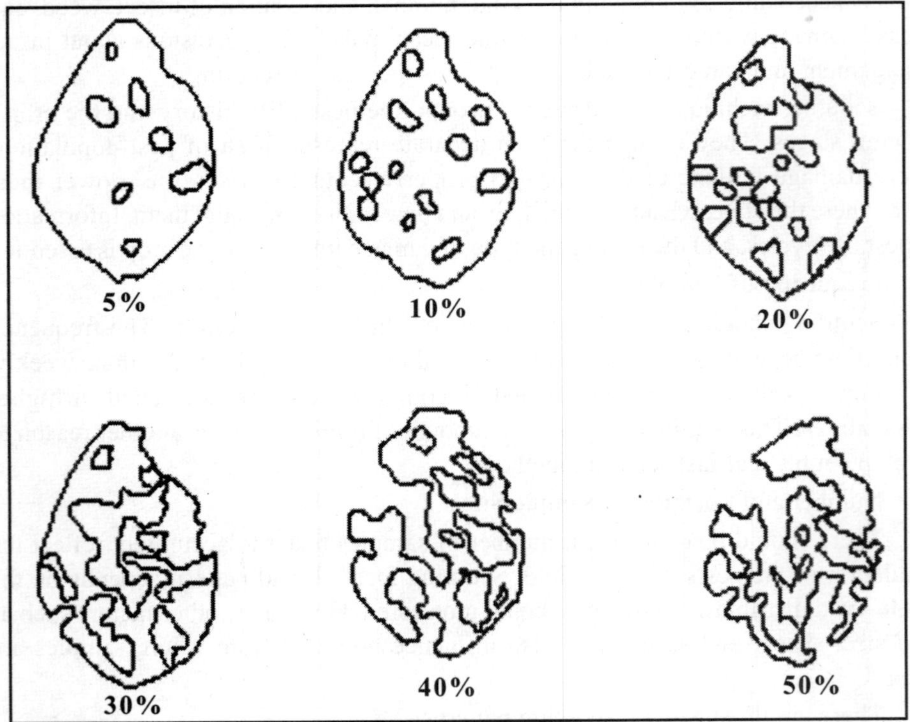

Fig. 26.1: **Defoliation Assessment Guide**

Soil inhabiting insects can be sampled using solar baits. To do this, dig a 4"-6" deep hole, about 10" in diametre, and fill it with a 1:1 mixture of corn/wheat seed (soaking the mixture for 24 hours facilitates germination). Place ½ cup of the mixture into the hole, cover with soil, and then cover the soil over the bait with a black plastic trash bag to warm the surface and speed germination. Cover the edges of the bag with soil to prevent wind from blowing away the plastic. Four traps per acre will give a reliable estimate of wireworm population, but this trap density may be unrealistic because of the time and effort involved in the scouting process. As a compromise, at least 10 traps should be used in each field. Collect the samples after one week, count the number of wireworms in each trap, and determine the average.

During emergence of soybeans, damage assessment is based on the potential for stand loss. Stand loss is estimated by checking 20 row feet of soybeans in at least 5 locations of the field and determining the percentage of plants cut or destroyed. If 20 per cent of plants are cut, and the stand has gaps of > 1 foot, or if at least one seedling per row foot is destroyed, treatment is economically beneficial.

After trifoliolate leaves have formed, damage assessment is based on estimates of defoliation. To estimate defoliation, the following procedure is recommended:

1. Pick a trifoliolate leaf from the top, middle, and bottom third of 10 randomly selected plants. Place into a plastic storage bag and estimate damage to all leaves at one time (this decreases errors in defoliation estimates).
2. From each trifoliolate, discard the most and least damaged leaflets, leaving 30 leaflets to estimate defoliation.
3. Compare the selected leaflets to Fig. 26.1 and record the average level of defoliation.

27

Disease Management

Overview

A serious problem for Minnesota soybean producers is underestimation of disease-incurred yield reductions. This portion lists and describes diseases one should recognize in order to increase soybean profitability.

Sclerotinia Stem Rot *Sclerotinia sclerotiorum*

Flower petals are infected and mycelium colonizes the stem and pods. Stem tissue becomes tan or white and may be covered with white mycelium and black sclerotia (round, oblong, hard, black structures). The top of the plant dies and turns brown. This is often the first symptom observed. Stem lesions may increase lodging. Sclerotia on the stem fall to the ground and others inside the pith are released when seed is harvested. Sclerotia can be found with the seed. The fungus survives winter as a sclerotia and can remain alive in soil for many years. Sclerotia germinate in warm/wet spring, summer, or fall periods and release spores that are windborne. Soybean infection requires moisture on the flower petals, and is favoured by closely-spaced plants that form a dense canopy early.

Phytophthora Seedling Blight Root, and Stem Rot *Phytophthora megasperma*

Symptoms include stand reduction, root rots, and basal stem decay Seed rot and pre-emergence damping-off are often credited to water damage. Taproots are usually dark brown, and small feeder roots are rotted or missing, on plants that survive the seedling phase. Stem discoloration, dark brown surface from the soil line up 6 inches, is less common on more tolerant/resistant varieties. Leaves on older plants become chlorotic, stunted and may wilt, die, turn brown, and remain attached to the plant for some time. This fungus survives as an "oospore" in infected crop debris. The oospore germinates in wet soils and releases many "zoospores" that swim to developing soybean roots and infect. Disease and infection is favoured by wet conditions and soil temperatures near 60°F. Low, poorly drained compacted soils, or soils with high clay content, or sites that are normally well-drained but wet, increase disease severity.

Pythium Seed Decay, Seedling Blight and Root Rot *Pythium species*

Seed rotted in soil, commonly soft, wet, and overgrown by other fungi are usually killed before emergence by this fungus. Rapid death prevents accurate diagnosis. Roots are brown, watery, soft and often completely decayed. Limited infection may produce brown lesions on roots, hypocotyl, or cotyledons. Death of meristem tissue may result in a swollen hypocotyl. These species are often called "Water Molds." They survive in soil and in plant residue. Cool (50°F to 60°F) and wet soils favour release of "swimming" spores and infection develops rapidly. Younger seedlings are most susceptible because soybeans become more resistant as they age.

Rhizoctonia Root Rot and Lower Stem Decay *Rhizoctonia solani*

Post-emergence damage is a bigger problem than is pre-emergence death. Root symptoms are confined to lateral root decay and outer root surface damage only. A red-brown discoloration of the hypocotyl and lower stem does not extend above the soil line. Slow growing plants are damaged most, and symptoms, wilting, and death develop following warm, dry weather early in the season. This is another soil inhabitant that survives in soil as sclerotia or as "resting" mycelium in crop residue. Infection is favoured by wet and cool conditions followed by warm and dry periods that stress the plant. Young plants are most susceptible, but stressed older plants may die if moisture is limited.

Fusarium Root Rot *Fusarium oxysporum* & other F. species

A problem on seedlings and young plant roots that develop in wet, cool soils, below 58°F. Seedling growth can be slowed and plants usually are stunted and weak. Infection is often limited to lower taproots, and lower lateral roots which may be destroyed. New roots can develop from the upper taproot providing a shallow fibrous root system that is prone to fail in dry soils. The vascular system can be affected, turns brown or black, and this increases late season plant wilt under moisture limiting conditions. Stress from soybean cyst nematodes, or other nematodes, and DNA herbicides predispose plants to infection. These soil born-fungi survive as chlamydospores and as mycelium in plant residues. *Fusarium solani*, reported to be the cause of Sudden Death Syndrome (SDS), has been reported to be near Minnesota, but isolates of this "Blue Strain" from Minnesota soils have not been confirmed to be like the isolates from Iowa or Illinois. Symptoms of SDS are interveinal chlorosis, necrosis, and leaf defoliation. Petioles remain firmly attached. The central pith (when stems are split) should be white with no discoloration or decay. It is believed that certain isolates produce a toxin that translocates to the upper leaves causing the above symptoms. Others report this fungus can be isolated from cyst nematodes.

Brown Stem Rot - *Phialophora gregata*

Root infection precedes discoloration of water conducting vessels and at mid-season the vascular elements and stem pith show a reddish-brown colour. The brown color develops first at the stem base and moves up, often most evident at nodes. Yield reduction increases with greater discoloration. Leaf symptoms develop later in the season. Look for wilt, interveinal browning and green tissue over the vein, leaf drying, and early leaf drop. Plants do not mature normally, and appear to be frost damaged. This fungus survives in crop debris and increased inoculum levels are reported following tolerant varieties. Cool weather leads to more stem browning and warm dry conditions increase foliar symptoms, especially during the reproductive stage.

Pod and Stem Blight and Seed Decay - Diaporthe (*Phaseolorum* var. sojae)

Linear rows of brown to black fruiting bodies, "pycnidia," are seen on stems, but are scattered on pods. Infection of healthy plants is common, but the pycnidia are produced only on dead or dying tissue. Seeds in infected pods have a white, moldy growth, are wrinkled, smaller, and germinate poorly. Seed infection tends to be greater when warm wet or humid weather delays harvest. Plants that are killed early, or plants that are harvested late in wet or warm humid late summer, often have pycnidia present. Infected seed can produce infected plants, but most infection comes from inoculum in infested crop residue. Spores splash on plants during wet weather and infection is favoured by injuries, hail, or lesions caused by other pathogens.

Anthracnose *(Colletotrichum truncatum & C. destructivum)*

Symptoms appear at early reproductive stages on stems, pods, and petioles. Watch for leaf rolling, petiole cankers, veinal necrosis, and early leaf drop. Stem and pods have black fruiting bodies, "acervuli," with black hairs, "setae." Seed are shriveled, moldy, and stained brown or dark. Early season infection can be from seed inoculum, while infection during flowering is mostly from infected plant residue. High plant populations and wet canopies favour disease development.

Bacterial Blight *(Pseudomonas syringae)*

Small, angular, water-soaked spots on leaves turn red-brown to black as tissue dies and dries. Spots may have a water-soaked margin and a yellow halo. As leaves grow and flex, dead tissue falls out, and leaves may appear tattered and ragged. Seed may be colonized, becoming shriveled with sunken, discolored lesions. Infected soybean residue or seed borne inoculum is spread to plants by wind-driven rains. Early infections may appear severe, especially in wet weather, but hot dry conditions stop disease development.

Brown Spot *(Septoria glycines)*

Primarily an early season leaf disease. Cotyledons, primary leaves and lower trifoliolates show brown to red pinpoint spots up to 1/4 inch. Some may grow together and become irregularly shaped spots. Look for black dots, "pycnidia," in center of mature spots. Severe infection can cause leaves to yellow and drop early, especially the lower canopy. Spores are splashed or wind blown to wet leaves, mostly in mid-spring. It can develop in warm moist periods at any time. Hot, dry weather stops this disease, but it can develop again before plants mature.

Purple Seed Stain and Leaf Blight *(Cercospora kikuchii)*

Seed discoloration varies from pink to pale or dark purple and the area affected ranges from specks to blotches, possibly the entire seed coat. Infected seed may not show symptoms, but infected cotyledons shrivel, turn dark purple, and drop early. Plants can be killed or stunted. This fungus survives as mycelium on the seed coat or on crop residue. Spores from infected seed cotyledons are splashed or wind-borne to leaves and stems. Small, red-purple, angular lesions develop on both sides of sunexposed upper leaves during seed set. Leaf symptoms begin as a light purple color that extends over the leaf and develops a leathery appearance. Infection is favoured by high temperatures (80°F plus) and humid conditions.

Downy Mildew *(Peronospora manshurica)*

Pale green to light yellow spots on the upper surface of young leaves which, may enlarge, forming bright yellow lesions of indefinite size. Older infected spots turn gray-brown. Spots on the lower leaf surface, especially in moist weather, have tufts of gray mycelium and spores easily seen with a lens. Older leaves are more resistant, but young leaves are susceptible. Pods may be infected without any symptom, and seeds are partly or completely covered by white mycelia and oospores, which are easy to see. Seed from infected pods may be smaller and have cracks in the seed coat.

Powdery Mildew *(Microsphaera diffusa)*

White powderlike patches of mycelia and conidia are seen on all aboveground plant parts. Additional symptoms develop on some susceptible varieties, such as chlorosis, green islands, rusty patches, and defoliation. Disease develops in cooler than normal years with reduced plant growth.

Stem Canker *(Diaporthae phaseolorum var caulivora)*

Infection symptoms develop during early reproductive stages at nodes as a small red-brown lesion. Over time, the lesion expands, forming a darker brown, elongated sunken canker. Leaf tissue yellows between the veins and, with reduced water flow, death of leaves is common. At times, top growth ceases and a shepherd's crook curl develops. Girdling and toxin production are responsible for symptoms and death. Symptoms in Minnesota often are field and seedlot specific, and may have resulted from seed contamination. However, the fungus is reported to survive on infested debris. Most soybean cultivars can be infected, but only those that are susceptible allow the disease to develop.

Virus Diseases

Large numbers of viruses infect plants, and soybeans, have more than a hundred virus or virus strains reported. New virus problems are expected to be seen as soybean seed production occurs in many new environments.

Soybean Mosaic Virus or Crinkle

Infected plant leaves are spindly, narrower than normal, have dark green swellings along veins. Plants are stunted, petioles are short, as are the internodes. Infected pods are small, flat, have less hair, and are curved more. Seed germination may be reduced. This virus is seed-borne, can overwinter in perennial weeds, and is spread by aphid species.

Bean Pod Mottle

A mild-yellow mottling is seen on the youngest leaves during rapid growth in cool weather. The mottle disappears as plants mature and plants may be slightly stunted, with distorted foliage, misshapen pods, and smaller seeds. The virus overwinters in legumes, clover, or alfalfa and is spread by insect feeding; especially the bean leaf beetle. Symptoms are masked by high temperatures, and are not seen after pod set.

Nematodes

Large numbers of nematodes exist in soils, but only a few are of economic importance on soybeans. Nematode damage can be direct and/or indirect. Soybean nematode damage is significant and difficult to accurately diagnosis without proper sample collection, including soil and root samples.

Cyst Nematode - *Heterodera glycines*

Low levels of infection can remain undetected for some time as no diagnostic above ground symptom exists. Stunted, chlorotic, vigourless beans with reduced root systems and few nitrogen nodules are typical of low infection levels in high fertility sites. Egg numbers do increase and symptom severity increases, reducing soybean yields. Carefully dig and examine roots for white to tan females containing eggs any time after late June through September. The cysts are spread by soil movement from equipment, or with water or wind. Birds can carry the cysts considerable distances. Most farms have some level of infestation.

Lesion Nematode - *Pratylenchus* species

Lesion nematodes are found world-wide. They attack the root cortex. Roots develop dark lesions and an overall brown color. Loss of the epidermis and cortex decreases root growth nutrient and water uptake. Under stress, plants yellow, become stunted, and have reduced yields.

Sting Nematode - *Belonolaimus* species

Seedlings can be killed, reducing stands. Larger plants are not killed, but appear stunted, chlorotic, and gray-green as if moisture deficient. Small, dark, sunken lesions are present on roots to the tip. Terminal root growth stops and roots appear stubby or have abnormal root proliferation. Damage is usually found in sandy soils. Sting nematodes feed on many host plants, especially grasses, and can also attack corn.

28

Insect Pest Management in Soybeans

Soybeans can be attacked by pests at any stage from seedlings to close to harvest, but are most attractive from flowering onwards. It is important to note that soybeans are very tolerant of insect damage at many stages of crop development, and that noticeable damage (particularly leaf damage) does not necessarily translate to yield loss.

Soybeans can tolerate up to 33 per cent leaf loss (providing terminal and auxiliary buds are not attacked) without yield loss but their ability to compensate for pest damage decreases as pods develop. Soybeans set a large number of reserve pods and can compensate for insect damage during early podding by diverting energy to fill these reserve pods. If developing seeds are damaged the plant diverts more energy to undamaged seeds, making these bigger and heavier.

Seeds damaged by pod-sucking bugs during early pod-fill are often lost at harvest, or are graded out post harvest, as they are lighter than undamaged seeds. Seeds damaged from mid pod-fill onwards are similar in weight to undamaged seeds, not lost at harvest or able to be graded out without resorting to colour sorters.

Crops remain susceptible to late bug damage until the pods harden just prior to harvest. As a result, late bug damage is a major factor affecting seed quality. As a rule of thumb, only 2 per cent seed damage is tolerable for soybeans targeting the culinary market.

Major Pests of Soybeans

Helicoverpa (*Helicoverpa armigera, Helicoverpa punctigera*)

Helicoverpa can severely damage all crop stages and all plant parts of soybeans. Of the summer legumes, soybeans are the most attractive to helicoverpa during the vegetative stage and can even be damaged during the seedling stage. In sub-coastal and inland southern Queensland, summer legumes are at greatest risk from *H. armigera* from mid-December onwards. However, spring *H. armigera* outbreaks are more likely in coastal regions.

Identification

Helicoverpa larvae can be confused with loopers, armyworms or cluster caterpillars.

Damage

- *Helicoverpa* spp. defoliation is characterised by rounded chew marks and holes (loopers make more angular holes).
- *Helicoverpa* will also attack auxiliary buds and terminals in vegetative crops. High populations in seedling or drought-stressed crops can cause considerable damage if vegetative terminals and stems are eaten. This type of damage results in pods being set closer to the ground. Such pods are more difficult to harvest.
- In drought-stressed crops, the last soft green tissue is usually the vegetative terminals, which are thus more likely to be totally consumed than in normally growing crops.
- Once crops reach flowering, larvae focus on buds, flowers and pods. Young larvae are more likely to feed on vegetative terminals, young leaves and flowers before attacking pods.
- Small pods may be totally consumed by helicoverpa, but larvae target the seeds in large pods.
- Crops are better able to compensate for early rather than late pod damage, however in dry land crops, where water is limited, significant early damage may delay or stagger podding with subsequent yield and quality losses.
- Damage to well-developed pods results in the weather staining of uneaten seeds due to water entering the pods.

Monitoring

- Beat sheet sampling is the preferred sampling method for medium to large helicoverpa larvae. Small larvae should be scouted for by opening vegetative terminals and flowers.
- Inspect crops weekly during the vegetative stage - damage to vegetative terminals is often the first visual clue that helicoverpa larvae are present.
- Soybeans should be scouted for eggs and moths to pinpoint the start of infestations and increase the chance of successful control.
- Inspect twice weekly from early budding until late podding.
- Sample six widely spaced locations per field. Take five one-metre samples at each site with a standard beat sheet. Convert larval counts/m to larvae/m^2 by dividing counts by the row spacing in metres.
- Beat sheet sampling may only detect 50 per cent of small larvae in vegetative and podding soybeans, and 70 per cent during flowering, as they feed in sheltered sites such as leaf terminals. Many of these small larvae will be lost to natural mortality factors before they reach a damaging size and in most crops, and this mortality will cancel out any sampling inefficiencies.

Thresholds

In vegetative crops, thresholds for many leaf feeding pests are expressed as per cent tolerable defoliation or per cent tolerable terminal loss. Before flowering, soybeans can tolerate up to 33 per cent leaf loss without loss of yield. However recent data shows that helicoverpa populations inflicting less than 33 per cent damage can cause serious yield loss, because the larvae not only feed on leaves, but also attack terminals and auxiliary buds. The data indicates an economic threshold of approximately 7.5 helicoverpa larvae per square metre (7.5/m^2) in vegetative soybeans.

Helicoverpa thresholds for podding soybeans currently range from 1-2 larvae/m^2 (depending on crop value and pesticide cost).

Chemical Control

- Prior to flowering, biopesticides, particularly Helicoverpa nucleopoly-hedrovirus (NPV), are recommended in preference to chemical insecticides. This helps conserve beneficial insects to buffer crops against helicoverpa attack during the susceptible reproductive stages, and avoids flaring of other pests such as silverleaf whitefly and mites.
- For best results, all ingestion type products require thorough plant coverage. For biopesticides, addition of Amino Feed® or an equivalent product is recommended.
- For chemical control and current registrations refer to How to find the right insecticide.

Cultural Control

- Where possible, avoid successive plantings of summer legumes.
- Good agronomy and soil moisture are crucial as large, vigorously-growing plants suffer less defoliation for a given helicoverpa population and have less risk of terminal damage.
- In water-stressed crops, terminals are more attractive to larvae than wilted leaves. Vigorously growing plants with adequate available moisture are better able to replace damaged leaves and compensate for flower and pod damage.

Natural Enemies

The number of natural enemies or beneficials varies with crop age, from crop to crop, region to region, and from season to season. The combined action of a number of beneficial species is often required to have a significant impact on potentially damaging helicoverpa populations. It is therefore desirable to conserve as many beneficials as possible.

Natural enemies of soybean pests include predators of eggs, larvae and pupae, parasites of eggs and larvae and caterpillar diseases.

Predatory bugs and beetles that attack helicoverpa eggs and larvae include:

- Spined predatory shield bug
- Glossy shield bug

- Damsel bug
- Bigeyed bug
- Apple dimpling bug
- Assassin bug
- Red and blue beetle
- Predatory ladybird beetles
- Other important predators include ants, spiders and lacewings.

Parasites include:

- *Trichogramma* spp. - tiny egg parasite wasps
- *Microplitis and Netelia* (wasps) - caterpillar parasites
- Species of *tachinid flies* - caterpillar parasites.

With the exception of the egg parasites and Microplitis, most parasites do not kill helicoverpa until they reach the pupal stage. Predatory earwigs and wireworm larvae are significant predators of helicoverpa pupae.

Naturally occurring caterpillar diseases frequently have a marked impact on helicoverpa in summer legumes. Outbreaks of NPV (Nucleopolyhedrovirus) are frequently observed in crops with high helicoverpa populations.

Pod-sucking Bugs

Pod-sucking bugs can move in at budding but significant damage is confined to pods. While pod-sucking bugs start breeding as soon as they move into flowering crops, nymphs must feed on pods to complete their development. Pod-sucking bugs cause shrivelled and distorted seed, and can severely reduce yield and seed quality. Pod-sucking bugs can even damage seeds in pods that are nearing harvest maturity. Late bug damage reduces seed quality but not yield. As only 2 per cent seed damage is tolerable in culinary soybeans, bug thresholds are based on seed quality, not yield.

A number of pod-sucking bugs can attack soybeans and include:

- Green vegetable bug
- Redbanded shield bug
- Large brown bean bug
- Small brown bean bug.

The green vegetable bug (GVB) and the brown bean bugs are equally damaging to crops, while the damage potentials of the redbanded and brown shield bugs are 0.75 and 0.2 of that of a GVB respectively. Nymphs of all species are less damaging than adults. While first instar nymphs cause no damage, subsequent instars are progressively more damaging with the fifth and final instar being nearly as damaging as adults. To determine the damage potential of mixed bug species populations, convert all species (adults and nymphs) to GVB adult equivalents (GVBAEQ).

Green Vegetable Bug (GVB) (*Nezara viridula*)

Pest status: This species is the most damaging pod-sucking bug in soybeans due to its abundance, widespread distribution, rate of damage and rate of reproduction. Very high populations are frequently encountered in coastal Queensland.

Risk Period

- Adult bugs typically invade summer legumes at flowering, but GVB is primarily a pod feeder with a preference for pods with well-developed seeds.
- Nymphs are unable to complete their development prior to pod-fill.
- Soybeans remain at risk until pods are too hard to damage (i.e. very close to harvest).
- Damaging populations are typically highest in late summer crops during late pod-fill (when nymphs have reached or are near adulthood).

Damage

- Pods containing well-developed seeds are most at risk.
- While GVB also damages buds and flowers, soybeans can compensate for this early damage.
- Damage to young pods cause deformed and shrivelled seeds and reduce yield.
- Seeds damaged in older pods are blemished and difficult to grade out reducing harvested seed quality, particularly that destined for human consumption (edibles).

GVB can even damage seeds in 'close-to-harvest' pods (i.e. pods that have hardened prior to harvest). Bug damaged seeds have increased protein content but a shorter storage life (due to increased rancidity). Bug damage also reduces seed oil content. Bug damaged seeds are frequently discoloured, either directly as a result of tissue breakdown, or because of diseases such as *Cercospora* (purple seed stain), which may gain entry where pods are pierced by bugs.

Sampling and Monitoring

- Crops should be inspected for GVB twice weekly from flowering until close to harvest.
- Sample for GVB in early to mid-morning.
- Beat sheet sampling is the most efficient monitoring method.
- The standard sample unit consists of five one-metre non consecutive lengths of row within a 20 m radius.
- Convert all bug counts per row metre to bugs/m^2 by dividing counts per row metre by the row spacing in metres.
- At least six sites should be sampled throughout a crop to accurately determine adult GVB populations.
- GVB nymphs are more difficult to sample accurately as their distribution is extremely clumped, particularly during the early nymphal stages (1-3).
- Ideally, at least 10 sites (with five non-consecutive row metres sampled per site) should be sampled to adequately assess nymphal populations.

Thresholds

Pod-sucking bug thresholds in edible or culinary soybeans (destined for human consumption) are determined by seed quality, the maximum bug damage permitted being only 2 per cent. GVB thresholds typically range from 0.3-0.8/m^2 depending on the crop size (seeds per m^2) and when bugs first infest a crop. Because thresholds are determined by per cent damage, the larger a crop (the more seeds per unit area), the more bugs required to inflict critical (threshold) damage, and the higher the threshold.

Chemical Control

- Bugs should be controlled during early pod-fill before nymphs reach a damaging size.
- Pesticides are best applied in the early to mid-morning to contact bugs basking at the top of the canopy.

Cultural Control

- Avoid sequential plantings of summer legumes as bug populations will move progressively from earlier to later plantings, eventually building to very high levels.
- Avoid cultivar and planting time combinations that are more likely to lengthen the duration of flowering and podding.

Natural Enemies

- GVB eggs are frequently parasitised by a tiny introduced wasp *Trissolcus basalis*. Parasitised eggs are easily recognised as they turn black.
- GVB nymphs are attacked by ants, spiders and predatory bugs.
- Final (fifth) instar and adult GVB are parasitised by the recently introduced tachinid fly (*Trichopoda giacomellii)*.

Redbanded Shield Bug

The Redbanded shield bug (RBSB) (*Piezodorus oceanicus)* was previously classified as *Piezodorus hybneri* and more recently as *P. grossi*.

Pest Status

Major, widespread, regular. RBSB is 75 per cent as damaging as GVB in summer pulses but is usually not as abundant. However, it is more difficult to control with current pesticides. Adults are similar in shape to GVB but are smaller and paler, with pink, white or yellow bands.

Damage

Damage is similar to that caused by GVB, with early damage reducing yields, and later damage reducing the quality of harvested seeds.

Thresholds

Convert to GVB equivalents to determine damage potential.

Monitoring

As for GVB. Beat sheeting is the preferred sampling method. Look for the distinctive twin-row egg rafts which indicate the presence of RBSB.

Chemical Control

- No insecticides are specifically registered against RBSB in Australia.
- Recent trials suggest pesticides currently registered against GVB are ineffective against RBSB.

- Control can be improved, albeit to only 50-60 per cent, with the addition of a 0.5 per cent salt (NaCl) adjuvant.

Natural Enemies

- Spiders, ants, and predatory bugs are major predators of RBSB, particularly of eggs and young nymphs with mortality of these stages sometimes exceeding 90 per cent.
- Eggs may be parasitised by the tiny wasp, *Trissolcus basalis*.
- Adults are infrequently parasitised by the recently introduced tachinid fly.

BROWN BEAN BUGS

Large brown bean bug (*Riptortus serripes*)

Small brown bean bug (*Melanacanthus scutellaris*)

Pest Status

As damaging as GVB. More frequent on the coast.

Host Range and Risk Period

As for GVB.

Damage

Both large and small brown bean bugs are as damaging as GVB. Damage is similar to that caused by GVB, with early damage reducing yield, while later damage reduces the quality of harvested seed.

Monitoring

- Sample crops early in the morning.
- The beat sheet method is not totally satisfactory as both brown bean bugs are very flighty, particularly during the hotter parts of the day.
- Crop scouts should familiarise themselves with the appearance of flying brown bean bug adults and include these in sampling counts.

Silverleaf Whitefly

Silverleaf whitefly (SLW) (*Bemisia tabaci* biotype B) poses a threat to soybeans in tropical and subtropical coastal regions. However, the recently released SLW parasite *Eretmocerus hayati*, together with native parasites and predators, can reasonably be expected to stabilise SLW populations, provided they are not disrupted by the overuse of non-selective pesticides.

Pest Status and Host Range

Major risk in susceptible crops. Of the summer pulses, soybeans and navy beans are preferred SLW hosts. Significant populations of SLW adults are frequently seen in mungbeans but nymphal development on this crop is very poor.

Risk Period

Summer pulses maturing during late summer and autumn are at greater risk of attack because invading SLW have had more time to increase from low over-wintering populations. As a rule, the earlier crops are infested, the greater the risk. Crops remain attractive to SLW until mid pod-fill. As the crop matures, leaves become unattractive to SLW and adults leave the crop to find more attractive hosts.

Damage

- SLW can reduce plant vigour and yield by the sheer weight of numbers removing large amounts of plant photosynthate from the leaves.
- Severe infestations in young plants can stunt plant growth and greatly reduce a crop's yield potential.
- Later infestations can reduce the number of pods set, seed size, and seed size uniformity, thus reducing yield and quality. As a rule, the impact of SLW is worst in drought stressed crops.
- In heavily infested soybeans, both pods and seeds are often unusually pale. While seed colour is unlikely to be of concern in grain soybeans (harvested seeds being naturally pale), pod and seed discolouration are a major marketing problem where pods are picked green (e.g. vegetable soybeans and green beans).
- SLW can also secrete large amounts of sticky honeydew. Adult females produce more honeydew than other stages and nymphs produce more honeydew when feeding on stressed plants. Honeydew is not a major problem, but the sooty mould which develops on honeydew shields leaves from sunlight and reduces photosynthesis.
- The impact of sooty mould is greatest during early to mid pod-fill when SLW activity is greatest at the top of the canopy, i.e. on the leaves with the greatest photosynthetic activity. Rain and overhead irrigation wash honeydew off leaves, lessening the risk of sooty mould.

Monitoring

- SLW eggs, nymphs and resting adults are mainly found on the underside of leaves.
- Flying SLW adults are readily observed when crops with high populations are disturbed.
- The presence of honeydew and sooty mould may also indicate SLW attack, but can be due to aphid feeding.

SLW eggs are laid on younger leaves, so by the time eggs develop to large nymphs in crops with high growth rates, leaves with the greatest visible SLW nymphal activity are further down the plant. This may be as many as 5-7 nodes below the plant top. As vegetative growth slows, however, plant nodes with greatest nymphal activity move progressively upwards to the canopy top.

Thresholds and Chemical Control

There are no validated thresholds for SLW and no pesticides are specifically registered for SLW control in summer pulses in Australia. Use the softest options possible for other pests early in the life of the crop, to encourage SLW parasites and predators.

Cultural Control

- Where possible, avoid successive plantings of summer pulses to prevent movement from early to late crops.
- Avoid planting summer pulses in close proximity to earlier maturing SLW hosts such as cotton and cucurbits.
- Where damaging SLW populations are evident in other crops early in the season (early summer), or in regions with a history of consistently damaging widespread SLW activity, consider planting a pulse type less attractive to SLW (e.g. mungbeans or adzukis) (*Vigna* sp.), rather than soybeans.
- Control SLW weed hosts such as rattlepod and milk thistle.
- Irrigate crops to reduce moisture stress which makes crops more susceptible to SLW damage. Overhead irrigation also washes off sooty mould and drowns adult SLW.
- Narrow leafed and smooth leafed (less hairy) cultivars may be less attractive to SLW. However, the latter attribute may leave crops more vulnerable to aphid attack.

Natural Enemies

SLW nymphs are parasitised by native species of *Encarsia* and *Eretmocerus* (both very small wasps). In 2005 CSIRO released the exotic parasite *Eretmocerus hayati* in the Bundaberg and Childers region. It has successfully established and spread up to 20 km from the original release sites, with high levels of parasitism reported. The parasite has now also been released in other areas and in conjunction with native SLW parasites, will hopefully help stabilise SLW populations.

MINOR PESTS

Brown Shield Bug *(Dictyotus caenosus)*

Pest Status and Damage

- Minor pest in Australia.
- The BSB damages only 20 per cent as many seeds as the GVB (i.e. BSB = 0.2 GVB).

Monitoring and Control

- Beat sheeting is the preferred sampling method.
- Sample crops early to mid-morning when bugs are likely to be at the top of the crop.
- Look for the distinctive egg rafts (small twin rows or small irregular rafts containing 10-16 eggs), which indicate the presence of BSB.
- When possible avoid sequential plantings of summer legumes.

Caterpillars

Cluster caterpillar *Spodoptera litura,* often referred to as 'spods'

Pest Status and Damage

As damaging as helicoverpa but less frequent.

- Can cause significant damage to coastal soybeans during flowering and podding.
- Small larvae window leaves, but older larvae chew holes in leaves.
- Older larvae may also attack flowers and pods.

Monitoring and Control

- As for helicoverpa.
- Look also for egg masses and clusters of young larvae.
- In pre-flowering crops, control is warranted if defoliation exceeds (or is likely to exceed) 33 per cent.
- Tolerable defoliation drops to 15-20 per cent once flowering and podding commences.
- Cluster caterpillars are not controlled by NPV and are difficult to control with *Bt* (*Bacillus thuringiensis*) unless very small.

Natural Enemies

As for helicoverpa and loopers.

Bean podborer (*Maruca vitrata*)

Pest Status and Damage

Not usually a pest in soybeans, but tunnelling has been reported in soybean stems in coastal regions such as Bundaberg.

Monitoring and Control

- Look for tunnelling and associated larval frass in soybean stems
- No thresholds are set as this pest is not regarded as a problem in soybeans.
- Report any unusual heavy podborer infestations in soybeans to The Department of Employment, Economic Development and Innovation's Entomology (Field Crops) team.

Etiella (lucerne seed web moth) *Etiella behrii*

Risk Period and Damage

- Spasmodic but important pest of specialist soybeans in drier regions (e.g. natto soybeans on the Darling Downs) due to near zero damage tolerance.
- Crops may be infested from flowering onwards, but are at greatest risk during late podding.
- Because etiella larvae consume far less than larger caterpillar species such as *Helicoverpa*, seeds are usually only partially eaten out, often with characteristic pin-hole damage.
- This damage is difficult to grade out and its unattractive appearance reduces seed quality.

Monitoring and Control

Techniques are being developed to monitor moth activity with light traps or lures, as the moth is this pests' most vulnerable stage. No pesticides are currently registered.

Loopers

- **Green loopers** - Soybean looper (*Thysanoplusia orichalcea*), Tobacco looper (*Chrysodeixis argentifera*), Vegetable looper (*Chrysodeixis eriosoma*).
- **Brown loopers -** Bean looper or Mocis (*Mocis alterna*), Sugarcane looper (*Mocis frugalaris*), *Mocis trifasciata* and *Pantydia* spp.

The following applies equally to green and brown loopers:

Risk period and damage

- Crops can be attacked at any stage but are greatest risk during flowering and podding.
- Summer legumes such as soybeans are least tolerant of defoliation at these stages.
- Loopers do not attack the flowers and small pods of soybeans.
- Looper leaf damage is different to helicoverpa damage, with the feeding holes being more angular rather than rounded.

Monitoring and Control

- Use a beat sheet.
- Inspect crops weekly during the vegetative stage and twice weekly from very early budding onwards until crops are no longer susceptible to attack.
- In pre-flowering crops, looper control is warranted if defoliation exceeds (or is likely to exceed) 33 per cent. Tolerable defoliation drops to 15-20 per cent once flowering and podding commences.
- Loopers are not controlled by products containing *Helicoverpa* NPV.
- Small loopers (under 12 mm) can be controlled with Bt.

Natural Enemies

- Loopers are frequently parasitised by braconids (*Apantales* sp.) with scores of parasite larva developing per looper host.
- Predatory bugs, tachinid flies and ichneumonid wasps also attack loopers.
- The use of *Bt* will help preserve beneficial insects.
- Outbreaks of looper NPV are frequently observed in crops with high looper populations. However, larvae are usually not killed by virus until they are medium-large (instars 4-5). Looper NPV is not the same as helicoverpa NPV.

Soybean Moth

Soybean moth (*Aproaerema simplexella*) is common in soybeans but is usually only present in low numbers with only the occasional leaf slightly webbed and folded to provide a shelter for larvae. However, they can occur in very high numbers and on rare occasions can destroy crops by denuding all the leaves.

Damage and Control

- Larvae initially feed inside leaves (i.e. mine leaves) for about four days, and then emerge to feed externally, folding and webbing leaves together.

- The most obvious symptom of damage is the webbing and folding together of leaves. The larvae normally only cause cosmetic damage.
- Infestations are favoured by hot, dry weather, with crops under severe moisture stress most at risk.
- Scout crops regularly for the early warning signs of rare plague events - numerous small, pale patches (leaf-mining) on the leaves and large numbers of soybean moths around lights at night.
- Indicative threshold is based on defoliation (i.e. 33% pre-flowering and 15-20% during early pod-fill).
- Control will rarely be required and no specific registrations exist for soybean moth.

Legume Leafspinner

The Legume webspinner is also known as the bean leafroller (*Omiodes diemenalis*).

Risk Period and Damage

- Widespread in coastal regions but rarely at damaging levels.
- Crops are usually at greatest risk during early podding.
- Larvae are leaf feeders, webbing leaves together.
- Silken webs and frass are indicative of webspinner attack, but other leaf webbers cause similar symptoms.

Monitoring and Control

- Larvae will be sometimes detected when beat sheet sampling.
- Inspect webbed leaves and look for the characteristic frass.
- The threshold is based on tolerable defoliation, i.e. 33 per cent pre flowering and 15-20 per cent during early pod-fill.
- Control is rarely required.

Red-shouldered Leaf Beetle

The Red-shouldered leaf beetle is also known as Monolepta (*Monolepta australis*).

Risk Period and Damage

- Common in sugar cane areas. Can arrive suddenly in large numbers, inflicting rapid defoliation and flower loss.
- Soybeans are at greatest risk during flowering.
- Infestations are most likely after heavy rainfall events.
- Monolepta attack leaves and flowers, high populations (e.g. more than 50/m^2) will shred leaves and denude crops of flowers.

Monitoring and Control

- Monolepta are readily assessed visually or with a beat sheet but can be difficult to count as they are extremely flighty. Estimate the number of groups of 5 or 10 beetles on the sheet to get a ′ball park′ population estimate.

- Check crops after heavy rainfall that may trigger the mass emergence of adults.
- Thresholds are not yet established but populations greater than $20/m^2$ can cause significant damage in flowering crops.
- Defoliation thresholds are the same as for leaf feeding caterpillars.
- Plant legume crops away from larval hosts of Monolepta such as sugar cane.
- Spot treatment of borders may be sufficient.

Lucerne Crownborer

Lucerne crownborer (*Zygrita diva*)

Risk Factors and Damage

- Soybean crops in the tropics, or growing in abnormally hot' summers, or in close proximity to lucerne are at greatest risk.
- Proximity to lucerne increases the risk of early infestation
- Larval feeding has little impact on yield but prior to pupating, plants are internally ringbarked or girdled above the pupal chamber causing plant death above the girdle and plants in thin stands may lodge before harvest.
- In southern Queensland, this usually occurs after seeds are fully developed with no yield loss. In tropical regions, larval development is more rapid and there can be considerable crop losses.
- Crownborers are very damaging to 'edamame' soybeans where green immature pods are harvested by mechanical pod pluckers. The stems of infested plants are weakened and snap off, contaminating the harvested product.

Monitoring and Control

- Break open stems to look for larvae and eaten out and brown discoloured pith.
- There are no effective chemical controls as larvae in the stems are protected from insecticide.
- Avoid planting susceptible crops close to lucerne.
- If in an at-risk region, consider later plantings to shorten crop development.
- In the tropics, consider winter plantings.
- Avoid thin plant stands to reduce the lodging of damaged plants.
- Currently there are no pesticides registered for lucerne crownborer in soybeans. Trying to control the only vulnerable stage, i.e. the adults in early vegetative crops, would greatly increase the risk of silverleaf whitefly attack.

Soybean Aphids

Soybean aphid (*Aphis glycine*)

Damage

- Not a major threat to soybeans but populations should be monitored. In the unusually cool summer of 2007-08 severe aphid outbreaks occurred in the Bundaberg region.
- More prevalent on the coast than inland.

- Cast off (white) aphid skins are evidence of past infestations.
- Heavily infested plants may be covered in sooty mould growing on honeydew secreted by the aphids.
- Heavy infestations can reduce yield significantly and delay harvest maturity.
- Infested plants can have distorted leaves.
- Crops become less attractive to aphids after early podding.
- The adult, winged-form of the aphid is able to travel long distances on prevailing wind currents.

Monitoring and Control

- Look for aphid colonies on the upper stems, leaflets and terminal leaves.
- In heavily infested crops, cast off aphid skins, sooty mould, and large ladybird populations are indicative of soybean aphids. The latter two can also indicate significant whitefly activity.
- Chemical control is rarely required due to the significant impact of natural enemies, especially ladybird beetles and hoverfly larvae.
- Soybean aphids can be controlled with systemic pesticides but no products are specifically registered for this pest in soybeans.
- In the United States, the soybean aphid threshold is set at 250 aphids per plant from budding to podding. As a rule of thumb, once soybean aphids are present on the main stem, populations are in excess of 400 aphids per plant.

Two-spotted or Red Spider Mite (*Tetranychus* sp.)

Damage

- Can cause severe damage, particularly during hot, dry weather.
- Mite outbreaks are often the result of using 'hard' pesticides to treat other pests, where the killing of their natural enemies flares mite numbers.
- Heavy infestations at pod-fill lead to leaf drop and early senescence.
- Seed size and yield may be reduced by as much as 30 per cent in severe cases.
- Mites first occur on the lower leaves and gradually move to the top of the plant as the population builds up.
- They make fine webbing on the underside of the leaves, and feed by a rasping and sucking action.
- Infested leaves take on a speckled appearance.
- In severe cases the leaves turn a yellow-brown before they wither and drop from the plant.

Mirids

Green Mirid (*Creontiades dilutus*) and Brown Mirid (*Creontiades pacificus*)

Risk Period and Damage

- Budding, flowering and early-podding crops are at greatest risk while no damage has been observed in more advanced pods.

- Low populations (less than 1 per m^2) of green mirids are often present in vegetative crops but there is no evidence they cause 'tipping' of vegetative terminals or yield loss.
- Mirids attack buds, flowers and small pods.
- Soybeans are less susceptible to mirids compared to other pulses due to the synchrony of flowering and because they produce up to four times as many flowers as are necessary to set enough pods to produce a high yield (4 t/ha or more).
- Trials have shown no yield loss in crops with up to 5 mirids/m^2.

Monitoring

- Mirids are very mobile pests and in-crop populations can increase very rapidly.
- Crops should be inspected twice weekly from budding onwards until post flowering.
- In row crops, the preferred method is beat sheeting, as this method is the most effective for helicoverpa and pod-sucking bugs.
- Sample five one-metre lengths of row (not consecutive) within a 20 m radius, from at least six sites throughout a crop.
- Avoid sampling during very windy weather as mirids are easily blown off the sheet.
- Thresholds for soybeans are 3-4 mirids/m^2.

Control

- Shortening a crop's flowering period reduces the risk of mirid damage.
- Flowering periods can be shortened by planting on a full moisture profile and by watering crops just before budding.
- Consider planting crops in at least 50 cm rows (as opposed to broadcast planting) to facilitate easier pest sampling.
- Spraying for mirids is unwarranted in most crops unless populations are in excess of 5/m^2. Unnecessary spraying for mirids in soybeans increases the risk of flaring silverleaf whitefly.
- Trials have shown that the addition of salt (0.5% NaCl) as an adjuvant can improve chemical control of mirids at lower chemical rates. Reducing pesticide rates (typically by 50-60%) reduces their impact on beneficials and reduces the risk of flaring helicoverpa.

Natural Enemies

Spiders, ants, predatory bugs and predatory wasps have been observed attacking mirids in the field. Naturally occurring fungi (e.g. *Beauvaria*) may also infect and kill mirids, but are rarely observed in the field.

29

Manage Soybean Diseases with Planting

Unlike the weather in recent years, this spring has been wet so far. There is a lot of moisture in the soil, which affects corn and soybean planting. Soybean diseases are affected by planting dates and planting conditions. Early or delayed planting may increase, reduce, or not affect a soybean disease, depending on when the disease infects soybean and soil conditions after planting. The table below summarizes how planting dates may affect major Iowa soybean diseases. Knowing this information can help you make planting decisions and anticipate what to look for during crop scouting. If you have experienced soybean diseases in your fields in the past, this table may be useful to avoid future disease problems.

Reduced Risk by Later Planting

For diseases in which infection occurs at the seedling stage, planting dates directly affect disease risk. Sudden death syndrome (SDS) caused by *Fusarium solani* and seedling blight caused by *Pythium* require cold soil temperatures when soybeans are in the seedling stage. Therefore, soybeans will have a higher risk of the two diseases if planted early in cool, wet soils. If these diseases were severe in the past, delay planting until the soil warms up to reduce disease risk significantly. In Iowa, severe SDS is more likely to be found in early-planted soybean fields than in late-planted fields. Be aware that the fungi will not cause much damage if soil moisture is not excessive. When spring conditions are not unusually wet, diseases may not be a concern.

Reduced Risk by early Planting

Contrary to *Pythium* damping off and SDS, seedling blight by *Rhizoctonia* and *Phytophthora* may be reduced by early planting because optimum conditions for infections by the two fungi are warm soil temperatures. If planted early, soybeans may grow out the susceptible seedling stage and escape damping off.

Effects of Planting Date on Soybean Diseases for Fields where Disease is a Concern

Disease	Conditions for Infection	Growth Stage for Infection	Planting Date Effect
Damping off by Pythium	Cool and wet soil	Before V2	Later planting reduces risk
Damping off by Rhizoctonia	Wet and warm soil	Before V2	Early planting may reduce the problem
Damping off by Phytophthora	Wet soil	Seedling stage	Early planting may reduce the problem
Sudden death syndrome	Cool and wet soil at planting	Early seedling stage	Later planting reduces risk
Brown stem rot	Cool and wet weather during the season	All vegetative growth stages	Varies; often more severe in late, mature soybeans
White mold	Cool and wet at and after flowering	Flowering stage	Varies with weather in flowering stage
Pod and stem blight Foliar diseases	Cool and wet after pod form Above normal rains after July	Pod setting Reproductive stages	Varies with weather during pod setting Higher risk in later planted and late MG varieties
Bean pod mottle virus	Warm and dry season	All season	Later planting reduces risk

No Effects

Some diseases—bacterial blight, brown spots, and stem canker—are not affected by planting dates because infections of these disease do not have critical stages.

Indirect Effects

Planting date also indirectly affects occurrence of white mold, pod and stem blight, and brown stem rot. Infections of the first two diseases do not occur in seedling stages, but there is a certain window of time during which soybeans are susceptible to these pathogens. Soybeans planted at different times in the spring will reach a disease-susceptible stage at different times in the summer—some early, some later. A planting whose window of susceptible stages overlaps with disease-favourable weather conditions will have higher risk of developing disease than a planting whose window misses the disease-favourable weather. For example, in 1996, more white mold was observed in late-planted soybeans because the cool, wet weather came late in the season. Similarly, the susceptible growth stage for pod and stem blight is in the pod-setting stage, and favourable weather during this growth stage affects the level of this disease.

Seed Treatment

This spring appears not to lead a dry planting season. If weather forecasts favour wet weather, use of seed treatments with fungicides in the grounds that had seedling diseases in the past could be beneficial. If you experienced damping off by *Phytophthora*, *Pythium*, or *Rhizoctonia* for a particular ground that is to be planted, consider use of treated seeds. Research has shown that early planting increases the possibility of achieving maximum yield and that the level of success decreases as planting is delayed. Because of narrow planting windows for high yield, especially in northern Iowa, one should not hold back the planting date just for fear of diseases. Knowing your grounds is the key. For instance, if you farm a large acreage and have fields that have disease problems, arranging planting order works in reducing disease risk. For example, if you have six fields and one of them had SDS in the past, you can reduce its risk by designing a planting route with the problematic field planted last and choosing a tolerant variety.

Glossary

Apothecia (sing. apothecium) - Saucer-shaped, mushroom-like fungal structures that produce spores.

Chlorotic - The yellowing of a plant's normally green leaf tissue, due to the absence of chlorophyll.

Conservation tillage - Any tillage or planting system that leaves 30 percent or more of the soil surface covered with crop residue after planting, to reduce soil erosion by water.

Cotyledons - The first emerging pair of leaves of the soybean seedling.

Damping off - Seedling collapse due to rot of seeds before or after germination, generally due to fungal infection.

Epidermis - The outer surface of a leaf, stem or root.

Hypocotyl - Component of a seedling soybean stem located beneath the cotyledons.

Longitudinal - Running lengthwise.

Microsclerotia (sing. microsclerotium) - Tiny, dark bodies (masses of hyphae with a thick rind) formed by certain fungi as survival structures.

Mosaic - A pattern of light and dark areas in a leaf that is frequently a symptom of a virus infection.

Mottle - Irregular light and dark-colored areas on plant parts that are frequently caused by a virus.

Necrotic - Dead; chlorotic areas may become necrotic as disease progresses.

Oospore - Thick-walled survival spore of some fungi.

Partial resistance - A term used to describe resistance made up of more than one gene. Also known as horizontal resistance or field resistance.

Pathotype - A classification system used for *Phytophthora sojae*. Similar to race, but better suited to the increasing pathogen diversity of *Phytophthora sojae*.

Pycnidia (sing. pycnidium) - Spore containers that are the fruiting structures of some fungi, visible to the naked eye as tiny dots or bumps on the plant surface.

Race - A distinct population within the same species with relatively small morphological and genetic differences. Races differ in their ability to colonize potential host plants.

Sclerotia (sing. sclerotium) - Seed-like structures formed by some fungi to survive winter or remain dormant until conditions are favorable for growth and/or plant infection.

Senescence - The natural decline and death of plant tissues due to aging.

Stomates - Natural openings in leaves that allow the exchange of air.

Toxin - When pertaining to plants, this is a chemical compound that causes damage to plant cells. Sometimes released by disease-causing organisms.

Zoospores - Spores that can swim in water.

Bibliography

Abney, T.S., Melgar, J. C., Richards, T. L., Scott, D. H., Grogan, J., and Young, J. 1997. New Races of *Phytophthora sojae* with *Rps*1-d Virulence. *Plant Dis.* 81:653-655.

Anderson, T.R. 1986. Plant Losses and Yield Responses to Monoculture of Soybean Cultivars Susceptible, Tolerant, and Resistant to *Phytophthora megasperma* f. sp. *glycinea. Plant Dis.* 70:468-471.

Anderson, T.R., and Buzzell, R.I. 1982. Efficacy of Metalaxyl in Controlling Phytophthora Root and Stalk Rot of Soybean Cultivars Differing in Field Tolerance. *Plant Dis.* 66: 1144-1145.

Apt W J, Caswell EP. 1988. Application of Nematicides via Drip Irrigation. *Annals of Applied Nematology* 2: 1-10.

Apt W Jr. 1976. Survival of Reniform Nematode in Desiccated Soils. *Journal of Nematology* 8: 278 (Abstract).

Ayala A, Ramirez CT. 1964. Host-range, Distribution, and Bibliography of the Reniform Nematode, *Rotylenchulus reniformis*, with Special Reference to Puerto Rico. *Journal of Agriculture of University of Puerto Rico* 48: 140-160.

Ayala, A. and Ramirez, C.T. 1964. Host-range, Distribution and Bibliography of the Reniform Nematode *Rotylenchulus reniformis* with Special Reference to Puerto Rico. *J. Agric. Univ. P.R.* 48:140-161.

Balasubramanian P, Ramakrishnan C. 1983. Resistance to the Reniform Nematode *Rotylenchulus reniformis* in Tomato. *Nematologia Mediterranea* 11: 203-204.

Birchfield and Martin, 1968. Evaluation of Nematicides for Controlling Nematodes of Sweetpotatoes. *Plt. Dis. Rept.* 52:127-131.

Caswell EP, deFrank J, Apt WJ, Tang C-S. 1991. Influence of Nonhost Plants on Population Decline of *Rotylenchulus reniformis*. *Journal of Nematology* 23: 91-98.

Dela Cruz, C.S.1988. Reactions of Sweet Potato (*Ipomoea batatas* Lam.) Cultivars to Reniform Nematode, *Rotylenchulus reniformis*, and Determinants of Resistance Mechanisms. M.S. Thesis. UPLB. 68 p.

Evans, K,D. L. Trudgill and J.M. Webster. 1993. Plant Parasitic Nematodes in Temperate Agriculture. University Press, Cambridge. 648 p.

Faris, M.A., Sabo, F.E., Barr, D.J.S., and Lin, C.S. 1989. The Systematics of *Phytophthora sojae* and *P. megasperma*. *Can. J. Bot.* 67: 1442-1447.

Förster, H., Tyler, B.M., and Coffey, M.D. 1994. *Phytophthora sojae* Races have Arisen by Clonal Evolution and by Rare Outcrosses. *Mol. Plant-Microbe Interact.* 7: 780-791.

Galano, C.D., R.M. Gapasin and J.L. Lim. 1996. Efficacy of *Paecilomyces lilacinus* Isolates for the Control of Root-knot Nematode (*Meloidogyne incognita* (Kofoid and White) Chitwood) in Sweet Potato. *Annals of Tropical Research* 18: 4-12.

Gapasin, R.M. 1984. Resistance of Fifty-two Sweet Potato (*Ipomoea batatas* (L.) Lam.) Cultivars to *Meloidogyne incognita* and *M. javanica*. *Annals of Tropical Research* 6: 1-19.

Gapasin, R.M. and R.B. Valdez. 1979. Pathogenicity of *Meloidogyne* spp. and *Rotylenchulus reniformis* on sweet potato. *Annals of Tropical Research* 1: 20-26.

Hansen, E.M., and Maxwell, D.P. 1991. Species of *Phytophthora megasperma* Complex. *Mycologia* 83: 376-381.

Inserra RN, Dunn RA, McSorley R, Langdon KR, Richmer AY. 1989. Weed Hosts of *Rotylenchulus reniformis* in Ornamental Nurseries of Southern Florida. *Nematology Circular 171*. Florida Department of Agriculture and Consumer Services, Division of Plant Industry, Gainesville.

Inserra RN, Dunn RA, Volvas N. 1994a. Host Response of Ornamental Palms to *Rotylenchulus reniformis* in Florida. Supplement to the *Journal of Nematology* 26: 737-743.

Inserra RN, Lehman PS, Overstreet C. 1994b Ornamental Hosts of the Reniform Nematode, *Rotylenchulus reniformis*. *Nematology Circular 209*. Florida Department of Agriculture and Consumer Services, Division of Plant Industry, Gainesville.

Kinloch RA, Sprenkel RK. 1994. Plant-parasitic Nematodes Associated with Cotton in Florida. *Journal of Nematology* 26: 749-752.

Linford MB, Oliveira JM. 1940. *Rotylenchulus reniformis*, nov. gen. n. sp., a Nematode Parasite of Roots. *Proceeding of the Helminthological Society of Washington* 7: 35-42.

Mai WF, Mullin PG. 1996. *Plant Parasitic Nematode. A Pictorial Key to Genera*, 5th Ed. Cornell University Press, Ithaca, New York.

Martin. 1960. The Reniform Nematode may be a Serious Pest of the Sweet Potato. *Plt. Dis. Rept.* 44: 216.

McSorley R, Campbell CW, Parrado JL. 1982. Nematodes Associated with Tropical and Subtropical Fruit Trees in South Florida. *Proceedings of Florida State Horticultural Society* 95: 132-135.

McSorley R, Parrado JL, Conover RA. 1983. Population Buildup and Effects of the Reniform Nematode on Papaya in Southern Florida. *Proceedings of Florida State Horticultural Society* 96: 198-200.

McSorley R, Parrado JL, Stall WM. 1981. Aspects of Nematode Control on Snapbean with Emphasis on the Relationship Between Nematode Density and Damage. *Proceedings of Florida State Horticulture Society* 94: 134-136.

McSorley R. 1980. Nematodes Associated with Sweet Potato and Edible Aroids in Southern Florida. *Proceedings of Florida State Horticultural Society* 93: 283-285.

Ploper, L.D., Athow, K.L., and Laviolette, F.A. 1985. A New Allele at the *Rps*3 Locus for Resistance to *Phytophthora megasperma* f. sp. *glycinea* in Soybean. *Phytopathology* 75: 690-694.

Radewald JD, Takeshita G. 1964. Desiccation Studies on Five Species of Plant-parasitic Nematodes of Hawaii. *Phytopathology* 54: 903-904.

Rebois RV, Epps JM, Hartwig EE. 1970. Correlation of Resistance in Soybeans to *Heterodera glycines* and *Rotylenchulus reniformis*. *Phytopathology* 60: 695-700.

Robinson AF, Inserra RN, Caswell-Chen EP, Vovlas N, Troccoli A. 1997. *Rotylenchulus* Species: Identification, Distribution, Host Ranges, and Crop Plant Resistance. *Nematropica* 27: 127-180.

Roman J. 1964. Immunity of Sugarcane to the Reniform Nematode. *Journal of Agriculture, University of Pueto Rico* 48: 162-163.

Sasser, J.N. 1989. Plant Parasitic Nematodes: *The Farmer's Hidden Enemy. University Graphics*, North Carolina State University, Raleigh, N. C. 115 p.

Sasser, J.N. and C.C. Carter. 1985. An Advanced Treatise on *Meloidogyne*. Vol. I: Biology and Control. North Carolina State University Graphics. 422 p.

Schmitthenner, A.F., and Bhat, R.G. 1994. Useful Methods for Studying *Phytophthora* in the Laboratory. Ohio Agric. Res. Dev. Cent. Spec. Circ. 143.

Schmitthenner, A.F., and VanDoren, D.M., Jr. 1985. Integrated Control of Root Rot of Soybean Caused by *Phytophthora megasperma* f. sp. *glycinea*. pp. 263-266 in: *Ecology and Management of Soilborne Plant Pathogens*. C.A. Parker, A.D. Rovira, K.J. Moore, P. T.W. Wong, and J.F. Kollmorgen, eds. American Phytopathological Society, St. Paul, MN.

Schmitthenner, A.F., Hobe, M., and Bhat, R.G. 1994. *Phytophthora sojae* races in Ohio over a 10-year Interval. *Plant Dis.* 78: 269-276.

Sipes BS, Schmitt DP. 2000. *Rotylenchulus reniformis* Damage Thresholds on Pineapple. Acta Horticulturae 529: 239-245.

Starr JL, Page SL. 1990. Nematode Parasites of Cotton and other Tropical Fibre Crops. pp. 539-556. *In*: *Plant Parasitic Nematodes in Subtropical and Tropical Agriculture*. Luc M, Sikora RA, Bridge J (eds). CAB International, Oxon, UK.

Tooley, P.W., and Grau, C. R. 1984. Field Characterization of Rate-reducing Resistance to *Phytophthora megasperma* f. sp. *glycinea* in Soybean. *Phytopathology* 74: 1201-1208.

Tyler, B.M., Förster, H., and Coffey, M. D. 1995. Inheritance of Avirulence Factors and Restriction Fragment Length Polymorphism Markers in Outcrosses of the Oomycete *Phytophthora sojae*. *Mol. Plant-Microbe Interact.* 8: 515-523.

Walker, A.K., and Schmitthenner, A.F. 1984. Heritability of Tolerance to Phytophthora Rot in Soybeans. *Crop Sci.* 24: 490-491.

Wang, K-H, McSorley R, Fasulo TR. (2006). Root-knot and Foliar Nematodes as Pests of Ornamental Plants. *Bug Tutorials.* University of Florida/IFAS. CD-ROM. SW 188.

Index